ALLAH MADE US

New Directions in Ethnography is a series of contemporary, original works. Each title has been selected and developed to meet the needs of readers seeking finely grained ethnographies that treat key areas of anthropological study. What sets these books apart from other ethnographies is their form and style. They have been written with care to allow both specialists and nonspecialists to delve into theoretically sophisticated work. This objective is achieved by structuring each book so that one portion of the text is ethnographic narrative while another portion unpacks the theoretical arguments and offers some basic intellectual genealogy for the theories underpinning the work.

Each volume in *New Directions in Ethnography* aims to immerse readers in fundamental anthropological ideas, as well as to illuminate and engage more advanced concepts. Inasmuch, these volumes are designed to serve not only as scholarly texts, but also as teaching tools and as vibrant, innovative ethnographies that showcase some of the best that contemporary anthropology has to offer.

Published volumes

1. *Turf Wars: Discourse, Diversity, and the Politics of Place*
Gabriella Gahlia Modan

2. *Homegirls: Language and Cultural Practice among Latina Youth Gangs*
Norma Mendoza-Denton

3. *Allah Made Us: Sexual Outlaws in an Islamic African City*
Rudolf Gaudio

ALLAH MADE US

SEXUAL OUTLAWS IN AN ISLAMIC AFRICAN CITY

RUDOLF PELL GAUDIO

WILEY-BLACKWELL

A John Wiley & Sons, Ltd., Publication

This edition first published 2009
© 2009 Rudolf Pell Gaudio
Blackwell Publishing was acquired by John Wiley & Sons in February 2007. Blackwell's publishing program has been merged with Wiley's global Scientific, Technical, and Medical business to form Wiley-Blackwell.

Registered Office
John Wiley & Sons Ltd, The Atrium, Southern Gate, Chichester, West Sussex, PO19 8SQ, United Kingdom

Editorial Offices
350 Main Street, Malden, MA 02148-5020, USA
9600 Garsington Road, Oxford, OX4 2DQ, UK
The Atrium, Southern Gate, Chichester, West Sussex, PO19 8SQ, UK

For details of our global editorial offices, for customer services, and for information about how to apply for permission to reuse the copyright material in this book please see our website at www.wiley.com/wiley-blackwell.

The right of Rudolf Pell Gaudio to be identified as the author of this work has been asserted in accordance with the Copyright, Designs and Patents Act 1988.

Wiley also publishes its books in a variety of electronic formats. Some content that appears in print may not be available in electronic books.

Designations used by companies to distinguish their products are often claimed as trademarks. All brand names and product names used in this book are trade names, service marks, trademarks or registered trademarks of their respective owners. The publisher is not associated with any product or vendor mentioned in this book. This publication is designed to provide accurate and authoritative information in regard to the subject matter covered. It is sold on the understanding that the publisher is not engaged in rendering professional services. If professional advice or other expert assistance is required, the services of a competent professional should be sought.

Library of Congress Cataloging-in-Publication Data

Gaudio, Rudolf Pell.
  Allah made us : sexual outlaws in an Islamic African city / Rudolf Pell Gaudio.
    p. cm. — (New directions in ethnography ; 3)
  Includes bibliographical references and index.
  ISBN 978-1-4051-5251-8 (hardcover : alk. paper) — ISBN 978-1-4051-5252-5 (pbk. : alk. paper) 1. Sexual minorities—Nigeria—Kano. 2. Prostitution—Nigeria—Kano. 3. Sex role—Nigeria—Kano. 4. Sex customs—Nigeria—Kano. 5. Islamic law—Social aspects—Nigeria—Kano. 6. Muslims—Nigeria—Kano Region—Social life and customs. 7. Hausa (African people)—Nigeria—Kano—Social life and customs. 8. Kano (Nigeria)—Social life and customs. 9. Kano (Nigeria)—Religious life and customs. 10. Kano (Nigeria)—Biography. I. Title.

  HQ73.3.N62K364 2009
  306.76088'2970966978—dc22

                                                                         2008051206

A catalogue record for this book is available from the British Library.

Set in 11.5/13.5pt Bembo by Graphicraft Limited, Hong Kong
Printed in Singapore

For my parents, Christina and Alexander Gaudio, and my *oga*,
Phil Shea.

CONTENTS

List of Figures   viii
Acknowledgments   ix
Notes on Orthography, Translation and Transcription   xiii

1   Introducing 'Yan Daudu   1
2   People of the Bariki   29
3   Out in the Open   61
4   Women's Talk, Men's Secrets   89
5   Playing with Faith   117
6   Men on Film   143
7   Lost and Found in Translation   175

Epilogue: May God Keep a Secret   196
Glossary of Hausa terms   206
Bibliography   210
Index   228

LIST OF FIGURES

1.1	Approximate extent of Hausa city-states since 1810	4
1.2	Nigeria	5
2.1	City of Kano just after Nigeria's independence	30
3.1	A 'mother,' her 'daughters,' and their friends in Sabon Gari, 1997	68
5.1	The author (a.k.a. Sani) in Rijiyar Kuka, 1994	130
6.1	Packaging for the video cassette for the film *Ibro Dan Daudu*	144
6.2	Alhaji Damina outside his own restaurant in Rijiyar Kuka, 2002	162
6.3	Invitation to a biki hosted by Hajiya Asabe in Sabon Gari, 1996	164
6.4	Dancing at a biki in Zakawa, 1993	167
7.1	Invitation to Madhuri Mairawa's biki, 1994	177

ACKNOWLEDGMENTS

Ma sha' Allah. This project took shape over great stretches of space and time thanks to numerous people who (like myself) often had only a vague sense of the form it would ultimately take. Their contributions are especially remarkable given the many delays, miscommunications and cultural breaches that I committed on both sides of the Atlantic. Whatever positive value lies in these pages is due largely to their efforts; the faults are all mine.

Because of the stigma and ambiguity attached to gender-nonconformity, homosexuality and prostitution (not to mention laws against such practices), making these acknowledgments raises some of the same rhetorical problems discussed elsewhere in this book. One associate in Kano confided that, despite my intentions, some audiences might even view this text as an act of ingratitude towards the people who helped me and towards Hausa Muslim culture itself. Thus, while I am anxious to thank the individuals and agencies that supported me while I was carrying out this research, I must emphasize that they have not necessarily endorsed the course it has taken. Many of those who were most helpful to me placed a premium on discretion and must remain anonymous. These individuals, known as 'yan daudu, independent women, and masu harka, welcomed me into their social worlds, offered me food, drink and fellowship, and tolerated my social and linguistic missteps, as well as unusual and inconvenient requests for assistance. In my attempts to describe their words, deeds and lives, I have tried to respect my friends' values and reputations, and I ask for forgiveness where I have fallen short.

I extend sincere thanks to the faculty and staff of the Department of Nigerian Languages at Bayero University, Kano (BUK), especially Professor Abdullahi Bature; the Centre for the Study of Nigerian Languages at BUK; the Kano State History and Culture Bureau, especially its former research director, Malam Auwalu Hamza; and Arewa House Centre for Historical Documentation and Research. I am indebted to Dr. Salisu A. Abdullahi, Professor Abdalla U. Adamu, Alhaji Muhammad Munzali Muhammad (CEO of Yoko Films), Professor Tijjani Isma'il and Hajiya Binta Tijjani, Alhaji Aminu Sharif Bappa, Alhaji Malam Sa'idu, Professor M.S. Abdulkadir, Professor Thomas K. Adeyanju, Hajiya Aisha Rufa'i, Mr. David Jowitt, Sani Bello Mai Tafari, and the staff at the former U.S. Consulate in Kaduna. Special thanks to Usman Aliyu Abdulmalik, who helped me with transcribing and countless other things; to Professor Fatimah M. Palmer, for the cultural and culinary lessons; and to Sunusi Ibrahim, Bashir Umar, Haruna Abubakar, and Sunusi Shu'aibu. *Allah ya saka da alheri, amin.*

Fieldwork in Nigeria was funded by a Fulbright Junior Research grant administered by the Institute for International Exchange; research and travel grants from the Department of Anthropology at the University of Arizona; faculty support awards from Purchase College, State University of New York; and a professional development award from the Purchase chapter of United University Professionals. Funds for completing earlier versions of the project were provided by the Stanford Institute for Research on Women and Gender and a DOE Title VI grant administered by the Stanford Center for African Studies; subsequent funding was provided by Purchase College.

My academic mentors and colleagues in the northern Nigerian/ Hausa studies 'mafia' – especially Clifford Hill, Joe McIntyre, Susan O'Brien, Matthias Krings, Esther Morgenthal, Katja Werthmann, Douglas Anthony, Louise Lennihan, Steven Pierce, Heidi Nast, Adeline Masquelier, Moses Ochonu, Sean Stilwell, and John A. Works – offered intellectual, moral and practical assistance. Murray Last and Renée Pittin gave critical feedback on earlier drafts; Jonathan Reynolds furnished archival materials for Chapter 2; and Jack Tocco made sense of my own archives. Special thanks to Alaine S. Hutson, for repeatedly helping me find my way; to Brian Larkin, Conerly Casey, and Shobana Shankar, for encouraging me to trust my ethnographic instincts; and to Deborah Pellow, for taking me under her wing and keeping me there.

The dissertation that this book grew out of was caringly guided by Shirley Brice Heath, John Rickford, Penelope Eckert and Will Leben of the Stanford Linguistics Department, where I also enjoyed the collegial support of Renée Blake, John Baugh, Jen Roth-Gordon and others; these relationships continue to enrich my work. The same can be said of my colleagues at the University of Arizona, especially Jane H. Hill and Susan U. Philips, on whom I have relied extensively for professional support and scholarly advice. Kira Hall, Anna Livia, Mary Bucholtz, Sara Trechter and Bonnie McElhinny gave painstaking editorial commentary on articles that furnished parts of Chapters 4, 5 and 6, and Sandro Duranti, Candy Goodwin, Chuck Goodwin, Bill Hanks, Miyako Inoue, Judith Irvine, Chaise LaDousa, Erez Levon, Bruce Mannheim, Barb Meek, Leila Monaghan and Bonnie Urciuoli gave critical feedback on work presented in other forums.

Henry Abelove, Cesnabmihilo Dorothy Aken'ova, Zehra Arat, Niko Besnier, Christa Craven, Catherine M. Cole, Donald Donham, Deborah Elliston, Wolfram Gleichmar-Hartmann, Lorraine Herbst, Janet Jakobsen, Miranda Joseph, Suzanne Kessler, Bill Leap, Ellen Lewin, Martin Manalansan, Shaka McGlotten, Stephan Miescher, Steven Murray, Esther Newton, Maisa Taha, Niels Teunis, David Valentine and Luise White offered incisive observations about sexuality, gender, nation and race in Africa and elsewhere. Deb Amory led me to many interesting places. Jacqui Ambrosini, Sima Belmar, Martha Fenn, Kathleen Hill, Brad Holland, Marie J. Palluotto, Leland Pitts-Gonzalez, Marianne Villanueva and Anne Wolf shared their experiences and insights on the creative process. Special thanks to Greg Gaudio for his critical feedback on my opening chapters, and to my great Aunt Louise Iorillo for her biscotti and her prayers.

For their guidance, encouragement and extraordinary patience, I thank my editor at Wiley-Blackwell, Rosalie Robertson, my former editor, Jane Huber, and their assistants/mavens, Deirdre Ilkson and Julia Kirk, whose unflagging attentiveness and enthusiasm kept me on track. Ben Soares, two anonymous reviewers, and the students in my Global Sexualities class at Purchase gave generous, detailed commentary on earlier drafts. Hassane Boukary and Isma'ila Maigyara patiently answered my linguistic questions. Rob Scarpa spent many hours designing the photographs, maps and other images, amazing me with his artistry and boundless generosity.

Marla Berman, Dana-ain Davis, Sid Donnell, Adriana Estill, Helen Gremillion, Marco Last, Bonnie McElhinny, Patrick Mead, Denise Morgan, Leslye Obiora, Roopali Mukherjee, Teresa Picarazzi, Carolina Sanin, Michelle Stewart, Jennie Uleman, Char Ullman and Jess Weinberg helped me navigate the ethical and emotional relationship between academics and "real" life. Towfiq Awwal, Emory Fry, Mike Hall, Gerard Ilaria, Marvin Peguese, Wai Poc, Thomas Uldrick and Case Willoughby let me kvetch. Stefanie Jannedy gave me solace and the space to compose myself. Steve Bialostok knew just what I needed. Jeff Maskovsky kept me honest. Norma Mendoza-Denton was my rain in the desert. Galey Modan reminded me to tell the story, and helped me see the point.

I thank my parents, Christina and Alexander Gaudio, and the whole Gaudio clan for supporting me from a distance and giving me a loving home to return to. This book is dedicated to them, and to my mentor and friend, Philip J. Shea, whose knowledge of northern Nigerian history and culture was surpassed only by the generous enthusiasm with which he shared it, often with a plate of food and a glass of lemonade. Phil inspired countless students in Kano and elsewhere. We miss him.

NOTES ON ORTHOGRAPHY, TRANSLATION AND TRANSCRIPTION

Orthography

Hausa is usually written using a modified form of the roman alphabet that includes three special 'hooked' letters to represent sounds that do not exist in European languages: Ɗ/ɗ and Ƙ/ƙ are glottalized (pronounced like their unglottalized counterparts, but with a supplemental constriction of the glottis), while Ɓ/ɓ is implosive (pronounced with a sudden in-breath of air). Other consonants are pronounced approximately as in English, with the following exceptions: *ts* is glottalized; *c* is pronounced like English *ch*; *r* is trilled or rolled.

Hausa vowels are pronounced roughly as in Spanish, and are either long (*aa*) or short (*a*); they are also pronounced with a distinctive tone: high (*ú*), low (*ù*) or falling (*û*). Although distinctions of vowel length and tone do affect word meanings, they are not marked in standard orthography. In this book I generally use standard spellings, indicating distinctive vowel qualities only when necessary – e.g., to distinguish the words *bábà* ['mother'] and *bàbá* ['father']. Excerpts from published texts are reproduced with idiosyncratic spellings intact.

I have chosen to treat the words *Shari'a* and *Bori* as proper nouns, capitalizing them to emphasize their special religious and cultural significance.

In accordance with the normal convention, single quotes indicate a gloss.

Translation

In translating from Hausa to English, I have attempted to strike a balance between literal and idiomatic interpretation. Arabic expressions used in everyday Hausa speech are sometimes translated (e.g., *Wallahi* ['by God']), sometimes not. Where the Hausa original is provided along with an English translation, <u>underlining</u>, **boldface** and *italics* are sometimes used to indicate matching passages, e.g., an Arabic expression with its English translation, or a Hausa proverb with its English translation.

The word *Allah* is sometimes translated as 'God' and sometimes left untranslated; this choice follows the practice of English-speaking Muslims in Nigeria and elsewhere, who use both names more or less interchangeably. (Note that Hausa- and Arabic-speaking Christians also refer to God as *Allah*.)

All singular Hausa nouns, pronouns and adjectives are grammatically feminine or masculine; plural forms are unmarked with respect to gender. When grammatical distinctions of gender and number are relevant to my analysis, they are indicated in English translation using superscript forms, e.g., *ke* ['you^f'], *kai* ['you^m'] or *ku* ['you^{pl}']; *dogo* ['tall^m'] or *doguwa* ['tall^f'].

Transcription

Where a verbatim transcript of Hausa speech is provided along with an English translation, punctuation marks (period, comma, question mark, exclamation mark) are used as in colloquial written English. Other transcription conventions are as follows.

= indicates latching, i.e., a quicker-than-usual transition between speaker turns unaccompanied by a conversational pause.
[indicates the beginning of a conversational overlap, with the open-bracket being located as closely as possible to the point in the first speaker's utterance at which the second speaker started talking.
] indicates the end of an overlap.

( ) indicates uncertainty regarding the accuracy of the transcription inside the parentheses.

(xx) indicates indiscernible speech.

(..) or <..> indicates that speech has been omitted from the transcript.

(( )) or < > indicates my commentary about the interaction (as an analyst, not as a participant).

1

INTRODUCING 'YAN DAUDU

Hajiya Asabe had a feminine name and a handsome, mustached face. In the room he rented in Kano's infamous Sabon Gari neighborhood, he received a daily stream of visitors: girlfriends stopping by to gossip, out-of-town relatives seeking financial assistance, flirtatious boyfriends, hopeful suitors. People knew they could count on finding Hajiya Asabe in his room because, as a self-described *karuwa*, or 'prostitute,' he woke up late most mornings and stayed close to home during the day. Most evenings he spent at a nearby nightclub where a modestly upscale, male clientele came to listen to live performances of Hausa and Arab music, to drink beer or a nonalcoholic alternative, and to socialize with the women and *'yan daudu*, feminine men like Hajiya Asabe, who served as the club's unofficial hosts. (Regular customers had to pay a door fee; women and 'yan daudu did not.) Among the 'yan daudu who frequented the club, Hajiya Asabe stood out with his stylish dress and a graceful, self-confident demeanor that was both charming and haughty. It was this demeanor that had made me notice him during my earliest visits to the club, and that made him so alluring to the men who sought his company.

One day late in the dry season in 1994, I went to pay Hajiya Asabe a visit. As I entered the cement courtyard, I found him kneeling on a small mat outside his room. Not wanting to disturb him as he performed the late-afternoon *la'asar* prayer, I took a seat on a nearby bench while the compound's other residents – most of them non-Muslims from southern Nigeria – went about their regular activities. Once he finished praying, Hajiya Asabe joined me on the bench and called for Mama Ayo, the middle-aged Yoruba woman who managed the compound, to bring me a cold beer. Hajiya Asabe did not drink alcohol, but he was unfailingly hospitable towards his guests, and in the early days of our friendship he always offered me a bottle of Gulder, the most expensive beer on the market, whenever I came by to visit. Although Hajiya Asabe and I had been casually acquainted for almost a year, we had only recently begun spending time together, so we were still getting to know one another. After the usual exchange of greetings and small talk, he complimented me on my command of Hausa, the major language of northern Nigeria, and suggested that all that remained for me to become a 'complete Hausa' [*cikakken Bahaushe*] was to embrace Islam. He even offered to slaughter a ram in my honor if I were to convert. Hajiya Asabe's religious zeal astonished me. After all, the social milieu in which I knew him was hardly one that most people would characterize as Islamically devout.

"But how could I become a Muslim?" I asked him, clutching my bottle of Gulder. "I like this," I reminded him, pointing to the beer. "And I like *harka*" – the 'deed' – that is, sex between men.

"Come now, Sani," Hajiya Asabe replied, addressing me by my Hausa name. "Muslims do these things too. They do them more than anyone!"

My first interpretation of this surprising exchange was that, for Hajiya Asabe, being a Muslim was less important than being Hausa, and had more to do with the performance of cultural rituals than it did with accepting the moral precepts of Islam. His irreverent claim that Muslims engaged in forbidden acts like drinking and homosexuality "more than anyone" was clearly facetious, yet I knew it was based on his experiences in Nigeria and Saudi Arabia, where he had performed the *hajj*, the pilgrimage to Mecca, more than once. Like many other poor pilgrims, Hajiya Asabe had overstayed his visa on several occasions in order to live and work illegally in the port city of Jiddah. While most undocumented Nigerians take on menial jobs that are Islamically legal, Hajiya Asabe supported himself through what he called *karuwanci* ['prostitution'], providing social and sexual companionship to men, some of whom might also enjoy the company of female prostitutes as well as marijuana, cocaine, or even alcohol. His most recent sojourn had ended over a year earlier, when he was arrested, deported and forced to leave behind most of the wealth he had accumulated. The circumstances of Hajiya Asabe's expulsion from Saudi Arabia weighed heavily on him, yet his day-to-day practices signaled a decidedly positive attitude towards the country. He dressed in Saudi men's fashions, listened to cassette tapes of Arab music, and peppered his speech with expressions from Arabic. Though he was unable to read in any language, he kept Arabic-language magazines prominently displayed in his room, along with perfume bottles and other mementos. He also performed the five daily prayers more consistently, and more visibly, than most other 'yan daudu I knew.

Despite his apparent disregard of certain aspects of Islamic morality, I soon discovered that Hajiya Asabe's commitment to his faith was more sincere than I had initially thought; his irreverence had definite limits. Like many ethnographers, I learned of these limits accidentally, by transgressing them in a way that left me embarrassed but enlightened. On another visit to Sabon Gari, when Hajiya Asabe and I were sitting in his room to escape the midday sun, I sought to explain my ethnographic interest in the language practices of 'yan daudu. With my limited, graceless Hausa, I told him how I had initially come to Nigeria to learn about the speech of *malamai*, Islamic scholars, but that I had eventually lost interest in that topic. "Staying with them is not pleasurable," I said, "and their talk is not interesting." At this Hajiya Asabe's facial expression suddenly changed from that of a sympathetic listener to one showing hurt and indignation. "Sani," he reprimanded me quietly. "This is our religion."

Cultural and Sexual Citizenship in Northern Nigeria

In the Hausa-speaking region of Northern Nigeria, prevailing interpretations of *Shari'a*, Islamic law, mandate a strict separation of the sexes and different rules of behavior for women and men in virtually every facet of life. 'Yan daudu break those rules. As men who are said to talk and act 'like women,' they are widely perceived to be witty and clever, but they are also persecuted for their presumed involvement in heterosexual and homosexual prostitution. This book is about 'yan daudu (singular: *dan daudu*) in and around Kano,

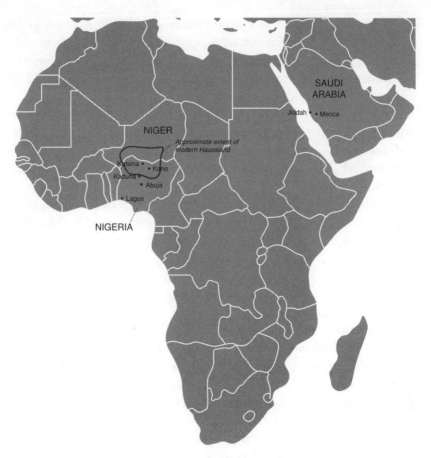

Fig. 1.1 Approximate extent of Hausa city-states since 1810 C.E.

the economic and cultural center of Hausaland, whose government joined that of eleven other northern Nigerian states in officially adopting Shari'a in 2000.[1] (See Figures 1.1 and 1.2.) An ancient Islamic emirate that grew rich from the trans-Saharan trade, Kano today is one of Nigeria's and Africa's largest cities. It is also the hub of a transnational network of 'yan daudu, independent women, and other gender and sexual minorities that links cities and towns throughout northern Nigeria with Hausa-speaking communities in other regions and countries.

'Yan daudu are most visible in urban markets and motor-parks (taxi and bus stations) where they cook and sell food to male workers and

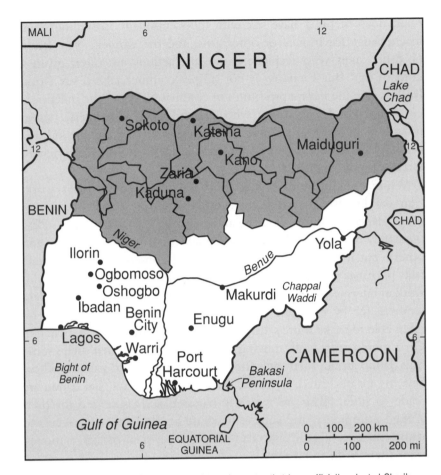

Fig. 1.2 Nigeria. Shaded area indicates the twelve states that have officially adopted Shari'a since 1999.
Source: Courtesy of User:Morwen according to GNU Free Documentation License
http://www.gnu.org/copyleft/fdl.html

travelers. Some 'yan daudu live or spend time at 'women's houses' where they and 'independent women' [*mata masu zaman kansu*, literally 'women who live on their own'] entertain male visitors. The term *gidan mata* ['women's house'] is often translated as 'brothel,' reflecting the popular image of independent women as 'prostitutes' and of 'yan daudu as their 'pimps' or as 'homosexual prostitutes' themselves. The translations are misleading. Some independent women, as they generally prefer to be called, and some 'yan daudu, especially younger ones, do sometimes have sex with (conventionally masculine) men in exchange for money or other gifts; and the women, 'yan daudu or other men who facilitate these interactions are often given a kind of tip.[2] But karuwanci is not simply commercialized sex work. Rather, like the malaya prostitutes in colonial Nairobi,[3] the independent women and 'yan daudu who live and work at women's houses provide a number of services other than sex: they serve food and drink, play cards and board games, and engage their visitors in friendly, flirtatious conversation.[4]

While cooking and serving food is considered women's work, 'yan daudu often describe their other feminine social practices – songs, dances, gestures, clothing and language – as 'play' [wasa]. 'Play' accurately reflects the pleasure these practices bring to 'yan daudu and others, but it belies their serious, material consequences. 'Women's talk' [maganar mata], for example, is useful for those 'yan daudu who work as intermediaries [kawalai] between male patrons and independent women, for by engaging men in flirtatious banter 'yan daudu are often able to make more satisfying, and potentially lucrative, matches. On a more covert basis, moving and talking 'like women' helps some 'yan daudu attract their own friends, sex partners and patrons. These benefits are mitigated, however, by the material ways 'yan daudu are made to suffer: they are regularly harassed and ostracized for their alleged immorality, and subject to abuse at the hands of police and young male hooligans, who can assault, rape, steal or extort money from them with impunity.

Nigeria – a member of OPEC – is rich with oil and other resources, but 'yan daudu, like other Nigerians, are overwhelmingly poor and illiterate, and they suffer from the economic deterioration wrought by years of corruption and mismanagement by politicians, military dictators, businessmen, multinational corporations and international lenders.[5] In addition to the impoverishment caused by this corruption, 'yan daudu and karuwai are often scapegoated for it – accused of conspiring with corrupt 'big men' [manyan mutane] who use their ill-gotten wealth to satisfy their legendary appetites for sex and other pleasures. From a cosmological standpoint, many Hausa Muslims believe their collective suffering is God's punishment for disobeying Him, and Muslim leaders commonly blame karuwai and 'yan daudu for promoting such disobedience. In the last half of the twentieth century, if not earlier, Northern Nigerian states, emirates and municipalities periodically enacted morality campaigns similar to the ones that accompanied the recent adoption of Shari'a; most of my 'yan daudu acquaintances had been arrested or worse at some time or other.[6] What was different in 2000 was that these campaigns were not confined to a particular territory or jurisdiction, and they did not quickly dissipate; rather, they constituted a broad, and seemingly more durable, movement to construct a Northern Nigerian public – a kind of nation, often termed simply *Arewa* ['the North'] – supposedly unified by its adherence to orthodox Islam.

While 'yan daudu have been subject to both official and unofficial persecution for at least several decades, with the adoption of Shari'a they became even more vulnerable. Why have 'yan daudu been targeted? How, in the face of these and other challenges (including poverty and HIV/AIDS) have 'yan daudu's social networks managed to survive? What do 'yan daudu's experiences tell us about gender and sexuality, culture and nationalism, religion and power in Northern Nigeria, in other postcolonial societies, and in the contemporary world at large? As this book will show, the answers to these questions lie to a great extent in the ways 'yan daudu use language, their bodies, and other media to 'play,' as they put it, with the boundaries of what it means to be male and female. For better and for worse, 'yan daudu attract the attention of many Hausa Muslims because, in the time since Nigeria received its independence from Great Britain in 1960, Islamic norms of gender and sexuality have come to be seen as symbols of Northern Nigerian culture – a culture that some people imagine is threatened by, and in competition with, other parts of Nigeria and the Judeo-Christian West.[7] Islamic reformists' ideas about how 'good' Muslim women and men should talk, dress and act are a central element of these norms, and it is to these ideologies that many people refer when they condemn 'yan daudu as 'bad' Muslims and 'worthless people' [*mutanen banza*].[8]

This book describes 'yan daudu's social practices as claims to and performances of *cultural citizenship*. The concept is similar to what is often called 'identity,' but I use it here to emphasize certain things. First, as defined in political theory, the concept of 'citizen' is defined in opposition to other social actors who do not enjoy full citizenship rights because of their age, gender, caste, race, disability, or other forms of embodied social difference. 'Citizenship' thus emphasizes the hierarchical nature of social constructions of identity, and the negotiations and conflicts that inevitably take place over who can do what, where, when, with whom and with what resources. Second, while legal citizenship is defined with respect to political units (states), 'cultural citizenship' calls attention to the fact that identities are embedded within particular social fields and institutions, including religion, commerce, work and leisure. Collectively, these (non-state) social fields are known in political theory as 'civil society' and in communication theory as the 'public sphere.'[9] Third, the term 'cultural' reminds us that participation in social life is not solely a matter of power relations, but also needs to be understood in terms of aesthetics, emotions and beliefs.[10]

'Cultural citizenship' thus refers to the things different people do in their day-to-day lives (as well as the things they don't or can't do), and the effects their actions have for them and for others.[11] These effects can be understood at various scales of social and spatial organization, from small-scale 'communities of practice' such as households, workplaces and neighborhoods, where social interactions are often face-to-face,[12] to large-scale 'imagined communities' such as nations, religions, political movements, classes, genders and races.[13] As an intermediate level of social-geographical organization, cities provide a focal point for empirical research and theorizing that link these smaller and larger scales.[14] Insofar as participation in the public sphere is constrained by and reproduces differences of gender or sexuality, we can speak of *sexual citizenship* as an integral aspect of cultural citizenship.[15]

As a linguistic anthropologist, I am especially attentive to the importance of language as both a medium of social participation and an object of criticism and control. At the same time, I am mindful that language is one of many media that human beings use to fashion and transform the relationships, communities and institutions that are meaningful to them. With respect to 'yan daudu, this book explores linguistic and bodily performances – 'masculine' and 'feminine', playful and serious – that challenge the arguments of Islamic reformists, African nationalists and others who insist that 'Islam' or 'African culture' is inherently hostile to, or devoid of, gender and sexual minorities. I also aim to show how 'yan daudu's citizenship claims challenge the arguments of Western-educated scholars and activists who assume that 'modern' and 'global' constructions of gender and sexuality are inevitably based on Euro-American models.

Who are 'Yan Daudu?

When I describe 'yan daudu as 'feminine men' to people from the USA and other Western societies, I am often asked, "Are they gay?" The answer is not straightforward. In the earliest days of my research, when all I knew about 'yan daudu was what other people had written or said about them, I imagined I might, as a gay man, be able to become involved in their largely hidden social world. I was intrigued the first few times that I saw 'yan daudu strolling and dancing at nightclubs and outdoor parties, and could not help but compare these images to gay life at home. Although subsequent events forced me to reconsider, but not to reject outright, the naive idea that 'yan daudu were men with whom I could communicate on the basis of a shared sexuality, my interactions with them introduced me to a thriving social world of men who acknowledged and acted upon their sexual attraction to other men. These men comprise what could arguably be called a Hausa homosexual community, though their social life differs in important ways from gay life in the West.

One comparison that seemed apt in the 1990s was that, as drag queens and 'fairies' did for straight-acting gays in mid-twentieth-century New York City,[16] 'yan daudu's visibility and social proximity to karuwai attracted conventionally masculine 'men who seek men' [*maza masu neman maza*] and permitted them to meet without blowing their cover. 'Yan daudu often call these men 'civilians' [*fararen-hula*], 'yan aras (an in-group term with no independent meaning), or simply 'men' [*maza*]. The men typically identify themselves as *masu harka* ['people who do the deed'], a 'secret' code term that embraces both 'yan daudu and 'civilians' and is preferred over the standard Hausa term, 'yan ludu ['sodomite,' literally 'people of Lot']. Many masu harka, including those who speak little English, also describe themselves as *homos*, especially when talking to outsiders like me. (The word *gay* tends to be used only by more educated urbanites.)[17] Some 'civilians' secretly self-identify as 'yan daudu – talking and acting 'like women' in private, while maintaining a masculine occupation and appearance in public. Such men are called 'yan daudun riga ['shirted 'yan daudu'], meaning they treat *daudu* – the practice of men acting 'like women' – like a shirt that can be put on or taken off at will. Unless otherwise noted, in this book 'yan daudu refers to 'men who act like women' openly and are publicly recognized as such.

Unlike most Western men who describe themselves as gay, masu harka do not see homosexuality as incompatible with heterosexual marriage or parenthood, or vice versa. At some point in their lives most masu harka, including a majority of 'yan daudu, marry women and have biological children. I have chosen not to use the term *bisexual* to refer to married masu harka because I understand bisexuality to refer to an individual's capacity to be sexually attracted to both women and men, and to pursue that attraction socially and physically; this implies a degree of choice regarding sex and kinship which is not widely recognized in Hausa society. Specifically, most Hausa people do not see marriage as a choice, but rather as a moral and social obligation; my own refusal to marry based on my lack of sexual desire for women typically did not follow the cultural logic of my homo acquaintances, who did not see a necessary connection between marriage and heterosexual desire. 'Bisexuality' is thus expected of all masu harka, whether or not they actually desire or enjoy sex with women. Although many masu harka say they enjoy sex with women, these men do not constitute a distinct subgroup, since men who do not desire women sexually are unlikely to admit this except to their closest friends.

I have also chosen not to refer to 'yan daudu as 'transgendered' or 'trans.' Although some writers and activists define *transgender* broadly, I generally hear it used to refer either to people who choose or feel compelled to embrace a gender identity 'opposite' or merely different from their ascribed biological sex (e.g., biological men who live as or become women).[18] With the exception of a male 'transvestite' in Kano whose story circulated on the internet in 2004, I have never met or heard about a ɗan daudu who tried to pass as a woman socially.[19] All the 'yan daudu I have known – even those who were consistently referred to by feminine names – saw themselves as 'real' men and enjoyed the privileges that come from that identity, even while they were stigmatized for being 'feminine.'

Another question I am often asked about 'yan daudu is, "Are they accepted?" Many Westerners, it seems, have heard that there are some non-Western societies in which feminine men, or gender and sexual minorities in general, are supposedly treated with more tolerance and respect than such individuals have historically found in 'the West.' The example of the *berdache*, an outmoded, colonial term for transgendered people in certain Native North American societies, is sometimes mentioned in this regard.[20] Another is the *hijra*, a term used in Hindi and other South Asian languages to refer to eunuchs and intersexed people who live as women.[21] Without making explicit comparisons with such groups (whose histories are too complex to be easily summarized), I generally answer that 'yan daudu's presence is universally acknowledged – no one denies they exist – but that their degree of social acceptance has varied according to time, place and situation. To make my explanation more concrete and up-to-date, I sometimes add that in recent years, Islamic reform movements have grown more powerful in Northern Nigeria, and this has made life more difficult for many 'yan daudu. "Oh," I am then likely to hear, "Northern Nigeria is Islamic?!" At this point in the conversation I often feel as if the pendulum of cultural assumption has swung to the other extreme, for if some societies are presumed to be more open and tolerant than 'the West,' others have the opposite reputation; and Islamic and African societies usually top that unfortunate list, especially when it comes to gender and sexuality.

Literary scholar Edward Said has described Europeans' long-standing fascination with gender and sexuality in the Muslim Middle East as *Orientalism*. In his book by that title and other works, Said argues that stereotyped images of belly-dancers, veiled women, sheikhs and terrorists, whether they appear in novels, travel writing or television news programs, have led people of European descent to imagine that they are part of a distinct culture – 'the West' – that is superior to the cultures of the Middle East; these images have been used to justify the efforts of Western governments and corporations to colonize Middle Eastern lands and exploit their resources.[22] In a similar vein, Leila Ahmed has examined the ways British government officials used reports about the supposedly subordinate status of Egyptian women to justify colonial rule in the late nineteenth and early twentieth centuries; yet many of those same (male) British officials opposed the granting of equal civil rights to women in their own country.[23] More recently, the US government used reports about the Taliban's mistreatment of women to justify the bombing of Afghanistan after the World Trade Center attacks in 2001; under US and allied 'protection,' however, the fate of most Afghan women has remained largely unchanged, and unnoticed.

US media coverage of Shari'a in Northern Nigeria shares many of the same Orientalist features. After the first Nigerian state (Zamfara) announced its intention to adopt Shari'a in late 1999, the *New York Times* published a photograph of a taxi with the image of a covered Muslim woman painted on its passenger door, indicating that the taxi was reserved for women only. The *Times* ran this photograph not once, but twice, reinforcing the equation of Shari'a with gender segregation.[24] Neither photograph was accompanied by a story documenting the difficulties women and other Nigerians face in finding adequate, safe and affordable transport of any kind. US media also gave prominent attention to the violence that erupted in Kaduna, a northern city with an ethnically and religiously mixed population, when Shari'a was introduced in early 2000, and again in 2002 when Nigeria hosted the Miss World beauty pageant in its capital, Abuja. In response to Muslim clerics who complained that the pageant objectified women's bodies, a non-Muslim journalist from southern Nigeria wrote, as a kind of joke, that the Prophet Muhammad himself would probably have enjoyed the show and might have taken one of the contestants to be his wife. More than 200 people died in the ensuing clashes between Kaduna's Muslims and Christians, the journalist received death threats and went into hiding, and the pageant was relocated to London. A few months later, the US magazine *Vanity Fair* ran a feature story detailing the events, with a focus on the experiences of the pageant's non-African contestants, though the rioting had occurred over 100 miles away from their Abuja hotels.[25]

Perhaps the most infamous story about Shari'a in Northern Nigeria was that of Amina Lawal, a divorced Hausa Muslim woman who was convicted of adultery by an Islamic court in her home state of Katsina and sentenced to death by stoning. The international attention generated by this case went well beyond press coverage to include a segment on *The Oprah Winfrey Show* and several petitions circulated on the internet, before Ms. Lawal was acquitted on a technicality in 2003. (The adultery trials of two other Northern Nigerian women also made headlines in the West, but not to the same extent.

Both women were acquitted.) Another international controversy erupted in August 2007 when 18 men were arrested at a hotel in the city of Bauchi for allegedly cross-dressing at a same-sex 'wedding.' Local protesters demanded that the men be prosecuted for sodomy (which, like adultery, carries the death penalty), while international gay-rights organizations sent representatives to assist in the men's defense.

These stories are important, for they highlight the degree to which gender and sexuality have become important and controversial sites of cultural citizenship in Northern Nigeria and in much of the contemporary world at large. At the same time, because they tend to focus on spectacular, exotic or horrifying events, stories like these construct a distorted image of Northern Nigerian social life – not because the details aren't true (though they sometimes aren't), but because they tend to leave out the more common challenges and pleasures that Northern Nigerians experience on a day-to-day basis, as well as the social and historical factors that have led to these experiences and make them meaningful.

Because of their wide circulation, such images, along with other exoticizing portrayals of Islam and of Africa, have the potential to influence the way people interpret my accounts of Northern Nigerian life. This makes it challenging for me to talk about my research in nonacademic settings, such as when I'm socializing with family or friends who don't use words like *exoticizing* on a regular basis. I face similar challenges in writing this book. In both cases my audience is similar: people educated in Western societies who are interested in other places and cultures, but who may have little or no scholarly training in African or Islamic studies, anthropology or linguistics. Whatever your background, in reading my stories about 'yan daudu and others, you will undoubtedly be reminded of things you have heard elsewhere about gender and sexuality, language and culture, Africa and Islam. Some of my stories might sound similar to what you've heard; some will clash. Keep track of these reactions. My aim is not simply to debunk or confirm what you've previously been told or believed to be true. Rather, my hope is that you will rethink those ideas, and reconsider their implications: Where do they come from? Who told you about them, and why? How can you know if they're true or false? And what difference does it make?

Encountering 'Yan Daudu

Gender and sexual diversity were not on my professional agenda when I first traveled to Nigeria in 1991 to take a Hausa-language summer course at Bayero University, Kano (BUK), and to do preliminary research for a doctoral dissertation on the language practices of *malamai* (singular: *malam*), Hausa Islamic scholars and teachers. Yet even before I arrived in Kano I knew that local ideologies of gender and sexuality would figure prominently in my day-to-day experiences there. The directors of the language program sent out a letter advising me and my fellow students (14 Americans and one Dutch) that we would be living in the *birni* (also called 'Old City' or just 'City') inside Kano's ancient walls, whose residents are known for their commitment to Islamic social norms. We were therefore instructed to show respect to our hosts by dressing modestly when we went outside – headscarves for women; no shorts or tank-tops for anybody – and to refrain from mixed-sex socializing. The women in our group were encouraged to get to know our female neighbors, most of whom were in seclusion [*auren kulle*, literally 'locked-up marriage'] but could invite female guests into their homes. My female colleagues were also told that while they could greet our male neighbors, it would not be appropriate to shake hands. The men in our group were likewise encouraged to socialize with our male neighbors, but to refrain from greeting our female neighbors even in passing.

Outside the Old City these rules applied with varying consistency, depending on the religious, ethnic and generational affiliations of the people we met and the activities they were engaged in. At BUK, for instance, a predominantly Muslim campus on the outskirts of Kano, the majority of women (most of whom were students) wore colorful head-scarves and perhaps a shawl draped loosely over the head and shoulders; a small number wore their hair uncovered, sometimes with shape-revealing blouses and jeans; others wore a plain-colored headscarf pinned under the chin – a contemporary version of the Islamic *hijab* or 'covering.' (By the early 2000s, this kind of covering had become more prevalent.) Men at BUK displayed a similarly diverse array of clothing, head-coverings and facial hair (or lack thereof). And students of both sexes mingled, or refrained from mingling, in ways that did not correlate with dress in any obvious way.

I returned to Kano in 1992 to embark on my fieldwork with mala-mai. With the help of scholars and staff at BUK (where I taught one course) and the Kano State History and Culture Bureau, I set out to establish contacts with malamai throughout the city, whom I interviewed on the relative value of Islamic and Western-style education and on the pedagogical use of Arabic, Hausa and English. All these contacts were with men, but it did not occur to me at first to question the gender arrangements of my fieldwork or of Hausa society in general. Various experiences, however, led me to reconsider both the methodological approach and substantive focus of my research.

Some of the malamai I interviewed brought up the subject of women even though I had not asked about it directly. Many of my questions dealt with what is often described as a gap in educational achievement between northern and southern Nigeria: northern Nigerians are said to lag behind southerners in the federal, English-medium school system, and this makes it hard for northerners to find salaried jobs in the civil service and private sector. The gap is usually attributed to northerners' traditional preference for Islamic education and their historical distrust of Western schooling, known in Hausa as *boko* (from English 'book'). When I asked one malam to explain the reasons for this distrust, he offered the following illustration. If you go to a business office or government agency here in Kano, he said, you will find southern women working as secretaries and the like, because they have more *karatu* ['reading,' from Arabic *qara'a*], by which he meant *boko*. But in the south, he continued, you won't find northern women working in offices, even if they've had some *karatu*. Why? Because northern women have *ilimi* ['knowledge,' from Arabic *'ilm*], by which he meant knowledge of Islamic scripture. According to this malam, Western schooling might yield practical, economically useful skills, but Islamic education was crucial to the maintenance of a moral social order; and gender segregation – keeping unrelated men and women separate – was a key symbol of that morality.

The prevailing practice of gender segregation affected my informal social interactions as well. Whereas, in the USA, I often spent time with women friends, in Kano, I initially found myself socializing almost exclusively with men, most of whom were, as I was, in their twenties and unmarried. I began to take notice of the ways these men talked about women. Speaking about marriage, for example, many of my acquaintances focused intensely on the issue of control. A man needs to 'control' his wife, they said; at the very least he must be made to feel as if he were in control. This notion of control, especially the controllability of a potential wife, lay behind many young men's preferences for the type of woman they said they wanted to marry: village girls are more controllable than city girls, uneducated girls are more controllable than educated ones, and so on.

Conversations about courtship and marriage were challenging for me in a number of ways. Though I had lived more-or-less openly as a gay man in the USA since my late teens, when I went to Nigeria for my fieldwork, I retreated into what I had learned to call 'the closet': I got a short, conservative haircut, removed my earrings, and answered presumptuous questions – like why I wasn't married and whether I had a girlfriend – with evasive headshakes and shrugs. Most ethnographers, it seems, develop doubts about the feasibility of their projects when they go out of the library and into the field. When I began to have doubts, I thought first about how I might be able to bridge the religious and cultural differences between me and the people I was working with; but I also felt a growing desire to do research that would not require me to suppress the philosophical and political commitments I had embraced as an out gay man. My experience was similar in many ways to the challenges faced by other researchers, especially feminists, lesbians and gay men, who have sought to maintain respect for the people and communities they were working with, even when some of those people said or did things that offended the researchers' own beliefs and values.[26]

As my circle of acquaintances grew and my relationships deepened over time, I made friends with whom I felt comfortable discussing culturally sensitive matters, and who helped me see that northern Nigerian society was far more diverse with respect to gender and sexuality than I had initially recognized. I was especially surprised to find out that Hausa society, and the city of Kano in particular, have a reputation for homosexuality. Many southern Nigerians, for example, deny that there might be men or women in their region who engage in homosexual behavior, and say it's only 'those Muslims' up north (along with decadent Westerners and Arabs) who do that sort of thing. For their part, Hausa people are less inclined to deny the existence of homosexuality in their society than they are to gossip about it, often but not always in disparaging terms. Living in Kano, I heard rumors about the homosexual proclivities of prominent local men, read sensationalistic newspaper stories about homosexual scandals in boarding schools, and heard reports of police raids on bars and nightclubs frequented by homosexuals.

These social experiences led me back to the scholarly literature on Hausa history, society and culture, where I found tantalizing references to 'yan daudu in relation to 'prostitution' [*karuwanci*] and *Bori*, the Hausa cult of spirit-possession whose practitioners are widely condemned by orthodox Muslims as 'pagan' [*arna*] or 'heathen' [*kafir*]. In most of these texts the term *'yan daudu* was translated as 'homosexuals,' 'transvestites' or 'pimps,' none of which turned out to be truly accurate, though they all convey a partial sense of 'yan daudu's activities and social identities. The most helpful source I found – and the only monograph devoted to 'yan daudu – was a master's thesis written by Salisu Abdullahi, a student of sociology at Bayero University, Kano, who later became a lecturer in that department.[27] With his encouragement and advice, I began to consider the possibility of changing the focus of my research from malamai to 'yan daudu.

Academic references and personal contacts thus pointed me to places and events that were far removed, socially if not spatially, from Kano's Old City, where I lived, and the largely conservative, scholarly circles I had been traveling in. I asked to be taken to Bori gatherings, which usually took place late at night in the outskirts of town; and I made my way to other parts of Kano, such as Sabon Gari, where 'prostitution' and mixed-sex socializing, along with alcohol and gambling, were more-or-less tolerated. These wanderings taught me a great deal about Hausa social and cultural geography – the ways people, institutions and activities were distributed in space, and the ways people talked about those places. From my previous visits and readings, I was already familiar with the basic distinction between Kano's *birni*, the area inside its ancient city walls, and the rest of the city, often called simply *waje* ['outside']. A more basic distinction is drawn throughout Hausaland between *gari*, a city or town of any size, and *kauye* ['village, countryside'].[28] (A territory with few or no human inhabitants is called *daji* ['forest, bush'].) These distinctions carry great moral weight, for it was in cities where Islam first established itself in Hausaland hundreds of years ago, while so-called 'traditional' [*gargajiya*] and 'pagan' [*arna*] customs continued to dominate in rural areas well into the twentieth century. In Arabic-Islamic terms, the city represents *dār al-Islām*, the abode of Islam, an oasis of restraint surrounded by *dār al-kufr*, the abode of unbelief, where wild, immoral practices prevail. The moral and aesthetic prestige of the city is also expressed in the lexical distinction between people who are said to be *nagari* ['urbane, sophisticated'; literally, 'of town'], while *kauyanci* ['countryness'] denotes poor manners and a lack of sophistication.

While the city is seen as the cradle of Islamic civilization, cities also bring people and things together in ways that can undermine that exalted image. As we will discuss in Chapter 2, for hundreds of years, Muslim leaders in Kano and other Hausa cities have periodically sought to cast out individuals and practices that they define as contrary to Islam. After the British imperial conquest in the early 1900s, activities like drinking, mixed-sex socializing, and spirit-possession [*Bori*] came to be tolerated in newly constructed 'outside' areas such as Sabon Gari [literally, 'New Town'], a residential neighborhood for poor men who were brought from various parts of British West Africa to work in factories, railway yards and other wage-earning occupations. As happened in other colonial African cities, these areas – known in Hausa as *bariki* [from English 'barracks'] – also attracted young rural women whose prospects for work and marriage were derailed by colonial policies that made traditional forms of farming, trade and family life difficult or impossible. 'Prostitution' (a term that often referred to concubinage or other long-term intimate relationships) was one way these women could support themselves and their families of origin; it was also a way to meet potential husbands.[29]

Sabon Gari was originally built in a rural, sparsely settled area east of the Old City, but as Kano continued to grow over the course of the twentieth century, its location became more geographically central. Only a few kilometers away from the Emir's Palace and the main Friday mosque, Sabon Gari today is adjacent to Kano's most commercially vibrant market and its busiest transportation hub. In addition to a diverse population of Muslim and Christian northerners, the area is home to a large community of migrants from neighboring countries and other parts of Nigeria, many of whom operate video stores, restaurants, barber shops (known in Nigerian English as *barbing saloons*), and auto-parts kiosks. The number of churches rivals that of mosques, and the sounds of Hausa commingle with those of Igbo, Yoruba, Pidgin English, French, Arabic and other languages; and it is not uncommon – even after the adoption of Shari'a – to see men walking outside in shorts or women with their heads uncovered. (Bariki areas in other cities and towns have become less free-wheeling.)

In spite of its association with cultural 'Others,' the bariki is a quintessentially Hausa construct, defined both spatially and socially in opposition to more respectable and homogeneous urban neighborhoods. In day-to-day Hausa discourse, a neighborhood's degree of moral respectability is often expressed in terms of the marital status of the women who live there. In Zakawa, for example, a roadside community on the outskirts of Kano with a high concentration of bars, hotels and women's houses, I was told many times that the number of married women (as opposed to 'prostitutes') was no greater than ten out of a population of several hundred. This improbable claim reflected the town's reputation, similar to Sabon Gari's, as a kind of sin city, where men could go to indulge in alcohol and drugs, attend performances of traditional music and Bori, or meet women, 'yan daudu or other men for companionship and sex. Barikis are said to be home to 'worthless people' [*mutanen banza*] – including karuwai, 'yan daudu, drug-dealers and thieves – while 'honorable people' [*mutanen kirki*], that is, married men and their families, live in areas where 'women's houses' are prohibited. If a married man is forced by poverty or other circumstances to set up his household in a bariki area, he may try to protect his own and his family's honor by painting the words MATAN AURE – BA'A SHIGA ['Married Women – Do Not Enter'] on the wall outside his home.

After my first personal contacts with 'yan daudu in the spring of 1993, I spent 12 months over the next year and a half visiting women's houses, nightclubs and restaurants in Kano. I also took periodic trips outside the city to attend *bikis*, festivities hosted by 'yan daudu and independent women that are modeled after the parties organized by married Hausa women to celebrate weddings and the naming of babies. All these places and events were open to the (male) public. Over time I established friendly relations with 'yan daudu in several locations that I began to visit on a regular basis. In addition to several spots in Sabon Gari, these locations included: a restaurant and some 'yan daudu's homes in Rijiyar Kuka, another 'outside' Kano neighborhood; a restaurant in the Old City of Katsina, a smaller but equally ancient Hausa emirate located north of Kano, near Nigeria's border with the Republic of Niger; and the market area of Madari, a small town located approximately 200 km southeast of Kano. The overwhelming majority of 'yan daudu I met were Nigerian Hausa Muslims, though some had other ethnic affiliations, especially Fulani. A small number were Muslim, Arabic-speaking immigrants from Chad or Sudan, or Christians with roots in southern or central Nigeria who had been born, raised or educated in the North. I also became acquainted with masu harka, 'men who do the deed,' whose sense of 'honor' [kirki] and 'shame' [kunya] sometimes made them hesitant to associate publicly with 'yan daudu. One mai harka who was not so hesitant was Mai Kwabo, a married 'civilian' who had many friends and acquaintances in the bariki areas in and around Kano. Because his regular job required his services only intermittently, and because he enjoyed spending time in the bariki, he agreed to work as my assistant in 1993–94.

Mai Kwabo introduced me to a number of the 'yan daudu who helped me in my research, and was instrumental in orchestrating most of the audiotape recordings that are transcribed and analyzed in Chapters 3–5. The number of recordings I was able to make (eight) was limited by 'yan daudu's sensitivity to outside interference in their affairs, and by my hesitation to arouse their suspicions by forcing the issue. Most of my collaborators had had little or no formal education in either the Islamic or Western [boko] school systems, and were therefore unfamiliar with the idea of original academic research, especially on topics that are unrelated either to Islamic scripture or to 'modern' subjects such as English, medicine or engineering, which are seen to have practical applications. The very word bincike ['research'] was understood by many people to mean government-sponsored spying. It was thus helpful and accurate to emphasize that my interest in 'yan daudu had to do with their celebrated linguistic expertise. Indeed, the tapes I made with my 'yan daudu friends, along with our many unrecorded conversations, did more than help me improve my ability to speak and understand Hausa; they also helped me learn how to use the language to play with and influence others.

When I started to test the waters with respect to changing my research topic from malamai to 'yan daudu, I was concerned about how my local scholarly contacts would react to a shift of focus from the most respected class of men in Hausa Muslim society to one of the most reviled. The process of changing my topic, therefore, involved not only trying to meet 'yan daudu, but also paying attention to the ways other people reacted to my new-found interest in them. Following the advice of several Nigerian friends (and the examples of men from my Old City neighborhood whom I occasionally ran into in the bars of Sabon Gari), I was careful not to appear 'too interested' in 'yan daudu, in order to avoid giving the impression that they were fixing me up with female karuwai, or that I was being sexually active with 'yan daudu themselves. In this context, too, it was helpful and appropriate to frame my research interest in linguistic terms – to say, for example, that I hoped to learn more about the Hausa language from listening to the clever ways 'yan daudu are said to use *karin magana* ['proverbs'] and *habaici* ['innuendo'] (see Chapter 4). As it turned out, my status as a foreigner made it relatively easy for me to move back and forth between places and social settings with different moral reputations. My white skin made me conspicuous, of course, but it often seemed to inoculate me from the social judgments that would likely be passed against a 'respectable' Hausa man who socialized openly with 'yan daudu and other 'people of the bariki' [*mutanen bariki*]. (I say 'seemed to inoculate' because my sense of my moral reputation sometimes turned out to be naïve. Still, I was repeatedly told by many Nigerian friends that as a white man and foreigner I could get away with morally questionable behaviors that they could not.)

I also became sensitive to the fact that some Hausa Muslims are wary of the interest many Western researchers seem to take in religiously sensitive topics like polygamy and wife-seclusion, or in stigmatized aspects of Hausa culture such as Bori and prostitution. In recent decades, there has been a profusion of research on the lives and experiences of Hausa women;[30] there has also been considerable research on practices and institutions that appear to defy orthodox Islamic norms, such as the occupational choices of independent women,[31] Bori spirit-possession practices;[32] charismatic and ecstatic religious movements;[33] youth gangs;[34] and controversial genres of popular culture, such as romance novels and video-films.[35] Like other researchers, I knew that my questions about Hausa Muslim cultural and religious norms, especially with respect to gender and sexuality, could easily come across as disrespectful – not only towards the society at large, but also towards the people who were helping me learn about it. This generated an ethical tension that lasted throughout my fieldwork and continues even today. While I have by no means resolved it, this tension has been intellectually and spiritually productive, for I came to see that many 'yan daudu (and others) had a similarly contradictory relationship with 'respectable' Hausa Muslim society, adhering to beliefs and practices that conformed to dominant cultural values, while sometimes saying and doing things that appeared to deviate from those values.

After completing my doctoral fieldwork in 1994, I returned to Nigeria four times, in 1997, 2000, 2002 and 2006. These visits ranged from one to two months each, and occurred during northern Nigeria's rainy season [*damina*] between the months of May and August. On each trip, I endeavored to revisit my earlier fieldsites in order to greet my friends and acquaintances, to find out how they were doing and how their lives and circumstances had changed. The changes I observed on these visits made me realize that the artifacts I had gathered in the early 1990s – audiotaped conversations, videotapes of bikis, newspapers, invitation cards, fieldnotes – were the products of a particular moment in the history of Kano, Northern Nigeria, and the world, and in the lives of particular individuals (including myself). With respect to the ethnographic statements I make in this book, therefore, when I use the present tense, I do so because it is my understanding that they describe Northern Nigerian social life at the moment of this writing. Otherwise, I use the past tense, in order to emphasize that my observations were historically specific, not timeless reflections of an unchanging Hausa Muslim culture.[36] I have also tried to refrain from referring to 'cultures' and 'societies' as naturally existing, monolithic entities ('Hausa culture,' 'yan daudu society,' 'Western culture,' etc.) except as these concepts have been imagined, talked and written about by others. When I do use such expressions, I hope not to overlook the fluid nature of 'societies' and 'cultures' or the diversity and inequality that inevitably exist within and between them.

One of the most important historical developments of the last decade, for 'yan daudu and for all Nigerians, has been the explosion of the HIV/AIDS epidemic. Unlike eastern, central and southern Africa, where HIV/AIDS began decimating communities in the 1980s, West Africa did not experience the ravages of the disease on a wide scale until the following decade. In the early 1990s, the Nigerian government was only beginning to address the epidemic and the topic was rarely discussed in the press or in everyday conversation. Among the 'yan daudu and masu harka whom I met at that time, I knew of only one young man who was said to have died of *kanjamau* ['slimming'], as AIDS is called in Hausa. (The word *AIDS* is also used.) By the time I returned in 1997, however, several of my friends and acquaintances had fallen ill or died with symptoms that seemed to indicate advanced HIV infection, though the cause of death was often described as emaciation [*rama*], tuberculosis [*tarin tibi*] or simply 'lack of health' [*rashin lafiya*].

Also in the last decade, historical developments occurred in two other social fields – politics and popular culture – that had a transformative effect on 'yan daudu and on Northern Nigerian society at large. In the political realm, the sudden death in 1998 of Nigeria's military dictator, Sani Abacha, paved the way for national elections in which Olusegun Obasanjo, an army general and former military ruler, was chosen to become the country's first civilian president since the last one had been overthrown by a coup d'état in 1983. Abacha, like most of Nigeria's previous heads of state, was a Hausa-speaking Muslim (born and raised in Kano), while Obasanjo is a Yoruba Christian. Less than five months after Obasanjo's inauguration in May 1999, the state of Zamfara adopted Shari'a, and within a year and a half, eleven other states had followed suit. Although a number of political leaders and commentators insisted that the adoption of Shari'a violated constitutional provisions against the establishment of a state religion, the Obasanjo administration did not formally challenge it. The federal government thus averted a political crisis that some feared could escalate into civil war.

I arrived in Kano in June 2000 shortly before the state government staged an elaborate public ceremony 'launching' Shari'a. As the largest state in the region, its ceremony attracted hundreds of thousands of people (including several 'yan daudu friends of mine) and a host of dignitaries from as far away as Libya and Saudi Arabia. In preparation for the ceremony the government mobilized police and posses of Shari'a-enforcers known as *hisbas* to go around the state warning bar-owners of the impending ban on alcoholic beverages and admonishing 'prostitutes' [*karuwai*] to get married or to leave the state. 'Yan daudu were also targeted by this moral purification campaign. According to the *New Nigerian*, a government-owned newspaper, ridding the state of 'yan daudu and karuwai would "boost morals" and "check vices," creating the social conditions necessary for the full implementation of Shari'a later that year; and the improvement of public morality along Islamic lines would lead to justice and prosperity for all.[37] A number of 'yan daudu and independent women were evicted from the 'women's houses' where they lived and worked. Some took refuge with family or friends, while others fled to states where Shari'a had not been adopted. Most remained in Kano, where they were vulnerable to harassment, arrest and occasional violence that was sponsored, or at least tolerated, by the state. Similar circumstances befell 'yan daudu and independent women in other Northern states.

When I returned to Nigeria in 2002, I was apprehensive about how Shari'a might have affected my friends who were 'yan daudu or independent women. Would I even be able to find them? In most cases, if they had left their old homes and places of work, I would have no easy way of tracking them down; they didn't have telephones or mailing addresses. As things turned out, I did not manage to find most of my old friends, but Shari'a was not the main reason. HIV/AIDS and other illnesses had killed some of them; others had moved to other parts of Nigeria or to Saudi Arabia, usually for economic reasons. The consequences of Shari'a were uneven and contradictory, and fell harder on independent women than they did on 'yan daudu. Independent women who ran restaurants in Kano and other large cities were generally left alone, while women who were believed to practice 'prostitution' had to get married or find a 'legitimate' occupation – no easy task for women who were poor, uneducated and estranged from their families. Independent women fared even worse in smaller towns like Madari, where they were forced to give up even 'legitimate' businesses.

Recent developments in media technology and popular culture have also proved challenging to the proponents of Shari'a. One such development is the Hausa-language film industry, which has grown exponentially since the late 1990s thanks to the widespread availability of inexpensive video production equipment, videocassette recorders and, most recently, digital video technology. Based in Kano, the Hausa video-film industry has produced hundreds of comedies and dramas and created a new class of film 'stars' [*taurari*] whose lives are a matter of intense public interest. The Hausa film industry's success is one result of the liberalization of Nigeria's economy that has taken place in the past 20 years, largely at the behest of international financial institutions and multinational corporations. In Northern Nigeria, these changes have enhanced the influence of wealthy local businessmen, many of whom subscribe to Islamic reformist ideologies that privilege individual piety, and individual success or failure, as opposed to older Islamic movements, like the Sufi orders, that emphasize group worship and loyalty to traditional hierarchies.[38] Yet capitalist competition requires producers to attract mass audiences through marketing strategies that cultivate consumers' aesthetic and emotional desires, which can clash with the sober norms of reformist Islam. Tellingly, much as their predecessors did with respect to movie houses in previous eras, some Islamic clerics have condemned Hausa films for promoting immorality and have called for the closing of commercial video parlors.[39] For their part, the industry's executives and artists consistently defend their films as socially enlightening and consistent with Islamic principles. These responses highlight some of the cultural contradictions that have surfaced in recent years, complicating efforts by Islamic reformists to construct a Northern Nigerian public unified by its commitment to normative Islam.

Outline of the Book

Subsequent chapters are organized as follows.

Chapter 2: People of the Bariki surveys how representations of 'yan daudu, 'prostitutes' and Bori practitioners changed in the decades before this project began, and connects these changes with the rise of Islamic Northern Nigerian nationalism.

Chapter 3: Out in the Open considers the relationship between daudu as an occupation and dan daudu as a public identity by examining dan daudu's stories about how they 'went into daudu' and the intimate relationships they formed with other 'yan daudu and with 'men.'

Chapter 4: Women's Talk, Men's Secrets describes how 'yan daudu use 'feminine' ways of speaking to convey 'secret' meanings about sex and other experiences, and relates these practices to the in-group code used by 'yan daudu and other 'men who seek men.'

Chapter 5: Playing with Faith describes how 'yan daudu use humor to 'play' with what it means to be Hausa and Muslim, and the ways they negotiate limits on what I call their 'faithful irreverence.'

Chapter 6: Men on Film compares representations of 'yan daudu in two audiovisual texts – a commercial feature film and videotape of a 'dan daudu's biki – and relates these to changing definitions of Northern Nigerian 'nationhood' and what it means to be a Hausa Muslim man.

Chapter 7: Lost and Found in Translation considers recent 'exposés' of 'homosexuality' in Northern Nigeria as evidence of a global trend toward sexual explicitness that is at odds with the playful, humorous practices of 'yan daudu.

Epilogue: May God Keep a Secret describes the fates of the people and places whose stories you have read. (Note that pseudonyms are used for all people and places, except for public figures, large cities and Sabon Gari.)

Notes

1   Of the twelve Nigerian states that have adopted Shari'a, native speakers of Hausa form the majority in nine (Bauchi, Gombe, Jigawa, Kano, Kaduna, Katsina, Kebbi, Sokoto, Zamfara). Hausa is widely spoken as a second language and lingua franca in the remaining three (Borno, Niger, Yobe) and in several neighboring states (especially Adamawa, Nassarawa, Plateau, Taraba).
2   Kleis and Abdullahi (1983).
3   White (1990).
4   See Pittin (2003) for a richly detailed account of the lives of independent women in the northern Nigerian city of Katsina in the late twentieth century.
5   Okonta and Douglas (2001).
6   Pittin (2003); Umar (1993); Pierce (2003).
7   I use 'Northern' (with a capital 'N') to refer to the ethno-regional community whose members are imagined to be unified by adherence to Islam and proficiency in Hausa (as either first or second language). The former British Protectorate of Northern Nigeria included this region along with others – many in what is now called the Middle

Belt – where the majority of residents were (and in many cases still are) neither Muslim nor native speakers of Hausa.

8 I use the phrase "Islamic reformist" to refer to social movements that seek to bring Muslims' social practices into conformity with the norms that prevailed in the earliest Muslim community during the lifetime of the Prophet Muhammad. To the extent that such movements advocate or engage in political action, I call them 'Islamist' (Soares 2005; Kane 2003; Umar 1993).

9 Habermas (1989); Gal and Kligman (2000); Calhoun (1993).

10 Hochschild (1983); Abu-Lughod (1986); Lutz and Abu-Lughod (1990).

11 Stevenson (1997); Rosaldo (1997).

12 Lave and Wenger (1991); Eckert and McConnell-Ginet (1992); Wenger (1998).

13 Anderson (1991).

14 Low (1999); Pellow (2008); Gregory (1999); Modan (2007); Harvey (2006); Sassen (2001).

15 Evans (1993); Kaplan (1997); Leap (2004a).

16 Chauncey (1994).

17 For other ethnographic treatments of the use of *gay* and related terms in cross-cultural settings, see Johnson (1997); Kulick (1998); Murray (2000); Manalansan (2003); Sinnott (2004); Boellstorf (2005); Valentine (2007).

18 Surgical transsexualism is not available in Nigeria and was unknown to many of the 'yan daudu with whom I talked about the issue. I never heard any 'yan daudu mention transsexualism as an option they would like to have available to them.

19 http://news.bbc.co.uk/2/hi/africa/3615082.stm

20 Roscoe (1991); Williams (1986); Whitehead (1981); Epple (1998); Gilley (2006).

21 Nanda (1990); Hall (1995a, 1997).

22 Said (1978, 1981, 1993).

23 Ahmed (1992). See also Stoler (1995).

24 The photograph, taken by Ryan Lash, accompanied articles written by Norimitsu Onishi on December 8, 1999, and January 29, 2000.

25 Bachrach (2003).

26 Leap and Lewin (1996); Kulick and Willson (1995).

27 Abdullahi (1984).

28 Yusuf (1974).

29 Cf. White (1990), Stoler (1995), Ferguson (1999).

30 Callaway (1987), Coles and Mack (1991); Hutson (1999, 2001); Werthmann (1997, 2000); Cooper (1997); Nast (2005).

31 Pittin (1983, 2003); Cooper (1995); Masquelier (1995).
32 Besmer (1983); Masquelier (2001); O'Brien (2007); Krings (1999).
33 Casey (1998); Watts (1999); O'Brien (2007).
34 Last (1991); Casey (2008).
35 Whitsitt (1998); Larkin (2002b; 2008); Adamu (2006); Furniss (2003).
36 Fabian (1983).
37 *New Nigerian* (2000). See Last (2008) for a historical–ethnographic account of the *hisbas*.
38 Grégoire (1993); Kane (2003); Mahmood (2003); Soares (2005).
39 Larkin (2002a, 2008); Bauchi (2005).

PEOPLE OF THE BARIKI

Like the 'women-only' taxis paraded before the international news media, the hisbas hired to enforce Shari'a were a spectacular symbol of the Northern Nigerian state governments' commitment to Islamic law and the promise of a new age of moral and social justice. Yet the service performed by the hisbas – the policing of public behavior by underemployed young men – was not a novel feature of Northern urban life. By the early 1990s, certain neighborhoods of Kano's Old City (see Figure 2.1) – not the ones I lived in – had become well known for their intolerant ways: where Nigerian Christians and other 'foreigners' might be looked at with suspicion; where a woman driving a car might be harassed by boys wielding rocks and yelling, "*Karuwar gwamnati!*" ['Government prostitute!']. In Sabon Gari and other bariki areas, young male hooligans would sometimes assault, rob or even rape independent women or 'yan daudu, whose status as 'worthless people' gave them little hope of legal redress. Indeed, the police themselves often acted outside the law, staging late-night raids on nightclubs or women's houses, where they would arrest independent women and 'yan daudu on charges of 'indecency' and 'vagrancy,' and hold them at the police station until someone paid the 'fine,' that is, a bribe. Other civilians – musicians, barmaids, janitors, or male customers – were less likely to be arrested unless they got in the way of the police or caused some kind of disturbance (e.g., because they were drunk).

Because I tended to go home early, I usually managed to avoid these raids. Sometimes Hajiya Asabe sent me home because he'd heard through the grapevine that someone had been tipped off about a

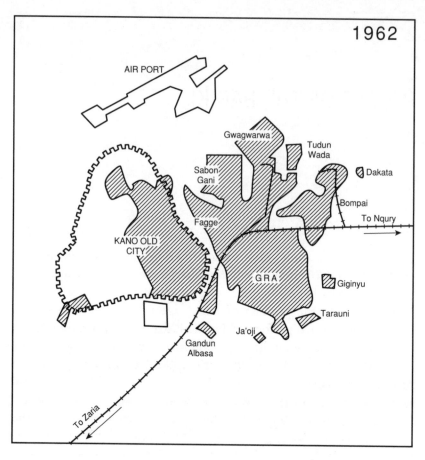

Fig. 2.1 City of Kano just after Nigeria's independence. GRA stands for Government Reserve Area, a neighborhood originally built for colonial residences and government buildings.
Source: Courtesy of J. Antwi and M. A. Liman, Dept. of Geography, Bayero University, Kano.

raid: "*Koma gida, Sani, wai za'a yi kame*" ['Go home, Sani, it's said arrests will be made']. On the few occasions when I was present for a raid, the police ignored me. One night I accompanied Hajiya Asabe and a group of his friends to the police station, where another friend of theirs was being detained. As we waited around for the 'fine' to be processed, I was struck by how calm and ordinary the scene appeared. Some sharp words were exchanged as Hajiya Asabe and his friends haggled with the police over the amount of the fine, but similar 'quarrels' were performed thousands of times every day as shoppers bargained with vendors at the nearby Sabon Gari market. Afterwards, when Hajiya Asabe's friend had been released and we were walking him home, I heard numerous curses and complaints about the police, but these too sounded routine.

But was this always the case? Had 'yan daudu always been subject to the stigma and persecution that I witnessed or heard about in the 1990s and early 2000s? Had they always associated with 'prostitutes'? Had they always been sought by men who appreciated their food, their charm, their graceful bodies? How long had 'yan daudu even existed as a named social category?

The historical record is exceedingly limited. As far as I know, neither the term ɗan daudu nor descriptions of men acting 'like women' appear in writing, in Hausa or in English, until the early twentieth century. When such references do appear, they were usually authored by people – Britons, Nigerians and Americans – who had little first-hand acquaintance with 'yan daudu. Many of these authors were scholars; some were colonial officers; others were seemingly ordinary Nigerians who had the privilege of being literate in Hausa or English. Most were men. Yet even within these narrow parameters (narrowed still further by the fact that I am not a trained historian), the range of representations is illuminating. Though it is not (yet) possible to ascertain the origins of daudu as a social practice, the available evidence suggests that the term ɗan daudu was in use before the British conquest, with some, but not all, of the cultural meanings it has today. In particular, all the texts I have found refer to 'yan daudu in relation to 'prostitution' [karuwanci] or spirit-possession [Bori], or both.

In surveying the texts excerpted below, this chapter aims to answer the following questions: Where, when and by whom have 'yan daudu been noticed? What places, people and activities have they been associated with? How have they been judged? And how have these representations changed over time? In particular, how is it that, by the late twentieth century, 'yan daudu had come to be identified in many people's eyes as sexual outlaws – people whose gender and sexual practices made them unfit for membership in Northern Nigerian society?

'Yan Daudu and Bori

Along with other 'people of the bariki' [*mutanen bariki*], 'yan daudu and independent women are often condemned as 'worthless people' [*mutanen banza*] and as *'yan iska*, an epithet that literally means 'children of the wind' or 'children of the spirit,' though its practical meaning is 'bad people' or 'rogues,' sometimes with the added pejorative force of the English insult *asshole*. By definition, *'yan iska* are said to engage in *iskanci*, literally 'spiritism,' used as a blanket term for immoral behavior. The association of the bariki with *iskanci* implicitly points to another group of people, *'yan Bori* ['Bori practitioners'], whose rituals revolve around communicating with 'spirits' [*iskoki*] in a way that violates orthodox Islamic norms. People who join the Bori society (or 'cult') typically suffer from physical or mental afflictions caused by spirits, and they let spirits 'mount' [*hau*] them in order to appease them. Initiation involves working with senior adepts to diagnose which spirit (metaphorically thought of as a 'horse' [*doki*]) has caused one's affliction and to learn how to prepare oneself to become that spirit's 'mare' [*godiya*]. It is not belief in spirits *per se* that troubles orthodox Muslims, for the Qur'an itself refers to *jinn*, or what Hausa call *aljanu* ['Muslim spirits']. Rather, it is Bori adepts' willingness to let spirits possess or 'mount' them that orthodox Muslims view as *shirk*, the sin of associating lesser beings with the supreme power of Allah. For their part, virtually all Bori practitioners today are Muslims and view their ritual 'play' [*wasa*] as compatible with God's will, for it was He who created the spirits and rules over them. Since the adoption of Shari'a, Bori has been banned from the public sphere, its members forced to perform their rituals surreptitiously, in remote villages or inside private homes.

Fremont Besmer's (1983) ethnography of Bori musicians, *Horses, Musicians, and Gods*, is one of the most widely cited references with respect to 'yan daudu. Based on fieldwork he conducted in Kano in the early 1970s, Besmer describes 'yan daudu as frequent participants in what he calls 'possession-trance' performances. According to him, Bori is a refuge for people considered 'deviants' in the wider Hausa society, "including prostitutes, male homosexuals, and the psychologically disturbed."[1]

One whose status identity is somewhat ambiguous, arising from some personal characteristic (homosexuality, transvestism, nymphomania, etc.) ... can seek either to have his social identity changed or his social status regularized and defined through participation in bori rituals. Marked by 'abnormality' and accepted as a candidate for membership in the cult through an identification of iskoki ['spirits'] as the cause of the problem, a person's behaviour becomes explainable, and simultaneously earns a degree of acceptability, after completion of the bori initiation.[2]

Besmer's study is frequently cited as evidence of a cultural association between homosexuality and spirituality not just in Hausaland, but in the 'traditional' religions of Africa, the Americas and the Pacific Islands. A common theme in these works is that in many (if not all) 'traditional' societies, male homosexuals and/or feminine men (the two concepts are often combined) enjoyed respect and authority because they were seen to have privileged knowledge of the supernatural realm. With the arrival of scriptural religions, especially Christianity or Islam, homosexuals supposedly lost these positions and were condemned as immoral.[3] Besmer gives qualified support to these arguments. Citing Beattie and Middleton's observation that "there is an association in some cultures between male homosexuality, with transvestism, and spirit-possession, especially where mediumship is mainly a female concern," Besmer adds, "The Hausa are a case in point."[4] Yet he also notes that he saw no 'yan daudu "fall into trance" themselves. Instead, they "appear at public bori performances where they dance in an effeminate manner." Like other onlookers, 'yan daudu also gave small amounts of money to cult members who did fall into trance.[5]

The 'yan daudu Besmer met were especially fond of a Bori spirit known as Dan Galadima. Galadima is a noble title, roughly akin to 'duke.' The term originally came from the Kanuri language spoken in Borno, a formerly powerful Muslim empire in what is now northeastern Nigeria. Galadima also seems to have been the indirect source of the term dan daudu. Besmer explains:

Daudu is a praise name for any Galadima (a ranked title), but it specifically refers to the bori spirit, Dan Galadima (lit. 'son of Galadima'; the Prince). The Prince is said to be 'a handsome young man, popular with women, a spendthrift, and a gambler.' ...

Informants were unable to provide a reason why male homosexuals should be identified with his name, and the association remains unexplained.[6]

Besmer thus gives two translations of *Dan Daudu*: 'male homosexual/ transvestite' and 'a supernatural spirit' in the Bori pantheon; much as I do with respect to the word *Bori*, he uses capital letters to mark this religious association. While this spelling is unarguable with respect to the spirit's name, it overstates the relationship between 'yan daudu and Bori in general. As Besmer acknowledges, the 'yan daudu he met had not been initiated into the cult, and they played other social roles outside Bori, namely, cooking and selling food and serving as intermediaries between 'courtesans' (i.e., independent women) and their patrons.[7] Thus, while Besmer's study has been used to support the argument that 'homosexuals' and/or 'transvestites' have played significant roles in certain 'traditional' religions around the world, his reported observations cast doubt on that argument with respect to 'yan daudu and Bori.

The connection Besmer notes between 'yan daudu and the spirit Dan Daudu points to other possible interpretations. In particular, it calls into question the degree to which both the spirit and the social category of 'yan daudu can be considered 'traditional.' As noted above, *Galadima* was originally a Kanuri title for a noble office. Its use in Hausa seems to derive from the political marriages and diplomatic alliances that used to take place between the Hausa and Borno royal families.[8] Since these families embraced Islam hundreds of years ago, it seems fair to suggest that the origins of *daudu* as a social practice should be sought not in the supposedly pre-Islamic traditions of Hausaland, but in the political, religious and sexual contacts that have historically taken place between the Hausa city-states and the wider Muslim world. As a number of scholars have shown, these contacts have had such a transformative effect on Hausa social life that it is now difficult, if not impossible, to distinguish 'pre-Islamic' from 'Islamic' beliefs and practices; even the religious practices of non-Muslim Hausa known as Maguzawa have been substantially influenced by Islam.[9]

When Hausaland was colonized at the start of the twentieth century, the Hausa city-states had existed for almost a millennium, and their rulers, known by the Hausa title *sarki* ['king'] or *sarauniya* ['queen'], had been at least nominally Muslim for about four hundred years. (When a city-state embraced Islam, it became known as an emirate, and its ruler took the Arabic title *amīr* ['emir'].) The oldest and largest of these cities were called the 'Seven Hausa' [*Hausa Bakwai*], and they traded, conspired and fought wars with one another and with other neighboring states, including Borno. Some Hausa cities, especially Kano and Katsina, grew rich from the trans-Saharan trade in gold, slaves, and other commodities, which attracted traders, travelers, and immigrants from near and far.

In the early 1800s, inspired by Islamic reform movements in North Africa and Arabia, local reformists waged a jihad against the Habe (ethnic Hausa) emirs, who were accused of betraying Islamic norms of governance and justice. Under the leadership of Usman dan Fodio, an ethnic Fulani Muslim scholar whose ancestors had migrated to one of the 'Seven Hausa' cities, the jihadists succeeded in overthrowing most of the Habe dynasties and replacing them with Fulani emirs who swore allegiance to a centralized Islamic Caliphate based in the city of Sokoto (in present-day northwestern Nigeria). Some Habe rulers escaped the jihad and fled north towards the Sahara, where they established emirates in exile. Public life in the Caliphate was dominated by the *ulama*, Islamic scholars, most of them men, who wrote treatises and sermons to ensure that Shari'a was observed by rulers and subjects alike. Most of these texts were written in Arabic, though some scholars also used an adapted version of the Arabic alphabet known as *ajami* to write occasional texts, especially song-poems [*waka*], in Hausa or Fulfulde (the Fulani language).[10]

One aspect of social life that was radically transformed as a result of the jihad was gender relations. The jihad's legacy is hotly debated. A number of feminist scholars have argued that under Caliphate rule, women lost much of the power they had previously wielded in the Hausa city-states. According to this narrative, before Hausa rulers embraced Islam, they relied on *bokaye*, 'priests' and 'priestesses' whose special abilities to communicate with the spirit world enhanced their worldly power; women are believed to have enjoyed privileged positions in these secret religious societies. Islam's establishment as the state religion supposedly replaced this egalitarian (or even matriarchal) system with a patriarchal one. Because many Hausa people (including those who had embraced Islam) continued to seek solace and power from spirits, however, Muslim Hausa kings (and at least one queen) generally tolerated these popular religious practices, and sometimes made tactical alliances with non-Muslim priests and priestesses. Some Hausa women also exercised power as royal wives, concubines and queen-mothers.

Usman ɗan Fodio and his successors sought to end these practices in strict conformity with Shari'a. Bori was an early and frequent target of the new regime's restrictive policies, though given the cult's continuing popularity, certain caliphs and emirs sometimes chose to make deals with Bori leaders rather than fight them.[11] In a more elite realm, Heidi Nast has documented how the jihadists' commitment to sexual propriety led to an extensive architectural restructuring of the Kano Emir's Palace, which had the effect of segregating palace women more strictly than they had been under Haɓe rule and greatly constraining their social, economic and political activities.[12] According to Usman ɗan Fodio, these measures were necessary in order to stamp out the supposedly un-Islamic 'innovations' that had been tolerated by the Haɓe emirs; these included "the staying of men at home and the going out of women to market, competing with men" which he condemned as "an imitation of Europeans."[13] While some feminist scholars lament the Caliphate's legacy, other observers see cause for celebration, insisting that the jihad emancipated women from the oppression they had suffered under the corrupt Haɓe emirs. Others, including a number of feminists, advocate a more balanced perspective, noting that, while Shehu Usman did restrict many women's activities, he also encouraged women to pursue Islamic education, allowing some women to achieve success and influence as Muslim scholars and teachers.[14]

In the so-called 'Scramble for Africa,' when the European powers divided Hausaland, they reproduced a geopolitical division that had existed for almost one hundred years: Great Britain was awarded most of the Caliphate, while the 'exiled' Hausa emirates became part of French West Africa (and later, the Republic of Niger). After proclaiming the 'Protectorate of Northern Nigeria' in 1900, British armies finally conquered the region in 1903. The united 'Colony and Protectorate of Nigeria' was created in 1914, with separate administrations for the Northern and Southern regions and for the capital, Lagos.

Colonialism was a fundamentally political and economic enterprise, motivated by competition among European governments and companies over land, resources and human labor. Over time, however, European elites came to justify colonialism in anthropological terms, as the natural and desirable outcome of their own racial and cultural superiority. Drawing on northern European scientists' theories of racial and cultural evolution, many Britons viewed colonization as a moral duty, or what Rudyard Kipling called 'the white man's burden' to 'enlighten' the world's 'primitive' races by exposing them to Christian European 'civilization' and 'modernity.' Those same theories also led British officials to look for racial, cultural and linguistic differences among the peoples they colonized, and to classify and rank each 'tribe' and language as more or less 'civilized.'[15] What counted as 'civilized' were those traits and practices that British observers saw as similar to their own. Hausa-speaking Muslims, with their traditions of literacy, scriptural religion and centralized government, were regarded as one the most 'civilized' races in all of sub-Saharan Africa, and lighter-skinned Fulani were considered especially 'evolved.'[16] By contrast, ethnic groups that had more 'Negro' features, or lacked writing, or whose political systems were more diffuse and egalitarian were deemed 'primitive.'

The cultural features that made Northern Nigeria seem more 'civilized' also made it an ideal location for the system of colonial governance known as Indirect Rule. Modeled largely after British imperial rule in India, Indirect Rule entailed appointing local African rulers to serve as the so-called 'Native Authority' on behalf of the British Crown. The system was designed to make colonial rule maximally effective at minimal expense, for it relieved the imperial government of the cost of setting up and staffing an entirely new administration. Additionally, by accommodating local customs, the British hoped to forestall the possibility of uprisings and revolts.[17] In most of Northern Nigeria, the Native Authority incorporated the administrative structures of the Sokoto Caliphate. In order not to antagonize the *ulama*, Christian missionaries were forbidden to evangelize, especially in urban areas where Muslim influence was strongest. Yet Indirect Rule did not mean that the British accepted Caliphate culture exactly as they found it; certain cultural practices were validated as 'traditional' while others were ignored or changed to suit the colonists' needs. For example, Hausa rather than English or Arabic was made the language of administration, and it now had to be written in roman script, not the Arabic-based *ajami*. This language policy revealed the colonists' ambivalence towards Islam: while it was certainly preferable to 'pagan' religious traditions, it was also regarded as less 'civilized' than Christianity and a potential source of resistance to imperial rule. Accordingly, the British often tried to emphasize 'Hausa' language and culture at the expense of Arabic and Islam.[18]

Mahmood Mamdani has described how the privileges bestowed on the Native Authorities often led to competing claims within a given 'tribe' over what its 'traditions' really were. The winning claimants – the people and institutions that were recognized as 'customary' – often used their power to suppress groups and activities that threatened their authority.[19] The 'Hausa' (or 'Hausa-Fulani'[20]) elites who sought positions within the Northern Nigerian Native Authority could point to a number of beliefs that they shared with the British in order to enhance their own power. For example, the notion that Hausa Muslims were more 'civilized' than non-Muslim Africans was compatible with an Islamic narrative of history that posits Islam as the most advanced state of human consciousness and social organization. Even the notion of Fulani racial superiority – though contrary to the egalitarian principles of Islam – echoed popular beliefs that Fulani or Arab blood was more prestigious and desirable than 'pure' Hausa (Habe) ancestry.

'Hausa' Muslim leaders also shared with the British a disdain for Bori. The energetic music and dancing, partial nudity and cross-dressing that accompanied spirit-possession struck Caliphate leaders and Christian colonizers alike as 'pagan' and 'uncivilized.' British colonial officers who studied the region's history were impressed to find out that in the late 1800s the last two precolonial emirs of Kano ordered certain Bori leaders executed, presumably because they were seen to pose a threat to the emirs' authority.[21] As documented by Susan O'Brien, while British officials had similar concerns about Bori's potential for political destabilization, they had trouble accepting the Muslim scholars' description of Bori as a pre-Islamic Hausa tradition. If that were true, the principle of Indirect Rule would compel the colonizers to accommodate Bori as a 'customary' practice in the same way that they were accommodating Islam.

An alternative explanation of Bori's origins would help them avoid this dilemma. Such an alternative presented itself when colonial administrators noticed that Bori was being practiced not just in rural villages, but also in urban areas where male workers indulged in alcohol and socialized with 'prostitutes.' This led some British observers to conclude that Bori was not a 'traditional' African custom, but a 'modern' problem that arose when Africans were detached from their traditional, rural roots and brought to live and work in colonial cities. In 1909, for example, a British official in Bauchi, an emirate southeast of Kano, reported:

> Bori is now most generally practiced in the "barrack" markets and small villages close to a Government Station where there are a large number of soldiers, police, servants, labourers etc. all of whom have money and a large capacity for amusement and sexual indulgence. The Bori man thus becomes merely a purveyor of whores and makes no inconsiderable income from his disgusting trade.[22]

A similar report was filed by one Mr. Rowe from Muri, a small emirate in what is now the east-central state of Taraba:

> Bori, prostitution and manufacture of liquor are all closely inter-related and it is lamentable to think that the place where liquor is sold and strumpets gather should now be known as "Gidan Governor" [Hausa for 'Governor's House'] from the fact of its being licensed . . . It is the bori men in female attire who particularly need to be suppressed.[23]

By "bori men in female attire," Rowe was probably referring to male adepts who were possessed by female spirits; such men may or may not have been 'yan daudu.[24] Whoever the men were, it is notable that he was troubled by their presence near the Governor's House, the primary site and symbol of British imperial rule.

The concerns expressed by Rowe and other officials reflect anxieties about gender, sexuality, nation and race that were prevalent among elite British men at the time. Back in England, Oscar Wilde had scandalized the public with his flamboyant style and open affection for boys, and was jailed for 'gross indecency' in 1895.[25] Male Bori practitioners had a similarly scandalizing effect on colonial observers, who described them as 'hysterical' and 'irrational,' implicitly comparing them to women. In both England and

Nigeria, male femininity, along with prostitution and other social problems, was seen as a symptom of moral decay caused by urbanization and modernization. Official responses to these problems differed according to race and location. In Britain, where the urban working classes were mostly white, the dangers they posed to social order were interpreted as the negative side-effects of economic progress, which could be remedied through a combination of policing, education and charity – the cornerstones of the modern fields of sociology and social work. In Nigeria, meanwhile, as in other colonized regions, colonial governments initially sought to prevent the 'natives' from becoming 'too urbanized' and 'too modern' on the grounds that they were constitutionally unsuited for the responsibilities and temptations of 'civilization.'[26] As Charles Temple, the lieutenant-governor of Northern Nigeria, wrote in a 1918 report entitled *Native Races and Their Rulers: Sketches and Studies of Official Life and Administrative Problems in Nigeria*, "The native in place of enjoying a robust constitution becomes fretful, excitable, and irritable, prone to tears. He becomes a ready victim to the vices of the white man."[27]

'Yan Daudu on the Eve of Colonial Rule: Baba of Karo Remembers

Whereas British colonists saw Bori as a sign of racial weakness brought on by modernity, Caliphate leaders saw it as an immoral throwback to pre-Islamic traditions. Both groups implicitly associated Bori with female power and saw it as a potential threat to their authority. But how did ordinary Hausa people view it? Here the historical record is especially slim, for it reflects the concerns of the people who wrote it, the overwhelming majority of whom (in Nigeria, Great Britain, and elsewhere) were elite men. It is partly for this reason that social historians use the method of oral history, for it provides access to observations and perspectives that might otherwise go unnoticed.

As far as I have been able to ascertain, the earliest recorded descriptions of 'yan daudu appear in *Baba of Karo: A Woman of the Muslim*

Hausa, a pioneering example of oral history that has been highly influential in the study and teaching of African and women's history. Baba was an elderly Hausa woman who agreed to tell her life story to Mary F. Smith, a British anthropologist, over a period of six weeks in 1949–50. Baba (whose name, pronounced *báabà*, means 'mother') was born and raised in Karo, a hamlet in the town of Zarewa in the southern part of Kano Emirate. (Today it is located in Kaduna state.) She was probably around 70 years old when she died in 1951, so her childhood memories – which include 'yan daudu – certainly predate the British invasion. Smith transcribed Baba's autobiography by hand and published an English translation in 1954; her husband, M. G. Smith, a renowned historian and social anthropologist, wrote the introduction. In 1991, Mary F. Smith published a Hausa version, *Labarin Baba: Mutuniyar Karo ta Kasar Kano* ['The Story of Baba: A Woman of Karo in Kano Emirate'], which purports to represent Baba's narrative "exactly as she dictated it"; by contrast, "the English version re-ordered the text for greater continuity."[28]

The following excerpts contain Baba's most detailed descriptions of the 'yan daudu she knew when she was 8 or 9 years old. Here, as elsewhere, she talks about 'yan daudu in relation to two social institutions: Bori and 'prostitution' [*karuwanci*].

> In the old days, Bori was prostitutes' work. But some men did it too. There were two [men who did Bori] in my family . . . Their Bori was good. But there were more women . . . In our neighborhood they didn't do Bori. Only in town at the prostitutes' compounds, we would go there and watch . . .[29]
>
> They would do their playing in the morning. After the [Muslim] mid-afternoon prayer they would do Bori. Sometimes if there were a lot of them, they would go to the market and do it there. One morning they went to the house of the Emir [of Zarewa]. He came out in his turban and appointed one of them Magajiya ['Chief of the prostitutes']. He said that if any man took a prostitute to his house and did not give her any money, she was to take a complaint to the Magajiya, who would make the man pay the woman her money and also fine him. That is, he gave her authority to do this. We would go and watch, their neighborhood was near to ours. When they did Bori, their drumming prevented us from sleeping.

There were some 'yan daudu's houses in the Illalawa neighborhood. As for prostitutes' houses, there was Auta's house at the North
Gate, Lemo's house at the South Gate, and the Magajiya's house
near the butcher's neighborhood. 'Yan daudu aren't healthy, they've
become like women, some of them even put on women's clothes.
They built and rented out rooms in women's compounds, and the
prostitutes would give them a little money. I remember Danjuma,
Citama, son of the blacksmiths, and Balarabe. 'Yan daudu, there
they were, very beautiful to look at, like women. But they weren't
healthy, they could not go to men or to women. They put on fine
clothes and ate nice food, that's all. The prostitutes would hire huts
from them and pay them money, and in the day they would go to
market and sell farm produce on commission, as the Chief Food-
broker does here – but he's healthy all right – he's always out chasing
women![30]

Keeping in mind that Baba recounted these events more than 60
years after she experienced them, and that we have no record of the
questions Smith asked her, Baba's narrative provides intriguing clues
about the social status of 'yan daudu, 'prostitutes' and Bori before
colonial rule. It is notable, for example, that as a child in a small
town, Baba knew several 'yan daudu by name, associated them with
'prostitutes' and Bori performances, and was not forbidden to interact with them.[31] Baba's account of 'yan daudu's participation in Bori
is especially interesting. Whereas Besmer describes 'yan daudu as
onlookers at Bori performances, Baba suggests that some 'yan daudu
got 'mounted' by spirits. In a subsequent part of her narrative,
she notes that the Emir of Zarewa appointed one ɗan daudu and
three 'prostitutes' as the town's official 'keepers' of Bori.[32] Finally,
although the spirit known as Ɗan Galadima did appear at the performances Baba witnessed, where he was addressed honorifically
as *Daudu*, she says nothing about 'yan daudu having any special
relationship with this spirit. (Interestingly, it was a woman – Baba's
aunt – who got 'mounted' by Ɗan Galadima.[33])

A comparison of the Hausa and English versions of Baba's life story
suggests that some of the choices Mary F. Smith made in the older,
English translation paint a somewhat different picture of 'yan daudu
from what Baba may have intended. In particular, in the English version Smith mistakenly renders the term *'yan daudu* as *'yandauda* ['sons
of dirt'], implying a negative moral judgment that Baba does not

seem to have shared. A question is also raised by the footnote in which Smith defines 'yandauda as "male homosexuals who associate with prostitutes, often acting as their agents."[34] This definition is different from Baba's, who describes 'yan daudu as "unhealthy," by which she seems to mean impotent, because, according to her, "they could not go to women or to men." (Note also that in the original Hausa version, Baba says, "*ba su iya zuwa wurin maza ko mata*" ['they could (or can) not go to men or women']; in the English translation Mary F. Smith switched the order of the sexes.)[35]

Because neither Smith nor Baba was likely to have had direct knowledge of 'yan daudu's sexual lives, both women's statements probably reflect assumptions based on what they heard people say about 'yan daudu or feminine men in general. Baba equates male femininity with impotence, a condition that she seems to view as unfortunate but not morally blameworthy. She also seems to take for granted that there are some men who 'go to men'; such men could presumably have been described in English as homosexuals or bisexuals, but Baba portrays them as neither feminine nor 'unhealthy.' By contrast, Smith's definition of 'yandauda as homosexuals seems to reproduce the stereotype of the effeminate homosexual that was prevalent among many mid-twentieth-century Western social scientists. Her definition may not have been entirely inaccurate, however, for if some men do 'go to' men, some men (like women) must be 'gone to.' Baba does not say who the latter might be, but it is possible, based on her account, that they include 'yan daudu. In any event, Baba's discretion on this topic stands in sharp contrast to Smith's performance of scientific confidence and clarity.

In the Hausa version of Baba's life story, the paragraph about 'yan daudu cited above appears in a section entitled "The Story of Ramatu" [*Labarin Ramatu*], in which Baba describes her father's marriage to a woman who had previously been a 'prostitute' [*karuwa*]. The translation of *karuwa* as 'prostitute' needs to be critically examined, for as a number of scholars have noted, the English term has connotations of impersonal, commercialized sexual encounters that do not accurately reflect *karuwanci* as it was historically practiced in Hausaland. In Baba's account, the defining characteristic of a *karuwa* is her autonomy. Before she married Baba's father, for example, Ramatu is said to have 'roamed the world' [*yawo duniya*]. This metaphor has long been used to describe the behavior of young people of both sexes who leave their family homes in search of autonomy and adventure; this behavior is widely assumed to include immoral activities, including 'forbidden' sexual encounters. In older Hausa-English dictionaries, *karuwa* is translated as a 'profligate person' – male or female – sometimes in addition to 'prostitute.'[36] This suggests a moral judgment that that was not limited to sexual immorality. Given the orthodox Muslim view of Bori as social and spiritual practices that deviate from Islamic norms, it is not surprising that *karuwai* – deviant people – should be associated with it. The fact that, by the late twentieth century, *karuwa* had come to refer specifically to 'prostitute' in the conventional, Western sense of 'sex worker' presumably reflects the increasing influence of patriarchal capitalism in Hausa society. This influence began in the precolonial period, when the Hausa city-states grew rich from the vibrant regional and trans-Saharan trade, but it intensified in the colonial and postcolonial periods.

'Yan Daudu, 'Prostitution' and Northern Nigerian Nationalism

As nationalist movements intensified across Africa following the Second World War, Northern leaders became anxious about the relative power they would wield in a postcolonial Nigerian state. Southern Nigerians, whose experience of British colonialism had been longer, generally had greater proficiency in English and were over-represented in the civil service. Discourses of Northern nationalism thus came to have two targets: the British and Southerners, who were often construed as the colonists' lackeys. These discourses oversimplified the cultural, linguistic and religious complexity of both regions; they also obscured divisions and struggles within the North's political establishment. In the periods before and after Nigeria's independence, the conservative Northern Peoples Congress (NPC) dominated the more radical Northern Elements Progressive Union (NEPU) in part by stressing the need for Northern unity in the face of Southern competition.[37] This political opposition was informed by class divisions, regional rivalries (especially between Sokoto and

Kano), and competition between Islamic Sufi orders, all of which had roots in the precolonial era.[38]

Gender and sexuality were implicated in this rising Northern nationalism, often with specific reference to the 'problem' of 'prostitution.' In his study of land and property law in colonial Kano, for example, Steven Pierce notes how concerns about a supposed increase in the number of 'prostitutes' led to changes in the Emirate's inheritance laws in the 1920s and 1950s.[39] The 'problem' of prostitution in Kano also featured prominently in newspaper articles that Jonathan Reynolds came across while doing archival research on northern Nigerian politics in the pre-independence era.[40] These articles (which Reynolds kindly passed on to me) report that, in the late 1950s, the Native Authority of the Northern Region ordered police to stage a series of raids on nightclubs where prostitution was said to take place; women who patronized such establishments were assumed to be prostitutes and were arrested. At first glance these raids seem consistent with the British government's long-standing concern over the moral deterioration of city life and the negative effects this had on social order and economic productivity. These concerns were evident in colonial officers' observations about bariki life in the early twentieth century; they were also evident in other colonial cities, such as Nairobi, Kenya, and Kitwe, Northern Rhodesia (now Zambia), where the British made repeated efforts to limit prostitution by making it difficult or illegal for unmarried women to live there.[41] An editorial in the Daily Comet, a Kano-based daily written primarily in English, asked, "Will driving away or arresting undesirable women solve the complex and intricate problem of prostitution?"[42]

Though their effects may have been questionable, campaigns against prostitution, and against immorality in general, enjoyed a fair amount of popular support. On July 6, 1959, the Northern Star, another Kano newspaper, published on its Hausa page a reader's letter asking the Emir and the Emir's Council to help solve a number of social ills, including "the stupid behavior of 'yan Daudu." The letter-writer also wanted to put pressure on prostitutes to get married.

Wipe Away Our Tears

From Kumbo, Kano.
After a thousand greetings I'm asking for a little space in your Prestigious newspaper, so that I might submit our complaint to our great leader the Emir of Kano, and his council, may they help us ban Banjo Dancing [*Rawar Banjo*], and Admonish prostitutes to get married, and other things, like *Dara* playing, and gambling, and the stupid behavior [*shashacin*] of 'yan Daudu.

The reason I'm submitting this complaint of ours is because no respectable Muslim [*musulmin kirki*] would want these kinds of immorality [*iskanci*] to take place in Muslim lands [*kasashen Musulmi*].

I hope the honorable Emir of Kano and his council will agree to wipe away these tears of ours.

In his effort to protect Kano's and Northern Nigeria's status as a 'Muslim land' [*kasar Musulmi*], the writer invokes two oppositions – Muslim vs. non-Muslim; respectable [*na kirki*] vs. unrespectable – both of which are indexed by the label *iskanci*, which I have translated as 'immorality.' In this case, the writer is criticizing behaviors he believes are incompatible with Islam: the Qur'an explicitly forbids gambling and prostitution, while banjo dancing and *dara*-playing were presumably objectionable because they were done in mixed-sex groups; *dara*, a board game known elsewhere in Africa as *mancala* or *bao*, may also have involved gambling.[43] "The stupid behavior of 'yan Daudu" presumably refers to their 'feminine' ways of acting.

Other letter-writers focused more specifically on 'yan daudu. A 1957 letter to the *Daily Comet* claims that 'yan daudu "do more damage [*barna*] than prostitutes, and transgress the limits set by God . . . But every day it's the thing that keeps spreading in this Islamic country of ours."[44] This writer also claims that the Prophet Muhammad had expelled 'yan daudu from the first Muslim community. There is, in fact, a *hadith*, or codified tradition, in which the Prophet is said to have identified four categories of people who "get up in the morning while they are under the wrath of Allah and they sleep in the night while they are under the displeasure of Allah": "Those men who try to resemble women and those women who try to resemble men (through dress and behaviour) and those who commit sex with animals and lastly those men who commit sex with men."[45]

Arresting Prostitutes, Donkey is Left Alone While Cargo-sack is Beaten: What about 'Yan Daudu? – By M. Muhammadu Korau

Dear Editor: –
Greetings, I would like a little space in your newspaper, which says the truth, to convey my complaint, and that of the Kano public [jama'ar Kano] in general, to the Kano Council with respect to the arrests of women that have been taking place these days.

It's a really difficult thing in this situation that we're in now that we're about to receive our independence in this country, various things keep coming up that make no sense.

Almost every day or every year there are preparations and orders to arrest women on the grounds that they supposedly cause the lack of rain and other problems. In my opinion however if anyone should be arrested it's 'YAN DAUDU because they are the ones who are spreading obscenity [asharranci] in this city along with other things that it would not be appropriate for me to say in this upstanding newspaper.

It's shameful to say that in a city like Kano every day women are frightened which doesn't happen in other cities, and if this happens it should now stop.

The kind of diabolical things [shaidancin] that 'YAN DAUDU do in this country are a thousand times worse than what women do, yet it's the women who are being punished. [Editor's note: Upper-case was used for emphasis in original text.]

Government campaigns against prostitution also faced opposition on political grounds. In July 1959, the *Daily Comet* reported accusations that the Native Authority, which was controlled by the NPC, had instructed its police only to arrest women who were associated with the opposition party, NEPU. In a letter to the editor that appeared on the paper's Hausa page, one reader claimed, "Today there are more than 100 NPC women in this city whose houses have not even been entered, while NEPU women have been arrested and carried off in cars."[46] The paper's editorial page admonished the Native Authority not to let political rivalries interfere with the fair enforcement of policies: "If we must allow a Halimatu to support the NPC we must at the same time allow a Gambo to pin her tent with the NEPU – that is democracy we inherited from democratic Britain." A spokesman for the Native Authority denied the accusation and affirmed that prostitutes were being arrested regardless of geographical origin, religion or political leaning.[47] In these newspaper articles and letters to the editor we read complaints about 'yan daudu, prostitutes and the general moral decline of Muslim Hausa society, referred to as *jama'a* ['people, public'] or *ƙasa* ['land, country'].

After Nigeria's independence in 1960, political and ideological conflicts within Northern Nigeria were compounded by the growth of Islamic reform movements which drew their inspiration from Saudi Wahhabism and the Iranian revolution.[48] Like the Haɓe emirs in the early 1800s, the Northern ruling classes responded to reformists' accusations that they were overly tolerant of un-Islamic 'innovations' and Western influence, and sought to defend their moral legitimacy by affirming their commitment to orthodox interpretations of Islamic scripture, leading to the eventual adoption of Shari'a by 12 Northern Nigerian state governments in 1999–2001.[49] The promotion of Shari'a can thus be seen as a response to political struggles within Northern Nigeria as well as between the imagined Muslim North and Christian (or pluralist) South.

Although 'yan daudu's legal and social circumstances have worsened in the wake of these developments, they faced ostracism and persecution long before the adoption of Shari'a. Consider, for example, the following excerpt from a song-poem by Aƙilu Aliyu, a well-known poet who was active in NEPU in the years before and after independence.[50] Entitled "Ɗan Daudu," the poem was published in a 1976 booklet entitled *Fasaha Aƙiliya* ['Aƙilu's Art'], which has been reprinted numerous times and continues to be sold in urban markets and college bookstores. Its polemical tone is typical of the *waka* genre as interpreted by politically minded poets.[51] (Line numbers, punctuation and capitalization are reproduced from the original publication.)

1	*Af! jama'a, ku bari in waigo,*	Ugh! people, allow me to take a look,
	In taɓa ɗan rakiyar Ta-Makwalla.	To walk along a bit with She-Who-Gossips.
2	*Shin kuwa ko kun lura da shi dai,*	Have you had a chance to look at him,
	Ko in fallashi jakin mata?	Or should I expose this women's donkey?
3	*Can wani shashashan daga gefe,*	There, that idiot off to the side,
	Wofin wofiyo, banzar banza.	Fool of fools, worthless worthlessness.
4	*Domin in nuna shi a fili,*	Let me show him out in the open,
	Har ma ai masa kallon banza.	So he can be seen in all his worthlessness.
5	*Ɗan-hamsin yake, ko Ɗan Daudu?*	Is he Ɗan-hamsin, or Ɗan Daudu?
	Wa ma zai kula garar kashi?	Who will even look at this gift of shit?
6	*Ba shi a tsuntsu, ba shi a dabba:*	He's neither bird nor animal:
	Jemage shi ke, mai ban haushi.	He's a bat, annoying.
7	*Babu fikafikkai gun dabba;*	An animal doesn't have wings;
	Tsuntsu shi kuwa ba shi hak'ori	A bird doesn't have teeth.
8	*Shi dai ya zama jakin-doki,*	But he's become a donkey-horse,
	Ya ɓata wa mazaje suna.	He's ruined the name of men.
9	*Ya ƙi mafi girman darajar tasa:*	He has refused his high status:
	Shi ya zaɓi ta ƙarshen baya.	He has chosen the least of the lot.
10	*Da ninki biyu ce daraja tasa:*	His rank was two-fold:
	Ya watsar, ya riƙe falle ɗai.	But he squandered it, he's kept only one.
11	*Amma dai kuwa ya yi hasara,*	Oh but he's really gone to waste,
	Tun da ya bar gaba domin baya.	Since he's forsaken the front for the back.
12	*Har yau shi kuma ya yi butulcin*	And he continues to show his ingratitude
	Kyautar mai-sama, Sarkin baiwa.	For the gift of the exalted one, the generous King.

13 *Ya ƙi rabon da Ta'ala yayyi,* He's refused the fortune bestowed by the Most High,

    Ya bijire wa umurnin Sarki. He's defied the order of the King.

14 *Ba na son Dan Daudu, haƙiƙa,* I don't like Dan Daudu, truly,

    Mai sha'awa tasa shi ma na ƙi. And anyone who does take an interest in him I also reject.

26 *Wai kuma shi ne Delu da Hansai!* And he calls himself Delu[f] and Hansai[f]!

    Ga shirme maganar ban haushi! Such nonsense, annoying talk!

27 *Ga shagwaɓa ta rashin shan kashi* See how spoiled from not being disciplined,

    Gun Dan Daudu abokin Larai. Dan Daudu, friend of Larai[f].

28 *Ga shewa a tsakanin mata,* See him doing *shewa* among the women,

    Har ya wuce gaba gun kai gara. He even leads the bridesmaids bringing gifts to the groom.

29 *Ban yi nufin zagi ba ga Daudu:* I didn't set out to abuse Daudu:

    Dan nan nasu akwai ɗan banza. It's just that some of them are really worthless.

30 *Ban da nufin Allah, da ƙala'i,* With due respect to God's plan, there's a saying,

    Gara ɓarinsa da haifar banza. Better to miscarry him than to give birth to worthlessness.

31 *Shi marabinsa da 'Alasambarka,'* He who parted from the Most Blessed,

    Tun kwanansa bakwai, ran suna. Since he was seven days old, his naming day.

32 *Ni da a ce ɗana ya zam shi,* If I were told my son had become one,

    Gara a ce mini ya zama gyartai. Better to tell me he'd become a calabash-mender.

33 *Ai da ya zam ɗandaudu, jinina,* Oh, if he were to become a 'dan daudu, my blood,

    Gara ya zam ajali ya sauko. Better his final day had arrived.

34 *Ai, wallahi, da dai ya yi, ni dai,* Oh, by God, if he did that, as for me,

    Gara ya mutu, shi yafi sauƙi. Better he should die, that would be easier.

Aƙilu Aliyu depicts the ɗan daudu as a traitor to God and man. His references to "the name of men," "the gift of the exalted one" and "the fortune bestowed by God" articulate a conviction that maleness is a God-given honor and privilege, the rejection of which is both sinful and absurd. The corollary to this androcentrism is misogyny, which the poet invokes when he mocks the ɗan daudu for calling himself by women's names, for being effeminate and spoiled, and for performing conventionally feminine activities such as gossiping; doing *shewa*, a loud, jeering form of laughter that women typically do in groups; and taking *gara*, the fancy foods and other presents that a bride's female friends bring to the groom on behalf of her parents. The final three lines provide a sobering glimpse of the animus directed against 'yan daudu. In comparing the ɗan daudu unfavorably to a calabash-mender (*gyartai*), one of the lowest-ranking occupations a Hausa man can have, the poet constructs the ɗan daudu as lower than low, unspeakably abject. In his parting salvo Aƙilu Aliyu declares, albeit hesitantly, that he would rather see his son die than become a ɗan daudu. This echoes earlier lines characterizing the birth of a ɗan daudu as "worthless" [*banza*] and worse than a miscarriage [*ɓari*].

Before his death in 1999, Malam Aƙilu (as he was popularly called) regularly performed this and other poems on the radio as well as in other venues. In an homage published on the internet in 2003, Mustafa Adamu fondly recalls listening to these radio performances as a child, and praises the aesthetic and moral contributions Malam Aƙilu made "to Hausa literature, to Northern Nigeria and to his religion."

> Another distinguishing quality of Aƙilu was the way he used his God-given genius in "enjoining what is good" and "forbidding what is bad" as commanded by his religion. He condemned anti-social vices like prostitution and its patronage (in "Yar Gagara" [Unruly Girl] and "Dangata" [Spoiled Child] respectively). He also unleashed his pen, and justifiably too, on the youth who copy the negative, alien cultures of the West.[52]

Because the waƙa genre is traditionally used to make public comments about important social issues, it is appropriate to read the poet's hostile sentiments as pertaining not just to his own household, but to Hausa Muslim society at large. The poem "Dan daudu" can thus be seen as both reflecting and reinforcing the social ostracism that 'yan daudu face and the persecution this leads to. Indeed, Aliyu's angry (hypothetical) rejection of his own son is iconic of the ways 'yan daudu have been, and continue to be, excluded from the Northern Nigerian public sphere.

Another excerpt comes from the end of a 36-stanza poem, "Waƙar Uwar Mugu" ['Song about the Mother of the Evil One'], by Yadudu Hamisu Funtuwa. The poem is primarily a polemic against prostitutes, accusing them of lying, seduction, and greed, and warning male readers not to be led astray by them. The excerpt is instructive for two reasons. First, it links 'yan daudu to prostitution, which in the 1970s was commonly thought to have become a major social problem, partly as a result of the Nigerian Civil War (also known as the Biafran War), which ended in 1970 and left many families impoverished, and partly because of the oil boom, which flooded the economy with cash, making people greedy and corrupt. It was widely assumed that, with their supposed connections to rich and powerful men, karuwai and 'yan daudu were cashing in on this boom. Second, Funtuwa links 'yan daudu to 'traditional' groups, especially Bori, that have historically been vilified by more orthodox Muslims. This linkage reproduces the rather confusing connection between 'modern' and 'traditional' vice that had been identified (and worried over) by the British colonizers and Hausa Muslim elites in the early twentieth century.

32 *Dandaudu wawa, maras mafadi,* Dandaudu, you[m] clown, maleducated,

   Ka tuba ga Allah, ka bar magudi, Repent before God, quit adulterating food,

   Shi ne fa kanwa, uwar 'yan hadi, That's the potash, the mother of adulterators,

   Ka bar daura gyauto, kana yafa shudi, Quit tying wrappers under your armpits and flinging dyed cloth over your shoulder,

   Ka zam sanya riga, kana yin nadi. Put on a man's gown and wear a turban.

33 *Allahu shi ya hallice ka namiji,* God created you[m] as a man,
   Ka bar bata kanka kana hardaji, Quit losing your way and mixing things up,

Da dai namiji bai zama mace, ka ji,	For a man can't become a woman, you hear,
Kaza mace ba ta zama namiji,	Just as a woman can't become a man,
Da dai tsamiya ba ta daidai da gamji.	And the tamarind tree is not the same as the gamji.

34 Ka bar binta boka, kaza masu bori,   Quit sponging off the soothsayers and bori practitioners,

Kaza masu duba, shakiyyan gari,   And the fortune-tellers, the rogues of the city,

Su kan karɓi taure da zakara fari,   With their castrated goats and white roosters [for sacrifice],

Kaza har ajingi, uban masu bori,   And the leader of the bori practitioners,

Wa dannan fa su me miyagun gari.   Those are the evil ones of the city.

35 Kowa ya yarda da su ya yi kuka,   Whoever agrees with them ['yan daudu] should suffer,

Da su da abokansu 'ya'ya na iska,   Them and their good-for-nothing friends,

Idan ka ga taronsu kauce abin ka,   If you[m] see them gathering, hide your things,

Ko sun kirawo ka ma kar ka tanka,   Even if they call you over don't take a step,

In ka ki jin shawarta, ruwanka.   If you refuse to listen to this advice, you're on your own.

36 Alhamdu lillahi na kare waka,   Praise be to God, I've finished the song,

A wannan wuri ne ta kai matuka,   This is where it comes to an end,

Hamisu Yadudu yai wagga waka,   Hamisu Yadudu has measured out the song,

Kar ku ga ban da fasaha ga waka,   Don't think I have no talent for singing,

Ku dai ku dubi nufi ba nifaka.   Pay attention to the message, which has no malicious intent.

Although Funtuwa does not mention the oil boom *per se*, he refers to it implicitly when he accuses prostitutes of traveling from city to city throughout Nigeria, and from bariki to bariki within Kano, assuming a different name in each location. Although prostitutes had long been stereotyped as people who 'roam the world' [*yawo duniya*], they and other Nigerians became even more mobile in the 1970s as the federal government used oil revenues to develop the country's transportation system, importing cars and buses and building intercity highways. Travel also figures prominently in the stories some 'yan daudu shared with me about their lives in the late 1970s and 1980s (see Chapter 3). This is not say the oil boom caused 'yan daudu, or the fictional karuwai in Funtuwa's poem, to migrate as far or as often as they did. But insofar as the civil war and the oil boom brought social and economic dislocations and heightened levels of migration, corruption and hedonistic excess, 'yan daudu and independent women certainly participated in these developments, and it is not surprising that, in some circles, they came to be blamed for exacerbating them. For their part, in the 1990s, I often heard 'yan daudu and independent women speak of the late 1970s and early 1980s as a kind of golden era, when men and money – and men with money – were readily available. Since then, my friends often told me, "Nigeria has been ruined" [*Najeriya ta lalace*].

This was also the era of Nigeria's Second Republic (1979–83), a period of democratic politics that the country had not seen since the First Republic was overthrown by a military coup in 1966. Democracy opened the political stage to a variety of actors. On one hand, 'yan daudu and independent women were recruited by mainstream political parties to enhance their popular support in urban areas.[53] Another group of political actors who benefited from democratization were Islamic reformers, like Sheikh Abubakar Gumi, who in 1978 founded the Society for the Removal of Innovation and Reinstatement of Tradition [Arabic: *Jamāʿatul izālat al-bidʾa wa iqāmat al-sunnah*], better known simply as Izala.[54]

A number of sources indicate that 'yan daudu's social status began to decline noticeably in the 1980s. In part, this may have been due to the long economic decline that set in after the oil boom went bust in the late 1970s. Since 'yan daudu and karuwai had come to be popularly associated with elites, their reputations declined as their elite patrons became increasingly vilified for corruption. But 'yan daudu's decline in status also coincided with the rise of reformist groups like the Izala, the Muslim Brothers [*'Yan'uwa Musulmi*], and others. Dorothy Aken'ova sees a causative connection between these developments.[55] Echoing accounts I've heard from a number of personal acquaintances, she cites interviews that describe how, until the 1980s, 'yan daudu throughout Northern Nigeria lived relatively peaceably with their neighbors; it was not uncommon for people to invite 'yan daudu (along with musicians, praise-shouters and Bori practitioners) to dance and entertain at parties [bikukuwa, sing. biki] celebrating weddings and naming ceremonies. With the rise of Islamic reform movements, these activities and the people associated with them became increasingly unwelcome in respectable society. Vilified for their association with both the (European) bariki and (African, pre-Islamic) Bori, 'yan daudu were thus cast in the para-doxical position of being both too 'modern' and too 'traditional' at the same time, a characterization that has striking parallels with British colonialists' attitudes towards Bori in the early 1900s, and with Northern Nigerian nationalists' xenophobic descriptions of non-Muslim southerners.

'Yan Daudu and the Academic Imaginary

As issues of gender and sexuality became increasingly politicized, academic research on 'yan daudu in the 1970s and 1980s focused largely on their association with karuwanci, translated by scholars as 'prostitution' or 'courtesanship,' in which their role was widely understood to be as intermediaries (kawalai, sometimes erroneously translated as 'pimps') who introduce male patrons to female karuwai. Based on research she conducted in Katsina in the 1970s, Renée Pittin describes 'yan daudu in terms that are similar in certain respects to Baba of Karo's – both observed 'yan daudu at women's houses, cooking food and wearing women's clothes – but they have different ideas about 'yan daudu's sexuality. In particular, Pittin notes that some 'yan daudu are "homosexual" or "bisexual" while others are "heterosexual."[56]

Salisu Abdullahi, writing in the 1980s with his mentor, Gerald Kleis, avoids making such direct claims about 'yan daudu's sexuality. Like Pittin, however, Abdullahi and Kleis argue that daudu is an occupational choice, that is, that young Hausa men become 'yan daudu because of the money they can make as kawalai. They point to Abdullahi's survey data which show that, when 'yan daudu were asked why they went into *daudu*, most of them, though not a huge majority, said it was because they lacked other economic opportunities.[57] Yet the answers 'yan daudu gave in response to Abdullahi's survey questionnaires should be considered critically, in light of the social context in which the questions were asked, rather than as absolute truths.[58] In particular, because 'yan daudu are so highly stigmatized, they are often legitimately wary of outsiders asking after their affairs. It is thus not surprising that a great number of 'yan daudu refused to participate in Abdullahi's survey, which consisted of questions printed in English, though few 'yan daudu are able to read in any language, and fewer still speak English.[59] Some of these questions touched on sensitive topics – such as the level and type of education achieved by the respondent and his parents, or what his father's occupation was – to which respondents could be expected to react with suspicion. Abdullahi also reports that on a few occasions the research assistants he had hired to administer the questionnaires – translating the questions into spoken Hausa, then translating 'yan daudu's responses back into English before writing them down – met with a hostile reception by 'yan daudu, and were verbally and even physically assaulted.

Abdullahi's ground-breaking research shed sympathetic light on 'yan daudu at a time when they were being increasingly ostracized and oppressed. However, the methodological problems he confronted in his research undermines his proposed explanation for why 'yan daudu exist and why they do what they do. Kleis and Abdullahi's claim, for instance, that the 'function' of 'yan daudu in Hausa society is to exercise authority over female prostitutes[60] ignores the fact that many 'yan daudu describe *themselves* as *karuwai*. Their portrayal of the ɗan daudu as a 'double-agent' who associates with prostitutes, and acts like them, as part of a patriarchal conspiracy to keep women under male control, likewise overlooks the extent to which 'yan daudu were being persecuted.[61] Indeed, Kleis and Abdullahi paradoxically reject any notion of 'yan daudu's agency when they allege that a young man's decision to become a ɗan daudu, which involves adopting overtly feminine behaviors whether or not he goes to work as a *kawali*, is determined almost entirely by structural forces external to him. By their reasoning, poor, uneducated Hausa men with no necessary inclination toward cross-gender or homosexual behavior are driven by economic circumstances not only into the world of prostitution, but also into adopting an identity as gender and sexual deviants, regardless of the social and psychological costs.

The ethnographic narratives presented in subsequent chapters challenge these claims on a number of counts, and describe a different relationship between *daudu* and *karuwanci* from that portrayed by previous researchers. Chapter 3 pays particular attention to how 'yan daudu talk about their own lives and work. While Kleis and Abdullahi, echoing popular accounts, cast 'yan daudu as men whose work involves controlling female karuwai, 'yan daudu themselves often describe the relationship between the two groups as being 'like Hassan and Husseini,' the traditional names given to (male) Hausa twins,[62] suggesting that they see themselves as the counterparts of independent women rather than as their social superiors. Furthermore, the fact that many 'yan daudu (covertly) describe themselves as *karuwai* suggests that 'yan daudu's experiences of gender and sexuality must be considered in relation to socioeconomic factors. Abdullahi's reluctance to make 'yan daudu's sexuality a focus of his research was doubtless motivated by the legitimate concerns he had as a young, local graduate student pursuing a highly sensitive research topic, as well as by his own presumed lack of familiarity with the subculture of Hausa *maza masu neman maza* ['men who seek men']. The personal narratives 'yan daudu shared with me, however, suggest that, while the practice of *daudu* and homosexuality are conceptually distinct, no discussion of *daudu* can be considered adequate if it focuses on 'yan daudu's economic activities while ignoring the subject of sexuality – and vice versa.

Notes

1 Besmer (1983: 47).
2 Besmer (1983: 122–123).
3 E.g., D. Greenberg (1988) and Murray (1987, 1997).
4 Beattie and Middleton (1969: xxv), cited in Besmer (1983: 18).
5 At the Bori performances I attended or heard about in the 1990s and 2000s, if a man was possessed by a female spirit, he was almost always a ɗan daudu. By contrast, in the Yoruba religious rituals observed by

Lorand Matory (1994) in southwestern Nigeria, male adepts who got mounted by female spirits were not perceived as feminine. Until very recently, there was apparently no recognized category of feminine men in Yoruba-speaking societies.

6 Besmer (1983: 30, n. 4). The description of 'the Prince' is from J. Greenberg (1946: 42). Note that Greenberg's study makes no reference to 'yan daudu *per se*, and he had no recollection of such a category when I spoke with him in person in Stanford, California, in 1993.

7 Besmer (1983: 18).

8 Bivins (1997).

9 J. Greenberg (1946); Trimingham (1968); O'Brien (2000).

10 See Last (1967) for an authoritative history of the Sokoto Caliphate and Hiskett (1975) on Hausa Islamic literary history.

11 O'Brien (2000).

12 Nast (1994, 2005).

13 Kaura (1990: 88), cited in Nast (2005: 17–18).

14 Boyd and Mack (2000).

15 Irvine and Gal (2000); Irvine (2008).

16 See, e.g., the racial descriptions contained in the colonial-era publication, *Nigeria, Our Latest Protectorate* (Robinson 1969), authored in 1900 by a British missionary who was also a lecturer at Cambridge.

17 In places where no centralized authority could be easily recognized, such as among the Igbo and other peoples in central and southeastern Nigeria, the British invented 'traditional' political offices so they could appoint local men – always men – to fill them (Crowder 1964; Mamdani 1996).

18 As noted by Moses Ochonu (forthcoming), the 'Hausa imaginary' promoted by the British also came at the expense of the many non-Hausa and non-Muslim peoples who inhabited the Protectorate of Northern Nigeria.

19 Mamdani (1996).

20 The term *Hausa-Fulani* reflects the fact that post-jihad elites in the Hausa city-states were (and are) considered ethnically Fulani because they had Fulani patrilines, but became ethnically and linguistically Hausaized through intermarriage, concubinage, and other practices. Today the term *Hausa* can be used narrowly to refer to someone with an ethnic Hausa (Haɓe) patriline, or broadly to refer to any Nigerian Muslim who speaks Hausa as a native language.

21 O'Brien (2000: 72) cites an early British colonial administrator who claimed: "that *bori* retained considerable vitality and importance right up to the eve of colonial conquest."

22 Cited in O'Brien (2000: 79). Much of the data in, and inspiration for, this section come from Susan O'Brien's masterful research on the history of Bori in the nineteenth and twentieth centuries.

23 O'Brien (2000: 80).

24 As noted in n. 5, at the Bori performances in the 1990s, if a man was possessed by a female spirit, he was usually a dan daudu. This seems not to have been the case in earlier historical periods.

25 Kaplan (2005).

26 Mamdani (1996); Ferguson (1999: Ch. 2).

27 Cited in O'Brien (2000: 99).

28 M. F. Smith (1991: iii).

29 M. F. Smith (1991: 15 and 1981: 64). The translation here is mine, adapted from Smith (1981).

30 Smith (1991: 36 and 1981: 64–65). The translation here is mine, adapted from Smith (1981).

31 By comparison, at many of the bikis ['celebrations'] and Bori perform-ances I attended in the 1990s, crowds of children – most of them boys – would stand by the sidelines and gawk as 'yan daudu performed 'women's dances.' If girls were present they had probably been sent to sell snacks on behalf of their mothers. Boys and girls also inter-acted with individual 'yan daudu at their food-stands and restaurants in market areas.

32 M. F. Smith (1981: 224).

33 M. F. Smith (1981: 116).

34 M. F. Smith (1981: 262, n. 13). Note that the English version more-or-less accurately transcribes the name Dandaudu. In the Hausa version, the term 'yan daudu is consistently rendered correctly.

35 M. F. Smith (1991: 36 and 1981: 65).

36 E.g., Bargery (1934: 574).

37 Reynolds (2001).

38 Paden (1973).

39 Pierce (2003, 2005).

40 Reynolds (2001).

41 White (1990); Ferguson (1999).

42 Daily Comet (1959a).

43 Banjo is presumably the American musical instrument, which in the 1950s would have been a relatively recent import, possibly introduced by soldiers who had fought in the British Imperial army alongside US troops (Barber et al. 1997: 10).

44 Namadi (1957).

45 Doi (n.d.: 28).

46 Korau (1959).

47 *Daily Comet* (1959b).

48 Umar (1993); Kane (2003).

49 Not all Islamists welcomed the adoption of Shari'a. Malam Ibrahim Zakzaky, for example, whose Islamic Movement gets support from Iran, insists that the postcolonial Nigerian state – including the Northern state governments – is fundamentally corrupt and therefore incapable of implementing true Shari'a. See Chapter 7.

50 Reynolds (2001).

51 Furniss (1996).

52 M. Adamu (2003).

53 Abdullahi (1984). Compare this to Barbara Cooper's (1995) account of Hausa women's involvement in politics in Niger.

54 Kane (2003).

55 Aken'ova (2002).

56 Pittin (1983: 296).

57 The survey data from Abdullahi (1984) were used in Kleis and Abdullahi (1983).

58 See Briggs (1986) for a relevant critique of interview and survey methodologies.

59 Abdullahi (1984: 18).

60 Kleis and Abdullahi (1983: 44).

61 Kleis and Abdullahi (1983: 46).

62 Female twins are called Hassana and Husseina.

3

OUT IN THE OPEN

"I was going to be a boxer," Jamilu told us, "until my accident." He raised his left hand to remind us of the two fingers he'd lost when his hand got caught in a grinding machine. He was in his mid-teens when it happened, living with his uncle in a village outside Madari where he'd come to help with the farm work, as he did every year during the rainy season. Jamilu was born in a small town near Kano, but like many city people his parents maintained close ties with their rural kinfolk. With his family unable to afford school fees, as a child Jamilu would spend several months a year at his uncle's compound, where he shared a room − a free-standing structure with mud walls and a straw roof − with his male cousins, whom he called 'senior brother' [wa] or 'junior brother' [kane]. (There is no Hausa word for 'cousin.') Having played and fought with Jamilu as boys, it was they who had noticed his strength and agility, and encouraged him to get training in *dambe*, a type of boxing that was popular throughout Hausaland, and a potentially lucrative profession. As a form of 'traditional play' [*wasan gargajiya*], boxing matches attracted large crowds of working-class men, and some wealthier ones, who came to enjoy the athletic competitions along with other performances such as live music and comedy skits. Another attraction were the independent women and 'yan daudu who sat in the audience, their flirtatious banter contributing to the festive atmosphere.

"So I went into *daudu*," he said. I sensed a hint of wistfulness in his voice.

By the time I met him in 1993, Jamilu was nearly 20 and was still spending rainy seasons at his uncle's. He was also a regular visitor at Madari's market, where he had many friends among the 'yan daudu and independent women who ran restaurants and food-stands.[1] Every Sunday, when the normally quiet town came to life for its weekly market-day, he would walk to the paved road and catch a ride on a minivan to join thousands of people who poured in from the surrounding countryside to sell farm produce, livestock, fresh milk, textiles and other crafts, and to buy foodstuffs, household supplies, and the occasional luxury like jewelry, perfume or second-hand clothes imported from Europe or North America. And, of course, to socialize.

Jamilu's best 'girlfriend' [ƙawa] was Kabiru, a short man with a wide smile who worked at a restaurant at the edge of the market, across from the main road. The proprietor, Hajiya Zara, was an independent woman whom Kabiru called 'mother' [uwa], and who had a few other young women working for her as well. Together, they helped her cook and serve meals to the dozens of men who would patronize her business over the course of the market-day. Some of these men were strangers who preferred to take their meals inside the restaurant, a modest-sized cement stall with a plastic mat on the floor and blue painted walls decorated with calendars commemorating the achievements of local politicians. Most of the customers were regulars who looked forward to relaxing under the large tree that shaded the outdoor fires where Hajiya Zara and her assistants cooked up rice and tuwo, a millet porridge served with a miya, or 'soup.' She always had at least two kinds of soup on offer – one made with baobab leaves, the other with okra – as well as variously sized pieces of beef and chicken. (Chicken was more expensive.) Sitting on benches or lounging on the plastic mat that had been laid out on the ground, Hajiya Zara's customers enjoyed joking and flirting with her, her 'daughters' and her 'son,' Kabiru, who amused and comforted them with his sassy attitude and gentle demeanor. To keep Kabiru company, Jamilu would sometimes help out at the restaurant – serving customers, picking up after them, washing their used enamel bowls and plastic cups. If he arrived early in the morning, he would assist in the food preparations: dicing tomatoes, chopping okra, slaughtering, plucking and disemboweling chickens, and keeping watch on the soups as they simmered over the fires.

Jamilu was adept at these culinary skills because he too had taken up the 'women's work' of cooking and selling food. Some time after his accident, a friend had referred him to an older ɗan daudu who ran a restaurant in Zaria, another of the original 'Seven Hausa' cities located about 100 kilometers south of Kano. Just as Hajiya Zara had done for Kabiru, the older ɗan daudu became a 'mother' to Jamilu, gave him a place to stay, and mentored him in the art and business of cooking. Every year at the end of the rainy season, when his labor was no longer needed on his uncle's farm, he went back to work at his 'mother's' restaurant in Zaria. Within a few years the money he earned there, combined with the gifts he occasionally received from male admirers, made it possible for him to open his own food-stand and eventually to get married. The last time I saw him, his wife had given birth to a baby girl.

Kabiru also struck out on his own. After a brief stint back in Kano, he returned to Madari to open his own stand just a few meters away from Hajiya Zara's restaurant. With his earnings and the assistance of Hajiya Zara, whom he continued to call 'mother,' he too was able to get married and to host a *biki*, a three-day-long party that attracted 'yan daudu and independent women from as far away as Kano; on the last day of the biki he received from his guests a tidy sum of donations, which he put away as capital so he could eventually expand his business. An investment opportunity presented itself when the state government adopted Shari'a, forcing Hajiya Zara and other independent women to give up their businesses. Kabiru couldn't afford the rent on Hajiya Zara's stall, so he took over the lease for an open-air structure by the side of the main road and paid the departing businesswoman for the supplies she left behind. His profits from the restaurant allowed him to start building a house on the edge of town. His wife and (eventual) children would live in part of it, and the other rooms would be rented out.

Narrating Gender, Sexuality, Kinship and Work

When the poet Aƙilu Aliyu compared *daudu* to the lowly occupation of calabash-mender, he highlighted the cultural importance of *sana'a* ['craft, trade, occupation'] in defining a Hausa man's social identity: among 'commoners' [*talakawa*], as opposed to 'aristocrats' [*masu sarauta*], a man is often known by what he does for a living.[2]

The equation of craft and social status [*daraja*] was especially salient when occupations were passed down from father to son. Although crafts like blacksmith and praise-shouter were not automatically inherited in the same way as social rank (aristocrat, commoner, slave), a man's social standing was greatly influenced by the work his father and grandfather did: Islamic scholars enjoyed great prestige, merchants were respectable, musicians and praise-shouters were low-status, while calabash-menders and other menial laborers, including farm workers, were even lower; thievery was at the bottom, an immoral pursuit that was not a true sana'a and that defined all the others as legitimate.[3] Colonial rule, which abolished slavery and imposed the capitalist system of work for wages, eroded lineage-based social and economic distinctions, but it did not eradicate them entirely. Lineage is still used to distinguish people socially, in ways that sometimes conflict with other forms of status.[4] Thus, a man whose father was of slave descent, or a calabash-mender, or a dan daudu, will always bear the stigma of those origins to some extent, regardless of how successful he may become. At the same time, the importance of an individual's occupation in determining social status has arguably been enhanced as middle-class notions of professional identity become more prevalent among educated urbanites.

The abolition of slavery was implemented incrementally over the first 20 years of British rule, and was widely blamed by colonists and Nigerians alike for the social problems that emerged in that period, many of which, as we saw in Chapter 2, were associated with the bariki. Chief among these was the perceived increase in the number of 'unattached women,' who were almost always assumed to be 'prostitutes.'[5] Another development attributed to the abolition of slavery was the growth in seasonal labor migration, or what Hausa speakers call *cin rani* ['eating the dry season'].[6] Seasonal migration had been practiced in the precolonial period, along with other forms of migration, as Baba of Karo illustrated when she described how Ramatu had 'roamed the world' as a 'prostitute' before she settled down and married Baba's father. But the economic consequences of colonial rule – dispossession of farms, coerced labor, expansion of the cash economy – made all kinds of migration more necessary, while new technologies of transport, such as railroads and automobiles, made long-distance travel more feasible, and even attractive.

The fact that 'roaming' and 'unattached' women were perceived to be 'prostitutes' rather than migrant laborers or businesswomen indicates the gendered nature of the concept of *sana'a* and its relationship to social status. Whereas men who leave the family farm can seek a variety of legitimate, albeit low-paying jobs, women are all destined for the same role in life as 'married woman' [*matar aure*], and their status is derived from their husband. This role entails work [*aiki*], but women's work is usually not considered a sana'a. Urban women who do practice a craft tend to be socially exceptional in terms of age, wealth, education, or rank: working-class girls who have not gone through puberty and post-menopausal women often engage in petty trade; highly educated and wealthy women can pursue careers; and very poor women often have no choice but to take on menial jobs. A few women pursue their father's sana'a, but these 'traditional' crafts, such as praise-shouting, are low-status. When 'yan daudu are referred to as 'men who cook food' or 'men who fry chicken,' therefore, they are not just being compared to 'women' in general, but implicitly to 'prostitutes' who turn 'women's work' into a sana'a.

By describing how he replaced boxing with daudu, Jamilu's narrative seems to confirm the popular belief, echoed by many of Salisu Abdullahi's informants, that boys choose to become 'yan daudu for economic reasons.[7] It also lends support to scholarly arguments that gender, sexuality, and other 'identities' should be seen as practices rather than essences, as things people do rather than things people are. The idea that identity is practiced, or 'performed,' encourages us to think about identities as fluid and variable, not static and fixed. It also encourages us to think about how the various identity categories we use – female, male, married, gay, karuwa, ɗan daudu – have come to be, and how their meanings might change or be subject to debate at different times and in different social settings.[8]

This chapter explores what it can mean to say that someone is, or has become, a ɗan daudu. As Jamilu's narrative implies, one of the key practices associated with daudu is the performance of 'women's work.' What his narrative does not tell us is whether daudu, for him, involved 'prostitution' [*karuwanci*] or 'procuring' [*kawalci*] women for male patrons. In fact, Jamilu and Kabiru rarely discussed such topics in my presence. This was undoubtedly due to the stigma attached to them, for karuwanci, like thievery, is generally considered an immoral way of making a living that does not qualify as 'work' [*aiki*] or a 'craft' [*sana'a*]. Jamilu and Kabiru's reticence may also have been due to my age, as I was roughly seven years their senior. 'Yan daudu who were about my age or older were more likely to talk with me about 'prostitution' and sex. By paying close attention to how various individuals narrated (or remained silent about) their experiences as youths with respect to 'women's work' and 'prostitution,' we can get a sense of the range of possible meanings that are attached to 'doing daudu' [*yin daudu*] and to *dan daudu* as a social identity; we can also gain insight into the tensions that exist within Muslim Hausa society generally with respect to gender, sexuality and work.

Readers who grew up or were educated in North America, northern Europe, or other places influenced by Anglo-American notions of sexual identity may be tempted to compare the narratives discussed in this chapter with the 'coming-out stories' recounted by many people who identify as gay, lesbian, bisexual, or transgender. Comparisons can be instructive, but they should be approached with caution. While a notion of disclosing a personal secret is common to people who 'come out of the closet' as well as to boys who 'come out in the open' as 'yan daudu, the kind of secret that is disclosed in each case, the way it is disclosed, and the meanings attributed to it are not identical. The most important difference is that, while 'coming out of the closet' typically refers to sexuality, among 'yan daudu 'coming out in the open' refers to gender – specifically, to the practice of acting 'like women'; the concept of publicly disclosing one's sexual desires or practices is virtually unheard of. In this sense, the category of *dan daudu* is comparable to the Anglo-American notion of 'transgender.' But whether one 'comes out of the closet' about gender or sexuality, the process is understood to be profoundly psychological, involving an isolated individual struggling with his or her inner feelings. The 'closet' is a metaphor for the psychological consequences of keeping one's stigmatized gender or sexual desires secret; to 'come out of the closet' is to liberate oneself from these consequences – to go from the dark, cramped space of secrecy into the bright, comfortable space of openness, freedom, and pride. This process is also fundamentally verbal: one 'comes out' by declaring that one is 'lesbian,' 'trans,' etc.; and the label one chooses (e.g., 'gay' vs. 'queer') can be a matter of discussion and debate in itself.[9]

By contrast, Jamilu's narrative and the others excerpted below focus more on actions than on thoughts, feelings, or identity labels. It is especially important to note that very few 'yan daudu ever explicitly told me that they had 'come out in the open' [*fito fili*]. That Hausa phrase is more often used in the third person ('he came out in the open') than the first ('I came out'), and it tends to refer more-or-less literally to the performance in a public setting of practices (e.g., acting 'like a woman') that used to be performed in secret. Additionally, the phrase often carries a negative or ambivalent moral judgment, suggesting that discretion or 'shame' [*kunya*] – keeping certain things secret – is more respectable than disclosure. This is not to say that narratives that describe 'coming out in the open' have no positive affective associations; as this chapter will show, some 'yan daudu did describe their experiences of publicly acting 'like women' in positive terms. But these are not the only or most important meanings, and they have not been codified (or 'entextualized') as a narrative genre in the way Anglo-American 'coming-out stories' have been.[10]

Another important difference between coming-out stories and the narratives excerpted here has to do with the interactional settings in which they were told. While coming-out stories can be elicited and recited in relative isolation from the flow of conversation, Hausa people are usually not inclined to inquire about other people's psychosocial development; such questions are generally considered intrusive, impolite and 'lacking shame' [*mara kunya*]. The positive moral value attached to 'shame' and discretion may explain why Jamilu never told me what factors – social, economic or psychological – led him to go into daudu instead of any of the other occupations that might have been available to a young man of his station. First-person coming-of-age narratives are more likely to be recounted in the course of a conversation where they serve to reshape speakers' social relationships in the immediate interactional setting.[11] Significantly, when Jamilu told me and Mai Kwabo how he 'went into daudu,' it was not because we had asked him about it. Rather, we had heard someone address him as "Boxer!" [*Dan dambe!*], and asked him what that meant. (Jamilu shared other details of what I would call his 'life story' at other times.[12])

As Jamilu's story illustrates, becoming a ɗan daudu in the overt sense of the term typically involves moving out of one's home to a bariki area in another city or town. Away from his kinfolk, a young man can more easily 'come out in the open,' that is, act 'like a woman' in public without having to face the judgments of his family and wider community, or the social and psychological consequences of those judgments. (Jamilu, like most 'yan daudu, never told me how his family had reacted to his becoming a dan daudu. If they did react negatively, they were apparently reconciled by the time I met him.) Leaving home carries risks, however, making neophyte 'yan daudu dependent on the hospitality of older and more established 'yan daudu and independent women. The relationships they are able to form in their new homes and places of work are thus key to their physical and emotional survival. This intimate dependence is indexed by the use of kinship terms, especially feminine ones such as 'mother' [*uwa* or *bábà*] and 'daughter' [*'ya*] and 'girlfriend' [*kawa*] (see Figure 3.1). When a young man 'comes out in the open,' therefore, he ideally enters into a network of 'people of the bariki' who will help and support him, and who will eventually rely on him to do the same

Fig. 3.1   A 'mother,' her 'daughters' and their friends in Sabon Gari, 1997. Hanging on the wall is a portrait of Ahmadu Bello, first Premier of Northern Nigeria and a descendant of Shehu Usman Dan Fodio.
Source: Photo by R. Gaudio.

for them. Of course, relationships don't always live up to ideal expectations; and it is precisely the problems that arise in their intimate relationships, along with other unexpected developments, that 'yan daudu, like other people, often focus on in their conversational narratives.

Daudu on the Move

While migration was an important part of both Jamilu's and Kabiru's experiences as 'yan daudu, their careers as they narrated them to me seemed relatively stable – geographically, economically and socially. Other 'yan daudu's narratives featured more dislocations. A few months after I started visiting Madari, a new ɗan daudu named Hamza showed up and opened his own food-stand in the market area. The other 'yan daudu and independent women received this new arrival cordially, but with suspicion, for he had arrived on his own, without a referral from anyone close to them in the bariki network of friends and acquaintances. With no one to host him, Hamza took a room in a small hotel, paying the equivalent of almost US$2 per night, more than many Nigerians could earn in a day. The hotel was run by a family of Christian Igbo migrants and had a bar that served beer and whisky – one of the few places in town where one could buy alcoholic drinks. (Years later, the bar had to close when the state adopted Shari'a.) Although the rent was cheap compared to the 'State Hotel' on the other side of town where 'big men' politicians were known to take their girlfriends, for full-time housing it was considered extravagant.

About a year after we first met him, Hamza agreed to let me and Mai Kwabo tape-record a conversation with him. One slow day at the market (not Sunday), he closed down his stand and took us to the bar at his hotel. After paying for a round of Gulders, I brought out my tape-recorder and turned it on. Mai Kwabo initiated the conversation with a customary exchange of greetings, then quickly shifted into a rapid, flirtatious banter that I found difficult to follow. Hamza didn't miss a beat. At some point he started reminiscing about his youthful days in and around Kano. The first place he mentioned was Zakawa, the town where I had been told that most of the women were 'prostitutes.' The following narrative recounts a segment of the conversation as I transcribed and translated it with Mai Kwabo's assistance. For the sake of clarity, I have omitted most of Mai Kwabo's nonverbal backchannels ("m," "mhm," etc.), as well as some false starts and segments that were inaudible.

"*Wallahi tallahi*," Hamza said to Mai Kwabo. "I know you go to Zakawa, don't you?" (*Wallahi tallahi* is a Hausaized Arabic interjection meaning 'By God, by God.')

"M," Mai Kwabo answered.

"Some day you should go and ask Shehu," Hamza instructed him. I knew from my own visits to Zakawa that Shehu was the proprietor of a 'women's house' and one of the town's oldest and most prominent 'yan daudu.

"Shehu," Hamza continued. "Tell him, 'Do you know a ɗan daudu called Hamza?' From way back even before the time of Shagari's administration. He'll say, 'Hamza?' Tell him, 'Yeah, him, the light-skinned one from Catako.' I hadn't gotten this facial tattoo yet." Hamza pointed to two green lines of hatch-marks running vertically down each temple on either side of his face. Such tattoos were common among older people of ethnic Fulani descent.

Hamza continued to imagine Mai Kwabo's hypothetical conversation with Shehu. "If you tell him, he'll say to you 'mhm,' he'll give you the history from a long long time ago –"

"When you were at Zakawa?" Mai Kwabo interjected. "Did you stay at Zakawa?"

"Absolutely," Hamza replied.

"At whose place did you stay?"

"Right at Shehu's house."

"What did you at the time?"

"I wasn't doing any kind of *sana'a*," Hamza answered. "Just *karuwanci*."

In rapid-fire speech Hamza proceeded to name all the neighborhoods in Kano that he'd lived, and the people he lived with, snapping his fingers to punctuate the list. (Note that Balaraba, Zainab and Farida are women's names; Namadi is masculine.)

"I was just doing a lot of *karuwanci*. When I was at Weatherhead [a street in Sabon Gari]. I wasn't doing any kind of *sana'a*. Ever since I came over to Brigade. I wasn't selling anything. I came over to

Adakawa and stayed. I wasn't doing any kind of *sana'a*. From Adakawa, I came over to Hausawa. From Adakawa I left Hausawa. I went back to Warure, I was living off my hosts, me and Balaraba. At Namadi and them's place. I spent six months at Namadi and them's room. I was just living *iskanci*, living off my hosts, living illicitly [*Zaman iskanci kawai nake, zaman cin siddan, zaman cin haram*]."

Hamza barely paused to take a breath. "Then I- I came back to the white house. Right! We were the first to move into the white house. The one in Unguwa Uku. I left that house, I went over to the house of the tamarind-tree, from the tamarind-tree house I went over to the pit house. At the time it was me and Farida and them, and short little Zainab. She had a boyfriend called Idi."

Like the fictional 'prostitute' in Hamisu Yadudu Funtuwa's poem "Waƙar Uwar Mugu" ['Song of the Mother of the Evil One'], Hamza portrays himself roaming from town to town, neighborhood to neighborhood, taking advantage of people's generosity wherever he went. Hamza's narrative is also set in roughly the same historical period: Funtuwa's poem probably dates to the 1970s, while Hamza's memories reach back to before the administration of Shehu Shagari, President of Nigeria between 1979 and 1983, when the country's economy was still flush with cash from the petroleum industry. Hamza would have been in his late teens or early twenties.

In regaling Mai Kwabo and me with this lively account of what he called the *zaman iskanci* ['frivolous, immoral living'] of his youth, Hamza almost seemed to be boasting. He seemed especially proud of the fact that he had supported himself entirely through 'prostitution,' implying that he had no trouble attracting male patrons and plenty of friends – 'yan daudu and independent women – who hosted him or helped him find lodging. Missing from Hamza's narrative is an account of why he kept leaving neighborhood after neighborhood. There are many possible reasons – legal or financial trouble, bad health, boredom, disagreements with housemates or neighbors – but whatever they were, their absence suggests they may not have been compatible with the image of rebellious glamour projected by the rest of his narrative.

The life Hamza claimed to have lived in Kano also contrasted with his relatively modest circumstances in Madari, where he was living alone in a hotel, trying to support himself by selling food. A few weeks after we made this recording, he abruptly left town in the middle of the night without saying good-bye or telling anyone where he was going. According to the bariki gossip, he had borrowed money from some 'yan daudu and independent women and ran away to avoid having to repay them. When I visited Madari again a few years later, my friends there said he had moved to a town that was more than an hour away by public transport. They would occasionally see him at bikis, but otherwise had nothing more to say about him.

Hamza's mobility may have been extreme, but it was not unheard of; many of the 'yan daudu I met in the early and mid-1990s moved a number of times over the following decade – to other towns in the North, to Abuja or Lagos, or back and forth to Saudi Arabia. His larceny was also not terribly unusual, for bariki people complained with some regularity about being robbed or duped by people they knew. What set Hamza apart from the other 'yan daudu in Madari was his ambivalent participation in *zumuncin bariki* ['bariki fellowship'], the bonds of solidarity and mutual support that 'yan daudu, independent women and their associates rely on to face the challenges of life in the bariki, and in general.

Girlfriends and Boyfriends

'Mothers' are not the only people young 'yan daudu rely on to host and to socialize them in the ways of the bariki. Peers play an equally, if not more important role. Like Kabiru and Jamilu, 'yan daudu who consider each other close friends typically call each other *kawa* (plural: *kawaye*). Less frequently, some 'yan daudu address independent women as *kawa*, and vice versa. In anthropological texts, the term *kawa* is translated as 'bond-friend,' referring to an intimate, enduring friendship between girls that carries mutual responsibilities of obligation and trust.[13] Adult women and 'yan daudu also use the term, but conventionally masculine men do not. (A man's platonic male friend is called *aboki* ['friend'] or *amini* ['trusted friend'], while a man's 'girlfriend,' in the sense of a romantic, heterosexual partner, is called 'his girl' [*yarinyarsa*].) I translate *kawa* as 'girlfriend' because this is the term I most often hear used in American English to describe women's close, platonic friendships with other women; 'girlfriend' is also used by some North American gay men to refer to their close, platonic friendships with other gay men.

('Girlfriend' in English can also refer to a woman's romantic or sexual partner. With respect to *kawa* this usage was unusual, or as linguists say, marked. The possibility of erotic relationships between female *kawaye* was taboo in polite conversation, though I did hear people gossip about it. In bariki circles, erotic relationships between 'yan daudu 'girlfriends' were also gossiped about, usually in disparaging terms that equated such relationships with 'lesbianism,' for which the standard Hausa translation is *madigo*, though 'yan daudu usually used colloquial, in-group terms such as *kifi* ['turning over']¹⁴ and *markade* ['mashing'].)

As enduring, intimate relationships, 'girlfriendships' were subject to numerous tensions. Many of these are superficially similar to the problems that beset all longstanding human relationships. But the form these problems took in 'yan daudu's relationships often reflected the particular contradictions that characterized life in the bariki. The most salient contradiction arguably lies in the conflicting imperatives faced by people in all stratified societies: on one hand, we are compelled to compete for social and economic advantages over others; on the other, we are compelled to collaborate and express corporate solidarity with the communities and institutions with which we are identified. Attempting to balance these conflicting imperatives is logistically and morally taxing for many people. But those who are poor, socially marginalized, and legally disenfranchised face material and psychological challenges that make it especially difficult to adhere to the ethical standards they believe in. In the bariki, these difficulties were often manifest in conflicts between 'girlfriends.'

Lami and Mansur were two 'girlfriends' whose relationship had lived through numerous challenges, and they shared some of these experiences — as well as more pleasant ones — in a tape-recorded conversation with Mai Kwabo and another friend in 1994. They were in their mid-twenties at the time and had known Mai Kwabo for several years. Lami operated a small restaurant — a cement stall with a mat on the floor, similar to Hajiya Zara's — in a central neighborhood of Katsina that had a high concentration of bars and women's houses.¹⁵ Another dan daudu, Haruna, ran a restaurant in the adjacent stall, and their cooking fires stood side-by-side in the dirt road outdoors. For lodging Lami rented a room in a nearby compound.

Mansur had no room or shop of his own, but often stayed with Lami and helped him out at the restaurant during the day. In the evening, he would often change into one of his many fashionable outfits and go out with men who came by on motorcycles, or the occasional car, to pick him up. Lami, on the other hand, usually spent all day at the restaurant, dressed in his dirty work clothes, cooking and serving customers until late at night. As he once explained to me, his responsibilities at the restaurant left him little time or energy to go out at night to meet men, and, in any event, he was not interested in having lots of boyfriends.

The first time Mai Kwabo brought me to the restaurant, I recognized Mansur from bikis I had attended at Shehu's house in Zakawa, where I had noticed his fine clothes and seen him dancing with other 'yan daudu and flirting with men. (I remembered one man in particular playfully calling Mansur 'my wife' [matata].) Mansur recognized me, too – I was always the only white person at the bikis, except once when I brought some guests – but we did not remember each other's names. It turned out that Mansur traveled regularly out of Katsina to visit friends and attend bikis. After his travels he would eventually return to Lami's place; in the year that I knew him he seemed to spend more time there than he did anywhere else. By contrast, Lami rarely went out of town to attend bikis, but he did make periodic day-trips to his home village outside Kano.

(Note that the name Lami is feminine; unless otherwise noted, the other names for 'yan daudu in this chapter are masculine. Like Hajiya Asabe, Lami was one of the few 'yan daudu I knew who was consistently addressed and referred to by a woman's name. I use masculine pronouns to refer to them, however, because that is how other people, including 'yan daudu, usually addressed them. This may sound strange to some Hausa speakers, just as some English speakers might find it strange to hear a person named Angela referred to as 'he.' When non-'yan daudu used feminine terms to refer to Lami or Hajiya Asabe, they generally did so in their presence, to signal intimacy or humor, or both. In other contexts, to refer to a ɗan daudu as 'she' would probably be interpreted as disrespectful.)

During the day, Mansur usually socialized in a playful, gregarious fashion with the people who worked or spent time near the restaurant: Haruna and other 'yan daudu who were cooking nearby; independent women who lived in the area; male customers, roving vendors, and other passers-by. Lami had a quieter demeanor, and seldom told jokes or made risqué comments as 'yan daudu and independent women were typically expected to do. He was also discreet about his intimate affairs. Sometimes, when the two of us were alone, he would tell me in hushed tones about the men he'd had sex with. One of these was Mai Kwabo, who had already told me that the two of them had had a sexual relationship some years earlier.

One weekend about a year after I first met him, Mai Kwabo and I traveled to Katsina to pay Lami a visit and, I hoped, to make some tape-recordings for my dissertation. On Saturday night we all stayed up late, chatting (on tape) in the restaurant with Haruna and a few other people, including Barbado, a teenage ɗan daudu who lived and worked elsewhere in town. (Some of that conversation is excerpted in Chapter 4.) Mai Kwabo, Mansur and Barbado then spent the night in Lami's room, while I slept at another friend's place down the road. Since Mai Kwabo had my tape-recorder, they made a new recording shortly after they woke up Sunday morning, while they were waiting for water to be delivered so they could bathe, get dressed, and go out. Haruna's wife had just given birth, and we had all been invited to the naming ceremony.

A substantial portion of the conversation consisted of Mansur and Lami telling stories about their relationships with 'yan aras, an in-group term that they and other 'yan daudu used to refer to conventionally masculine men (like Mai Kwabo) who had sex with 'yan daudu or with other 'yan aras. One story – in which Mansur got involved with a boyfriend of Lami's – brought these themes together in a volatile mix of jealousy and accusations of betrayal. The moral and social implications of this story led to another exchange of narratives in which Lami and Mansur described the history of their relationship as 'girlfriends.' It was in the course of those narratives that Lami and Mansur each described how they 'came out in the open' as 'yan daudu.

About halfway into the 90-minute recording, the four conversationalists are divided into pairs: Hajiya Lami and Mai Kwabo are discussing mutual acquaintances in Kano, while Mansur is gossiping with Barbado about an encounter that another ɗan daudu supposedly had with a ɗan aras. This story attracts the attention of Mai Kwabo and Hajiya Lami, and inspires Hajiya Lami to recount his own story about a dealer of second-hand clothes who supposedly seduced him into having sex and then gave him a shirt: "*Aka gama harka . . . aka 'dauko min riga, aka ba ni*" ['The deed was finished . . . a shirt was picked out and given to me.']

Continuing the theme of sex and gift-giving, Mansur tells a story about a man named Usman who pursued him and gave him a ring. The narrative is complicated by the fact that Usman had originally received the ring as a present from Hajiya Lami, who became enraged when he saw it on Mansur's hand and realized the infidelity of both his 'boyfriend' Usman and his 'girlfriend' Mansur. The setting of this love triangle was Kaduna, another large northern Nigerian city, where, as reported later in the conversation, both Mansur and Lami had lived before they moved to Katsina. In his opening line, or what William Labov calls the orientation,[16] Mansur refers to his job selling kolanut, a mild, legal stimulant that is commonly sold by roving vendors, including children of both sexes. This indicates that he had not yet started performing 'women's work' publicly. He had, however, started spending time at Lami's home, where he met Usman, a *dan aras* that Lami was then 'staying' with. ('Staying' [*zama*] with someone is an idiomatic expression for an ongoing erotic relationship, roughly equivalent to the old American English expression 'going steady.')

As Lami and Mansur take turns, or compete, in telling their stories, they periodically address Barbado by name and with certain phrases such as 'let me tell you^f [*in gaya miki*] and 'you^f hear, right?' [*kina ji, ko?*]. Most of these phrases, which linguists call discourse markers, contain a feminine second-person pronoun, which I represent as 'you^f.'[17] As in Arabic and Hebrew, to which it is distantly related, Hausa grammar requires speakers to choose a feminine or masculine form in the second and third person, but only when the referent is singular, thus: 'you^f' or 'you^m,' 'she' or 'he.' In reading the transcript, pay attention to how and when Lami and Mansur use feminine or masculine forms to refer to each other. For the benefit of readers of Hausa, transcribed excerpts of the original dialogue are provided along with an English translation. Arabic expressions and their English translations are underlined. Extraneous dialogue (greetings, requests for information, etc.) involving people who were passing by Lami's room has been omitted. Other transcription conventions are explained in the Notes on Transcription on p. xiv.

Mansur: Na gaya ma, lokacin ina tallan
goro ne, ga yadda na sami Lami,
tana zama da wani mutum
ana ce mar Usman.
Ina zuwa T, kawai sai muka sauka,
sai ya ɗaure min gindi (muka tafi).
Ni, ina zaune duk lokacin (nan),
ina zaune, da ma na zo wajen Lami.
Shi ke nan, ina zaune, na yi zama,
na yi shiru::, ina tunani,
ina tunanina.
Sai wannan mutumi, sai ya zo,
sai muka gaisa da shi.
Lami, (aka-) aka ba ni labari,
kin ga, Usman, ko Usman?

Da shi kuke zama.
Shi- ta nuna min wannan mutumin, a: yo
ni, Lami, ashe, zobuka duk
na hannunsa ma na Lami ne,
(su xx).
Ina zaune a cikin zobukan hannun naki,
sai ya zaro zobe.
Wanda da ma ko Lami ta ba shi.
Wanda take ji da shi=
Lami: =Wanda nake bala'in so.=
Mansur: =In gaya miki,
sai ya zaro wannan zobe,
sai ya ɗauka min a hannu.
Kin gani? La haula <illa> fi sa'atullahi.

M: I tell you[m], when I was selling
kolanut, here's how I met up with Lami,
she was staying with a guy
called Usman.
I was going to T, then we just got down,
then he took care of me (and we went off).
Me, I was sitting (this) whole time,
I was sitting, I had come to see Lami.
That's it, I was sitting, I'd sat down,

I was quie::t, I was thinking,
I was thinking my thoughts.
Then this guy, he came over,
and we exchanged greetings.
Lami, I'd (been-) been informed,
you[f] see, Usman, it was Usman, right?
That's who you[pl] were staying with.
He- she showed me this guy, so uh:

I, Lami, wow, I realized all the rings
on his hand were Lami's, (they xx).

I was sitting in the rings of your[f] hand,
then he took off a ring.
Which previously Lami had given him,
Which was her favorite=
L: =Which I liked terribly.=
M: =Let me tell you[f],
then he took off this ring,
then he took me by the hand.
You[f] see? There's no power <except> in the expanse of God.

By using an Arabic-Islamic oath about God's supreme power, Mansur implicitly diminishes whatever role he might have played in enticing Usman to give him one of Lami's rings. Mansur goes on to describe Lami's violent reaction to seeing the ring on Mansur's hand. The Arabic phrase *La'ila!* is short for the Islamic profession of faith which begins, *La ilaha ill-Allah* ['There is no god but Allah']; it is often used in colloquial Hausa as an expression of surprise.

Mansur: Lami dai, "Ki yi magana,"	*M:* To Lami, I said, "Say something,"
ba za ta yi ba. Ta yi magana, ba za ta yi ba.	but she wouldn't. I told her to say something, but she wouldn't.
Sai ta zo ta kalli zobe.	Then she came to look at the ring.
(xx) "La'ila:!"	(xx) She said, "<u>There's no go:d!</u>"
Ai, ba ta da haƙuri!	Oh, she had no patience!
Sai ta ji magana.	She insisted on hearing an explanation.
In ta zo, ta kalli zobe, (ta kalli zobe xx)	When she came over, she looked at the ring, (she looked at the ring xx)
Lami, sai ta kasa barci.	Then Lami, she couldn't sleep.
(xx) Wai, "Shin mafari-a ina kika sami wannan zoben?"	(xx) She said to me, "And the reason- where did you[f] get this ring?"
Ni na ce, "Ai, ina na sami zoben?	Me I said, "Oh, where did I get the ring?
Abokinka ne ya ba ni."	Your[m] friend gave it me."
Kawai in gaya miki,	Let me just tell you[f],
Lami sai: ta rufa ido,	then Lami, she just closed her eyes,
wai "ga ni a nan."	she said, "Well, look at me here."
Kawai sai ta dira wa mutumin nan.	Then she just swooped down on this guy.
Wai, watau, ita, ba ya ƙaunarta ke nan.	She said, that is, he must not love her.
"Ba ka ƙaunata! Ni, har zan cire abu a hannuna, in cire abu	"You[m] don't love me! Me, who'd take a thing off my hand, I'd take a thing off
da kankin kaina in ba ka, ka cire ka ba wani ɗan daudu	myself and give to you[m], and you[m] take it off and give it to another
a gabana!" Wai, in duba na ga fa,	ɗan daudu in front of me?!" She said, I should realize, see, it was because of
don Lami na zo gurin nan, kuma ita ce ƙawata fa.	Lami that I'd come to this place, and she was my girlfriend, see.
Ita ce ƙawata, don ita na zo gurin nan,	She was my girlfriend, it was because of her that I'd come to this place,

don Allah, don Annabi.	by God, by the Prophet.
Lami ta yi kawaici,	Lami got quiet, she got pensive, right?
ta ɗauke kai, ko?	
Sai na bar gurin su yi	Then I left the place so they could thrash
cashiyan nan.	
Lami dai, a nan gun	it out. As for Lami, right there
(ta cashe mutumin nan.)	(she thrashed the guy.)

As Mansur describes it, Lami implicitly accused him of violating one of the cardinal rules of "girlfriendship": girlfriends should not 'steal' [sata] each other's boyfriends. Against this accusation, Mansur consistently portrays himself as the passive object of Usman's advances, and therefore blameless. Thus, when Lami asked, "Where did you[f] get this ring?," Mansur replied, "Your[m] friend gave it to me." The masculine possessive pronoun in this statement is also significant, for with it Mansur implicitly ignored his "girlfriendship" with Lami and their concomitant moral obligations to each other. Additionally, by referring to Usman as Lami's 'friend' [aboki] rather than as his ɗan aras or 'boyfriend,' Mansur downgraded the moral imperatives of that relationship as well.

In contrast to his passive self-portrait, Mansur depicts Lami as active in ways that can be interpreted, according to dominant cultural values, as unfeminine and therefore unattractive. The simple assertion that Lami had given Usman a ring implies that it was Lami who pursued Usman, not vice versa. Although the idea of a ɗan daudu courting a ɗan aras is not unheard of, it is often assumed in such cases that the pursuer is probably too old or unattractive to be the object of a (younger) man's affection. In this story, which took place when Lami and Mansur were both quite young, Mansur implies that Usman found him more attractive than Lami. Lami, however, seems unfazed by this suggestion and focuses more on the moral obligations of "girlfriendship."

Lami makes an especially pointed effort to challenge Mansur's portrayal of him as lacking "patience." As he and Mansur each seek to get their point across, the conversation grows lively with considerable latching (talking one after another with no pause between utterances) and overlapping (talking at the same time). These features point to – or as linguists say, index – the competition that Mansur and Lami appear to be waging over the right to narrate their conflict;

at the same time, the structure of the conversation iconically reproduces the terms of that earlier conflict.[18] Whereas the two 'yan daudu
were once competing for the affection of Usman, they are now competing for Barbado's attention, and possibly for Mai Kwabo's as well.
(Note that Mansur uses two in-group expressions: *rayuwa* ['life'], which
I usually heard to refer to the social world of men who have sex
with men, and *aras*, referring to the physical act of sex between men.)

Mansur: Alkawalin Allah, idan ba
sai da
Lami ta cire wannan zobe daga
hannuna
ba, Allah ya tsinan.
Lami: Ni, abin da ya sa, kina ji ko?

Barbado=
Mansur: =Lami ta zare zoben nan
daga
hannuna, kuma <u>wallahi tallahi,</u>
wannan mutumin, wanda so yake
mu yi rayuwa da shi,
ko mu yi aras da shi, ko?

Ni a lokacin tsoron 'yan aras
nake ji,
saboda ni [(xxxxxxxxxx)
Lami: ['Yar Mansuriya, Barbado,
ƙawata ce,
[[tun ina yarinya]] a Kano.
Mansur: [[Tsoro nake ji.]]
Lami: Ko ba hujja [ba.
Mansur: [Ba ruwana=

Lami: =Kafin ki san duk wani
ɗan daudu da ke cikin garin
Katsina,
na san Mansur.

M: Promise to God, if Lami didn't
then
take that ring off my hand,

may God damn me.
L: Me, the reason was, do you[f]
hear?

Barbado=
M: =Lami took the ring off

my hand, and <u>by God by God,</u>
this guy, who wanted
me to do the life with him,
or for me to have sex with him,
right?

Me, at the time I was afraid of
'yan aras,
because I [(xxxxxxxxxx)
L: [Little[f] Mansuriya[f], Barbado,
has been my girlfriend,
[[since I was a girl]] in Kano.
M: [[I was afraid.]]
L: Isn't that [right.
M: [I had nothing to do <with
them>=
L: =Before you[f] knew any other
ɗan daudu in the city of Katsina,

I knew Mansur.

In response to Mansur's depiction of him as impatient and out of
control, Lami attempts to explain his angry outburst.[19] With feminine references to himself as a 'girl' [*yarinya*] and to Mansur as 'Little[f]

Mansuriya' ['Yar Mansuriya], Lami again justifies his actions with reference to the mutual obligations of 'girlfriends,' which are supposed to take precedence over 'boyfriends.'

Lami's appeal to the history of their friendship leads him to go back farther in time to describe how he and Mansur, after having lost track of each other for an unspecified amount of time were reunited in Kaduna. It is in the lead-up to that reunion that Lami, with Mansur's assistance, gives a brief account of how he 'went into daudu.'

Lami: Tun da ni ban girma a Katsina ba.
A Kano na girma.
(A Kanon ma) na san Mansur.

L: Since I didn't grow up in Katsina.
I grew up in Kano.
(And it was in Kano that) I knew Mansur.

Mansur: (xx)
Lami: Na zo daga makarantata, har na je yawon duniya.
Na yi ɗan shekara biyu haka Legas,
na dawo, sai katsam,
sai ga ni a Kaduna. Na kuma daɗe a wannan lokacin a Kaduna.
Ina nan, ina nan, ina nan, sai katsam, sai Ubangiji Allah ya haɗa ni
da Mansur a Kaduna.=
Mansur: =Ke [kin ɗauko] tallan doya ne=
Lami: [(Lafiya.)] =I!

M: (xx)
L: I came from my school, and went off to roam the world.
So I spent a couple years in Lagos,
and came back, then wham,
here I am in Kaduna. And I spent a long time in Kaduna at that time.

Here I am, here I am, here I am, then wham, the Lord God united me

with Mansur in Kaduna.=
M: =You[f], [you'd[f] taken up] selling yams=
L: [(All right.)] =Yes!

This excerpt summarizes the process whereby Lami became publicly identifiable as a ɗan daudu. It began when he left the Qur'anic school that his parents had sent him to and went off — like Baba of Karo's step-mother Ramatu — to 'roam the world.' (The level of schooling Lami had achieved was rare among 'yan daudu; his ability to read *ajami*, Arabic script, was mentioned to me admiringly by others on several occasions.) Just as Hamza did in Kano, in Lagos — Nigeria's largest city, in the predominantly Yoruba-speaking southwest of the country – we can presume that Lami stayed with other 'yan daudu and independent women in one of that city's sizable Hausa communities.

Lami's 'roaming' seems to have ended when he moved to Kaduna and began 'selling yams' [*tallan doya*], a phrase that is frequently used as a metonym for cooking and serving food in general. Note that Mansur uses feminine forms to report this activity, underscoring the idea that cooking and serving food is 'women's work.' Mansur, meanwhile, was living with relatives in Kaduna and working as a roving vendor of kolanut. In a part of the transcript not excerpted here, he describes how one day, when he and his junior brother were traveling about the city, he spied Lami from a distance.

"Hey," Mansur said, "I know that dan daudu."

"Oh, well," Mansur's brother replied, "he's a dan daudu. It's no surprise if you know him."

After a joyful reunion, Lami invited Mansur back to his place. Although Mansur had not yet assumed a public identity as a dan daudu, he became a regular visitor to the house, a 'women's house' where he enjoyed spending time with the 'yan daudu and independent women who lived there. One day, his employer, Alhaji Musa, came to the house to see his girlfriend, and discovered Mansur sitting with a group of 'yan daudu as they were doing *shewa*, a kind of jeering laughter that is stereotypically done by women in groups. As Mansur narrates it, this event had life-changing consequences for him.

Mansur: Duk lokacin da na dawo tallan goro, sai na biyo ta wurin Lami, kuma wannan gidan nasu ya zamo wurin hirata.
Lami: I.
Mansur: To, tun ina tallan goro, shi ubangidana na 'yan goro, in an ce min dan daudu ne, ina masifa. In an kira ni da sunan 'yan daudu. In ta bala'i, ina masifa. Barbado. Shi ke nan, sai aka yi- waye gari, yau ga shi, Allah, ya same ni a gidan Hassana Dan Daudu. Muna zaune a gun wannan-Alhaji

M: Whenever I came around selling kolanut, I'd stop by Lami's place, and this house of theirs became the place of my chatting <i.e., my hangout>.
L: Yes.
M: Okay, since I started selling kolanut, my boss, the one of all the kolanut sellers, if someone called me a dan daudu, I'd make trouble. If someone called me by the name of 'yan daudu. I'd make a stink, I'd make trouble. Barbado. That's it, then one- one day, there he was, <swear to> God, he saw me at the house of Hassana Dan Daudu. We

Aminu yake ko waye?

Mai sai da abinci–
Lami: m, Alhaji Aminu.
Mansur: An jere haka! In gaya
miki. Shi fa yake tare min faɗa,
Alhaji Musa na 'yan goro. Ya ce
ba za'a kira ni da ɗan daudu ba,
kawai sai ya zo ya tarar an jere,
ana ta ɗan ƙara shewa har da ni.
(xx) Barbado, wannan shewa da
ake, ina ganin (zuwan) Alhaji
Musa, kawai sai na kauce. Sai na
ɓoye. Shi ke nan, sai na ga- m-
Alhaji Musa ya shige cikin gida,
wurin yarinyarsa. Ni ma, saboda
in ɗebe kewa, kar ya [(xx)

Lami: [Ni dariya ma [[kake ba ni.
Mansur: [[Sai na bari, sai da ya
koma wurin yarinyar tashi. Ni
kuma, sai na tashi na je na
gaishe shi a nan wurin.
Tun daga rana mai kama ta
wannan- ta ran nan, na ce
"Allahna da manzon Allah, na
rufe tallan goron nan a Kaduna."
Tun da wannan mutumin ya zo
ya same ni cikin 'yan daudu ana
wannan shewa, na ce "to ni in
na koma, yaya zai ce min a
kasuwa?" Ni da ake dambe-
dambe da ni fa a kasuwa [(xx)
Barbado: ["Hasara," ko?=
Mansur: =I! In gaya miki. Na ce
"to,
ba zan fa koma ba" . . .

were sitting at Alhaji Aminu's place-
is that who it was?
The one who sells food–
L: Yeah, Alhaji Aminu.
M: We were lined up like this! Let
me tell you[f]. Alhaji Musa of the
kolanut sellers, it was he who
defended me from fights. He said no
one should call me ɗan daudu, and
then he came and found us lined up,
doing shewa over and over, me
included. (xx) Barbado, we were
doing this shewa when I saw Alhaji
Musa (coming), so I just ducked
down. I hid. That's it, then I saw-
m- Alhaji Musa went into the
house, to his girlfriend's place. And
I, to smooth things out, so he
wouldn't [(xx)
L: [Me, you're[m] making [[me laugh.
M: [[So I waited, till he went over
to his girlfriend's place. And I, then
I got up and went over to greet him
there. Ever since that very- that day,
I said "my God and the Prophet of
God, I'm done selling kolanut in
Kaduna." Since this guy came and
found me among 'yan daudu doing
this shewa, I said "Okay, if I go
back, what will he say to me in the
market?" I who get in to boxing-
boxing matches in the market [(xx)

B: [<He'd say> "What a loss," right?=
M: Yes! Let me tell you[f]. I said,
"Okay,
I won't go back" . . .

Afraid to face his boss again, Mansur went to Lami, who suggested
that the two of them should go to Katsina, where he had friends.
Since Mansur was in a rush to leave town, he ran away from home

– confiding only in his junior brother – and took a bus to Katsina, where he went about locating the 'yan daudu Lami had referred him to. Some of them treated him with disdain, but one dan daudu took him in, gave him room and board, and eventually introduced him to 'yan aras. By the time Lami arrived from Kaduna, Mansur was well established: "I was getting my money, Barbado. 'Yan aras. They set me up in this town" [*Ina samun kudina, Barbado. 'Yan aras. Sun daure min gindi gari wannan.*]

Judging from their narratives, Mansur and Lami seem to have had a sense of themselves as 'feminine' before they assumed public occupations and identities as 'yan daudu. In Mansur's case this is evident from his report that, while he was still selling kolanut, he enjoyed spending time with 'yan daudu, performed 'women's customs' like *shewa*, and had an intimate relationship with at least one dan aras (Usman, the ring-giver). It is also notable that while Mansur reacted violently when boys in the market called him a dan daudu, he did not hide his 'feminine' activities from his junior brother. Finally, Mansur's descriptions of his relations with 'yan aras suggest that he viewed sex with men, in the context of *karuwanci,* as an integral part of what it meant to do daudu, though not its determining feature.

Lami narrated his 'feminine' career somewhat differently. By referring to himself as a 'girl' in Kano, he indicated that he viewed himself as feminine when he was still in school studying the Qur'an, before he went off to 'roam the world' and 'sell yams.' This claim is comparable to the coming-out stories of Anglo-Americans who say they 'knew' they were gay or transgendered from a very early age. The historical truth-value of such claims may be unverifiable, but that does not diminish their value as 'life stories,' the purpose of which is to construct a coherent, intelligible sense of self in the present.[20] Like other constructs, a person's sense of self is likely to vary across social situations. On another occasion, when Lami and I were sitting alone in his shop, he described his move from Kano to Lagos by saying, "This *iskanci* took hold of me" [*Wannan iskanci ya kama ni*]. As noted previously, *iskanci* is a generic label for any activity considered frivolous and immoral, such as drinking alcohol, gambling, gossiping, etc. Although Lami did not practice Bori, by describing daudu as an immoral force that 'took hold of' [*kama*] him, he implicitly compared it to other unseen, malevolent forces that take hold of people, such as spirits. The negative moral judgment conveyed by this statement can be contrasted with the positive emotions indexed by Lami's references to being a 'girl' and his affectionate relationship with his 'girlfriend' Mansur.

Discourse analysts' observations about the role audiences play in influencing how speakers tell stories[21] compel us not to overlook the participation of Barbado and Mai Kwabo in the conversation. By addressing Barbado directly, Lami and Mansur made him their explicit target audience, and this in turn may have had a number of rhetorical effects. It could index efforts on each speaker's part to get Barbado to accept his version of the story. At the same time, Lami and Mansur may have been socializing their young companion, that is, educating him about the opportunities and problems of life in the bariki, and the ethical dilemmas he could expect to confront, especially with respect to 'girlfriends' and 'boyfriends.'[22]

Though he mostly remained silent, Mai Kwabo's conversational role should not be overlooked, for he was notably the only out-of-town guest, the only ɗan aras, and the one who had brought the tape-recorder. The attention Lami and Mansur paid to their relationships with 'yan aras was not lost on him; on several occasions he told me privately that his relationship with Lami was still intermittently sexual, and that he often sensed that Mansur was vying for his attention, too. Though I was not able to verify these claims with Lami and Mansur, the fact that Mai Kwabo and I had come from Kano with the express purpose of visiting Lami may well have conferred certain social advantages. For one thing, Mai Kwabo's visit affirmed that Lami was still attractive to 'her' former boyfriend. In addition, the fact that I had come along may have further enhanced Lami's social status, for my presence demonstrated Mai Kwabo's (and by extension, Lami's) potential access to the social and material benefits that presumably come from befriending and helping a *Bature*, or 'white man.' In this light, the moral values of loyalty and reciprocity that Lami invoked with his references to 'girlfriendship' were potentially relevant not only to his historical conflict with Mansur over Usman, but also to the current interaction, which featured a strikingly parallel triangle of gendered, sexual and affective relationships involving himself, Mansur and Mai Kwabo.

Conclusion

The 'life stories' of Jamilu, Kabiru, Hamza, Lami and Mansur demonstrate that there is no single way to 'go into daudu' or to be a ɗan daudu. Just as there is no single way of being a Hausa woman, acting 'like women' involves a flexible set of practices, relationships and cultural values with respect to gender, sexuality, kinship and work. The particular ways these elements are configured varies from one individual to another, from situation to situation, and changes over time. As with all social phenomena, this variation is not strictly predictable, but it does display certain patterns. Some of these patterns can be glimpsed in the ways different 'yan daudu narrated and evaluated their youthful experiences. In many cases, the path whereby a young man 'went into daudu' seems to have been marked by a painful psychological separation from home and kin. In Jamilu's case the pain was also physical, entailing the loss of his fingers as well as his dreams of becoming a boxer.

Participating in the social networks of 'people of the bariki' also played out in different ways, yielding emotional, erotic, and economic rewards for some 'yan daudu, but not for others. At its best, the bariki was a place of 'fellowship' [zumunci], where the friend of a friend might find kinship, a home, a livelihood, and even some fun. But as a popular Nigerian bumper-sticker says, "No condition is permanent."[23] The vagaries of Hamza's life were unfortunate but not unique, for life in the bariki – as in most socially marginalized spaces – was inevitably unstable and precarious. Poverty, illness, social discord, and the police kept many people on the move. Some quit the bariki altogether. An independent woman might get married and become 'respectable' (though she could always get divorced and come back to the bariki if things didn't work out).[24] And some 'yan daudu might 'leave daudu' [bar daudu] and return to living as a conventionally masculine man – or so it would seem.

One man I knew was said to have 'left daudu' to become a live-in servant for a middle-class family. In his spare time, he sometimes visited his old 'yan daudu friends who continued to sell food elsewhere in town. His former associates still considered him a 'girlfriend,' but they respected his need for discretion and refrained from visiting him at his employers' home. Like Mansur, when he was still selling kolanut, this man both was and was not a ɗan daudu. His gender identifications varied depending on where he was, who he was with, and the things he was doing at any given time. In the distinctive 'dialect' [*yare*] of 'yan daudu, he was known as a *ɗan daudun riga* ['shirted ɗan daudu'] – someone who kept his unconventional gender practices hidden from public view (and public hearing). But it is not only shirted 'yan daudu who have secrets. 'Yan daudu who 'come out in the open' have them too.

Notes

1 Madari is the seat of a local government area (LGA) that had a popu-lation of approximately 90,000 in the early 1990s; the town itself had roughly 20,000 inhabitants. When I first visited Madari in 1993, the market area had one restaurant and three food-stands run by 'yan daudu and at least four restaurants run by Hausa-speaking independent women. Several other restaurants were operated by male or (married) female migrants from southern Nigeria. A 'restaurant' [*gidan abinci*, literally 'food house'] had a covered dining area (with or without walls) and served proper meals featuring a starchy staple like rice or *tuwo*. A 'stand' [*tebur*, literally 'table'] was uncovered and usually served fried snacks, such as sweet-potatoes, white potatoes and chicken.

2 M. G. Smith (1959).

3 Barkow (1973).

4 Such status contradictions also occurred in the precolonial period, see, e.g., Stilwell (2004) and Nast (2005) on the status of palace slaves. My claim is not that colonialism generated such contradictions, but rather that it multiplied status contradictions and made them more frequent (Smith 1959; Hill 1972; Pierce 2005).

5 Pierce (2003: 469).

6 Barkow (1973); Rain (1999).

7 Abdullahi (1984); Kleis and Abdullahi (1983).

8 On the notion that gender and sexual identities are 'performed,' linguistic anthropologists often refer to the ethnomethodological work of Kessler and McKenna (1985) and West and Zimmerman (1987), and to later anthologies, including Hall and Bucholtz (1995); Hall and Livia (1997); Bucholtz, Liang and Sutton (1999); and McIlvenny (2002), which draw in part on the speech-act theories of Searle (1969) and Austin (1975) as interpreted by Butler (1990, 1993, 2004). For a lively debate on the merits of making gender and sexual 'identity' the focus

of linguistic-anthropological research, see Leap (1996); Kulick (2000); Eckert (2002); Cameron and Kulick (2003; 2005); and Bucholtz and Hall (2004).

9   For a careful ethnographic treatment of such debates in the United States (particularly New York City), see Valentine (2007).

10   Bauman and Briggs (1990); Plummer (1995).

11   Abu-Lughod (1993); Goodwin (1990).

12   Linde (1993).

13   E.g., M. F. Smith (1981: 259).

14   *Kífíi* ['turning over'] is unrelated to *kíifíi* ['fish'], though both words have the same standard spelling (*kifi*).

15   Most of Katsina's population, including 'people of the bariki,' still resided within the city-state's ancient walls. There was no colonial-era 'native quarter' outside the old city, such as Kano's Sabon Gari.

16   Labov (1972).

17   Some of the Hausa forms that I have represented with English pronouns are actually parts of verb phrases called aspect markers. Like the endings of Spanish verb conjugations (e.g., *hablo* 'I speak'; *hablamos* 'we speak'), Hausa aspect markers show grammatical agreement with a subject pronoun that may or may not be expressed. This is indicated as [m](masculine), [f](feminine), and [pl](plural).

18   Shuman (1986).

19   Charlotte Linde (1993: 90–94) describes 'explanation' as a device that storytellers use to repair apparent ruptures in the coherence of their 'life stories,' in order to construct an image of self that is consistently virtuous.

20   Linde (1993).

21   Shuman (1986); Duranti (1994: 159); Goodwin (1990: 234–237).

22   On the use of language to socialize young people, classic texts include Heath (1983); Ochs (1988); Schieffelin (1988); and the chapters in Schieffelin and Ochs (1986). On narrative socialization, see especially Heath (1986); Miller et al. (1990); and Ochs and Capps (2001).

23   Lawuyi (1997).

24   Pittin (2003).

WOMEN'S TALK, MEN'S SECRETS

Mansur had a knack for stealing his girlfriends' boyfriends. Not long after he ran away to Katsina, he got entangled in a new love triangle involving Mudi, the dan daudu who had taken him in, and Mudi's boyfriend, Abba. Mansur and Abba had apparently met while Mansur was working at Mudi's restaurant.

"Wow, that Mudi, was he jealous," Mansur told his young friend Barbado, as Lami and Mai Kwabo listened in. "It was like he was going to kill himself, he was so jealous. Abba was his dan aras, see. I'd been helping out at Mudi's restaurant, cooking pepper-soup with guinea-fowl meat. He took some soup to my Abba, let me tell you[f], but Abba swore the soup must have been made with a 'medicine,' so he refused to eat it. Abba and I really loved each other, see. Wallahi, Mudi must have brought him that pepper-soup seven times, but whenever she set it down, he refused to taste it. He knew it was made with a 'medicine.' He knew how Katsina people are, that's why he didn't eat the meat. Mudi – you[m] know – he was ready to kill himself. Mudi – you[f] know – she was ready to kill herself over Abba . . ."

Inspired by the idea of using a potion or 'medicine' [magani] to win a man's affection, Lami turned to Mai Kwabo and in a quiet, seductive voice, asked, "How about me, my father? If I made some pepper-soup for you[m], would you[m] refuse to eat it?"

"Of course I'd eat it," Mai Kwabo declared. "Wallahi, nothing would happen to me."

"You[m] know," Lami gently assured him. "I wouldn't give you[m] anything to eat that would kill you[m]."

"I wouldn't be afraid to eat anything you[m] brought me," Mai Kwabo insisted.

"Doesn't your[m] family make you[m] pepper-soup?" inquired Lami, coyly pretending to be jealous by referring to Mai Kwabo's wife.

Ever the flirt, Mai Kwabo shot back: "You're[m] right here, my bride."

"Oh, he doesn't have a wife," Mansur interjected, throwing water on the flames of Lami and Mai Kwabo's rekindled affection.

"Who doesn't have a wife?" huffed Lami, indignantly.

"Says who?" Mai Kwabo demanded.

"He's got a wife AND a mistress," Lami bragged, defending Mai Kwabo's masculine honor. "He's doing lots of mistressing these days." (The word dadaro ['mistress'] can refer to the person or the practice.)

"Is it someone with bowls, or what?" Mansur asked. ('Bowls' [koko] was the in-group term for 'breasts.' 'Someone with bowls' [mai koko] was slang for 'woman.')

"He's got someone with bowls and a meka," Lami replied, meaning that Mai Kwabo had two 'mistresses' – a woman and a ɗan daudu.

Mansur asked again: "Is it someone with bowls – a karuwa – or is it a meka?"

Lami was growing impatient. "One mistress is someone with bowls – a karuwa – she's got family here in town. But I'm sure he's got a ɗan daudu as his mistress in Kano, too, since I know he can't stay without one."

"Shegiya, Lami!" Mansur laughed. The epithet literally means 'female bastard,' though as used here it was roughly equivalent to the English insult, 'you bitch!'

Mansur and Lami's banter with respect to Mai Kwabo exemplifies the kinds of rivalries 'yan daudu often engaged in over the men they called their 'boyfriends' [samari], 'husbands' [mazaje], or 'yan aras. These rivalries typically revolved around suspicions that one ɗan daudu was trying to 'steal' another's boyfriend, sometimes by devious means such as 'medicine' [magani], i.e., charms or potions. Occasionally, as we saw in Chapter 3 in the story about Usman and the ring, these rivalries erupted into open conflict. More frequently, 'yan daudu competed indirectly, using a speech genre known as habaici, which consists of catty insults and innuendo. Habaici often incorporates other 'indirect' speech genres, especially proverbs, and is supposedly used to 'hide meanings' [*boye ma'ana*] that may be awkward or impolite to express openly.

Both habaici and proverbs [*karin magana*, literally 'folded speech'] are stereotypically associated with women, especially co-wives, i.e., women married to the same man in a polygamous household. According to dominant cultural norms, co-wives are supposed to treat each other like sisters, showing mutual affection and support while respecting hierarchies of age and marital longevity. (A man's senior wife is known as *uwargida* ['mother of the house'], while junior wives are known as *amarya* ['bride'].) In Hausa popular culture, however – folktales, novels, dramas and films – co-wives are invariably depicted as jealous, conniving and back-biting. The word *kishiya* ['co-wife'] is even derived from the word for 'jealousy' [*kishi*], and has the additional meaning of 'opposite.'[1] Women's reputation for using habaici and proverbs thus arises from the rivalries that are supposedly common in polygamous households. The co-wife's penchant for irony and sarcasm is itself the subject of numerous proverbs, for example: *Na taɓa ki da alheri, kishiya ta taɓa kishiya da bakin wuta* ['I touch you with good intentions, says one co-wife to another as she touches her with a burning piece of wood'].[2]

In the conversation excerpted above, Mansur and Lami could be compared to co-wives who were competing for the attention and approval of both a ɗan aras (Mai Kwabo) and a younger ɗan daudu (Barbado). When Mansur asserted that Mai Kwabo "doesn't have a wife," for example, he was not only insulting Mai Kwabo's masculine honor; he was also implicitly disparaging Lami, whom Mai Kwabo had just called his 'bride.' (Mai Kwabo did have one legal wife – the 'mother of his house' – who lived with him in Kano.) Even if Lami and Mai Kwabo were no longer sexually involved, their relationship clearly still had an erotic dimension and remained important to Lami, who rushed to defend Mai Kwabo's sexual prowess by bragging about his 'mistresses' [*dadaro*], who supposedly included both a woman and a ɗan daudu. In response to this rather outlandish claim, Mansur's laughing use of the feminine epithet *shegiya* ['female bastard, bitch'] suggests that any rivalry between him and Lami may have been more playful and affectionate than it was serious. Despite its popular associations with competition and conflict, therefore, 'the talk of women' can also be seen as an assertion of 'feminine' solidarity.

The above exchange exemplifies 'the talk of women' in other respects as well. Note, for example, how Mansur shifts between feminine and masculine grammatical forms in referring to Barbado (addressed as both 'you^m' and 'you^f') and Mudi (referred to as both 'she' and 'he'). Like names (e.g., *Lami*) and other labels (e.g., *shegiya*), gendered pronouns and other forms that refer to people are a linguistic resource that 'yan daudu sometimes use to represent themselves and others as 'feminine.'[3] Although the use of such forms is highly noticeable, it is also relatively rare; in day-to-day speech 'yan daudu usually refer to each other, and prefer to be addressed, with masculine forms. The use of gendered grammatical forms should thus be viewed not as a simple reflection of 'yan daudu's identities as 'feminine men,' but as a strategic means whereby they index their stances with respect to the activities and relationships that are relevant in particular social contexts. Because social contexts, relationships and stances shift, it is often helpful to speak of one's 'subject position,' which is relatively flexible and negotiable, rather than one's 'identity,' which is usually thought of as enduring, stable and even fixed.

'The talk of women' as performed by 'yan daudu – comprising feminine names and pronouns; 'indirect' speech genres; the laughter known as *shewa*; certain kinds of songs; and stereotypically feminine phonetic practices like speaking with a high-pitched, nasal or breathy voice – is often described by other Hausa people as annoying and shameless. At the same time, many people also find it clever and funny. This mix of aesthetic and moral responses seems contradictory, but it points to the ways in which 'yan daudu's uses of 'women's talk' play with norms of gender, sexuality and social space. For example, when 'yan daudu use habaici in a *bariki* setting, they take a speech genre traditionally associated with heterosexual domesticity and bring it into a public zone of illicit, lower-class sexuality, coming scandalously and (for some listeners) tantalizingly close to violating Hausa Muslim norms of privacy and shame.

Even more scandalously, the sight and sound of two men reenacting the sexual rivalry of co-wives implicitly raise the taboo subject of homosexuality. Notwithstanding their supposed 'shamelessness,' the 'yan daudu I knew were intensely private about their sex lives and normally discussed them only with other 'people who do the deed' [*masu harka*]. They also made use of a supposedly secret lexicon, or slang, which they called *yaren harka* ['harka dialect']. This 'dialect' included some terms adapted from standard Hausa, such as *harka* ['deed'] for 'homosexual sex' and *mai ƙoƙo* ['someone with bowls'] for 'woman'; it also included words that had no apparent meaning outside the 'secret' social world of 'people who do the deed,' such as *meka* and *ashi* for 'ɗan daudu' and *ɗan aras* for 'masculine man who has sex with men.' Other harka dialect terms included *lemo* ['citrus fruit, soda pop'] for 'penis' (presumably from the shape of a soda bottle); *birni* ['walled city'] for 'anus'; and *makaho* ['blind person'] for 'heterosexual.' For audiences who understood it, the harka dialect highlighted the sexual meanings 'hidden' in 'yan daudu's performances of 'the talk of women,' and was an additional source of aesthetic pleasure and social solidarity. The social solidarity of 'men who seek men' was limited, however, by the gender, class and moral hierarchies that distinguished 'yan daudu from 'civilians' [*fararen-hula*], that is, 'men who seek men' who are conventionally masculine. The social and spatial divisions between these groups is the focus of the last part of the chapter.

Playing and Laughing with Language and Gender

Alhaji Ado had a restaurant inside Madari's motor-park, a walled-in area about the size of a football field, where long-distance 'bush taxis' and minivans picked up and dropped off passengers and their cargo. With the assistance of a few younger 'yan daudu who usually called him 'father' [*bàbá*], Alhaji Ado prepared meals of rice and stew over an open fire next to a one-room structure with a corrugated metal roof in which he served his customers. Above the entrance into the restaurant someone – not Alhaji Ado, who could not read or write – had painted in black the words WASA DA DARIYA HOTEL / ALHAJI ADO. Once, when I asked Alhaji Ado about the name, he told me that *wasa da dariya* ['play and laughter'] was what 'yan daudu were known for: "We don't like fighting," he said, "just playing and laughing."

Sunday was Alhaji Ado's busiest day of the week, which he looked forward to not only because the weekly market was his main source of income, but also because of the visits he could expect from friends and acquaintances, some of whom would spend several hours chatting with him and helping him with his work. Before the adoption of Shari'a, the town regularly hosted visitors on other occasions as well, especially *wasan Bori* (spirit-possession performances) and *bikis* hosted by local 'yan daudu or independent women. These events usually lasted several days at a time and drew large numbers of participants and spectators, many of whom would come from long distances. Nighttime festivities were the highlight of these events, but visitors also enjoyed socializing during the day. With its secluded location at the back of the motor-park, the large shade-tree near Alhaji Ado's restaurant was especially popular as a daytime meeting place. Musicians, praise-shouters, Bori practitioners, 'yan daudu, independent women and other 'people of the bariki' would sit or lie for hours on large mats woven of plastic or grass, chatting, arguing, napping, smoking, playing board-games, and occasionally sharing in food or drink if someone had the money to spring for it. Every so often one of the musicians would take out his *garaya* (a string instrument) and sing an impromptu song, improvising the words to praise, flatter or tease someone present. At other times a group of younger 'yan daudu might get up and stand in a circle, clapping, dancing and singing 'women's' songs.

The following snippet, though not recorded in Madari, is typical of the songs I heard at such times. Like the conversation excerpted at the top of this chapter and in Chapter 3, this song was recorded in Katsina on a weekend in 1994 when Mai Kwabo and I had traveled from Kano with the hope of making some tape-recordings. We made the first recording close to midnight on Saturday, after Lami and Mansur had finished cleaning up and were ready to sit and relax in Lami's restaurant. Knowing that I was interested in hearing how 'yan daudu did 'the talk of women,' they asked two of their friends to join us: Barbado, a younger dan daudu who happened to be in the neighborhood, and Haruna, who operated a restaurant next door to Lami's and was said to have a clever way with words. A few men from the neighborhood – not 'yan daudu – were also present, looking on from the sidelines. (Another dan daudu who worked with Haruna was invited to join us, but he refused. The others told me he felt 'shame' [*kunya*] and 'fear' [*tsoro*] because he did not know me and was worried the tape-recording might be used to embarrass him.)

At the request of Haruna and Mansur, I gave them money so they could buy some whisky, which they shared with Mai Kwabo and Barbado. (Lami did not drink alcohol.) As the bottle got emptier, the conversation grew more lively; at one point, Mansur and Barbado spontaneously started to sing. The refrain at the bottom of each stanza (*E sakatile tillewa*) is a nonsense phrase akin to English 'Hi de hi de ho' and is typical of songs sung by Hausa girls.[4]

"Go back home"

Barbado: Daudunki ni bai birgen ba.
Yayinki ni bai birgen ba.
Gwadarenki ba ya birge ni.
Kwallinki ba ya birge ni.
Ki koma gida aikin lambu,
ko tomaturi ko tattasai,
ko allayahu, ma sha taushe.
E sakatile, tillewa

B: Your[f] daudu hasn't impressed me.
Your[f] turn hasn't impressed me.
Your[f] sweet-talking doesn't impress me.
Your[f] make-up doesn't impress me.
Go back home to tend the vegetables,
tomatoes or peppers,
or spinach, we want to drink *taushe* [soup]
E sakatile, tillewa

Mansur: Gafara kadan, gafara kadan,
gafara kadan, rada danni!
Daudunki ba ki birgen ba.
(xx)ki ma bai birgen ba.
Ki koma gida don ki soye
ko yakuwa, ko tattasai,
ko tomaturi.
E sakatile, tillewa.

M: Pardon me a little, pardon me a little,
pardon me a little, wallflower!
Your[f] daudu, you[f] haven't impressed me.
And your[f] [xx] hasn't impressed me.
Go back home so you[f] can fry
red sorrel or peppers
or tomatoes.
E sakatile, tillewa.

By contrasting the urban glamour of daudu with the tedious work of farming, this song presents an idealized version of the migrations that characterize the lives of many 'yan daudu and independent women. Insofar as it makes light of those experiences, the song exemplifies the 'playing and laughing' which Alhaji Ado identified as the trademark of daudu. As noted earlier, respectable Hausa men are not supposed to dance or sing unless it is part of their trade, and even this is acceptable only for certain traditionally low-status occupations. Otherwise, singing and dancing are restricted to women and girls at wedding parties or naming ceremonies. Moreover, the content of the song also displays feminine talents. The haughty refusals to be impressed and the catty way each ɗan daudu tells the other to go back to his home in the countryside, back to the unglamorous tasks of farming or frying vegetables, recall the catty competitions waged by stereotypical co-wives.

'Yan daudu's reputed skill with proverbs and habaici is frequently cited as evidence of their 'love of play' [son wasa]. While the Hausa term wasa can refer to behaviors that are seen to be frivolous and inconsequential, it also refers more generally to a variety of cultural practices associated with marginalized social groups. What counts as 'play' is a consequence of the unequal distribution of status and power in Hausa Muslim society. Gender is a key axis of such inequality, along with other social attributes such as wealth, rank, education and age. Thus, children's games and teenage boys' recreational sports are considered innocuous forms of 'play,' as are the dancing and singing performed by women and girls at bikis, traditional festivities commemorating weddings and namings. Such merry-making is considered undignified for men and older boys, who normally sit and talk quietly outside the home in which a biki is going on. A similar equation of play and profanity is evident in the fact that activities of the Bori spirit-possession society are referred to as wasa – even by Bori practitioners who self-identify as Muslims – though this label is never applied to orthodox Islamic rituals.[5]

The notion of wasa, therefore, invokes dominant discourses which label as frivolous, vulgar or morally suspect the cultural practices of marginalized social groups: children, women, the poor and uneducated, rural folk, social deviants and infidels. Many of these practices fall under the rubric of Hausa 'traditional customs' [al'adun gargajiya], which elite and aspiring Muslim urbanites typically view as distinct from, if not inferior to, their own more sophisticated lifestyle. Respectable Muslim men in particular are expected to focus their attention on serious matters and to have no time for 'play.' Many traditional oral-literary genres are likewise considered forms of verbal play unsuitable for elite adult men. Thus, kirari ['praise-epithets'] are composed and performed by maroka ['praise-shouters'], who are usually low-status males; women, elderly folk and older children narrate folktales [tatsuniyoyi] for the enjoyment of the very young; and the clever use of proverbs and habaici is associated not only with women and 'yan daudu, but also with other low-status groups, including butchers and *Maguzawa*, non-Muslim practitioners of Bori.[6] The only literary activities deemed worthy of the Muslim male elite have historically been religious treatises (often written in Arabic) and song-poems (*wakoki*) dealing with Islamic religious and political themes, most of which are composed, performed and published by educated male poet-singers. Respectable Hausa Muslim men can take these genres seriously because they see them as addressing issues of 'truth' [*gaskiya*], especially Islamic faith and practice, while more 'traditional' genres such as folktales are dismissed as mere 'play' because they traffic in 'lies' [*karya*] and are meant only to entertain. By openly engaging in 'playful' activities considered unseemly for respectable Muslim men, 'yan daudu explicitly align themselves with other low-status and 'traditional' groups, such as Bori practitioners, musicians and women, especially independent women. The latter qualification is especially important to make, because, although daudu is defined as the practice of men who act 'like women,' women do not constitute an undifferentiated class. Rather, the dominant Hausa conception of 'woman' is based on a binary moral distinction between married women and karuwai, between good women and bad. The ways in which 'yan daudu play with 'women's' language, therefore, not only destabilize the fundamental gender dichotomy between male and female; their play also highlights the unstable and fractured nature of the category of 'woman.'

Dominant Perceptions of Proverbs and Habaici

Academics have treated the subjects of Hausa proverbs and habaici very differently, in ways that reflect popular ideologies of language and gender. Proverbs have attracted literary and linguistic scholars' attentions because of the important position they are seen to have in Hausa oral traditions,[7] and because of their distinctive structural properties.[8] Yahaya and Dangambo echo the popular belief that women, praise-shouters and 'yan daudu use proverbs more often than other speakers do, but acknowledge that all kinds of people make use of them.[9] Their claim that the use of *karin magana* requires wisdom [*hikima*], skill [*fusaha*] and cleverness [*azanci*] also reflects popular ideas about language use: in high-school debates sponsored by the Kano

State History and Culture Bureau, for example, I noticed that girls and boys earned extra points for the skillful rhetorical use of Hausa proverbs.

While proverbs are used by a variety of speakers and enjoy a great degree of academic and popular respect, habaici has a far less exalted place in Hausa linguistic ideologies. Gidley (1967) and Furniss (1995), for example, refer briefly to the popular association of habaici with a speaker's malicious intent, while Rufa'i (1986) reports that habaici are widely considered a "women's domain" because they demonstrate "weakness."[10] Conversations with nonacademic Hausa speakers reveal similar negative attitudes about habaici as the linguistic symptom of (women's) 'powerlessness' [rashin ƙarfi], 'fear' [tsoro] and 'lack of sense' [rashin hankali]. Not surprisingly, habaici are in general not seen to have much literary value and do not appear in most scholarly discussions of Hausa oral traditions. One exception is Gidley's (1967) discussion of Hausa comedians known as 'yan kama, in which he describes habaici as a useful, albeit mean-spirited way of "using Hausa sayings" to mock someone indirectly. According to Gidley, 'yan kama make use of a "modified form" of habaici from which the usual "sting" is removed by the comedians' "skilful touches of humour."[11]

Yet humor does not always imply a lack of malicious intent; nor does it assure that the presumed targets of a habaici will not be offended. By way of example, one day I was sitting in a Madari bar with Mai Kwabo and another friend, Idris, who was also a young, conventionally masculine man from Kano; another man was seated alone at the table next to ours. The man was obviously drunk and had been trying, awkwardly and without success, to engage us in conversation, and became upset at our refusal to acknowledge him. Without turning to face us, he started muttering angrily under his breath, just loud enough for us to hear him. The more we tried to ignore him, the more he proceeded to taunt us.

"You[pl] haven't recognized who I am," he shouted. "I am the son of the emir of Madari." With this claim he implied that, despite his drunken demeanor, he was a person worthy of respect, and that we had behaved improperly towards him.

At this point, Idris, who had been biting his tongue, lost patience and turned to address the man. "You're[m] the son of the emir of Madari?!" he shot back. "Well, if that's so, then I'm the son of the emir of Kano. Between the emir of Madari and the emir of Kano, who's greater?" We all knew that the small emirate of Madari had historically paid allegiance to Kano, so it was the emir of Kano (and his son) to whom the royal family of Madari needed to show respect, not the reverse.

This example of men using habaici suggests its common association with women is based at least as much on ideological concerns as it is on objective facts about gender and language use. Indeed, the fact that habaici is reputed to be a feminine specialty not only reflects popular beliefs about women's speech; it also reflects normative ideas about how men should and should not talk. Several features of this exchange demonstrate why habaici is considered undignified for respectable Hausa Muslim men. First, the man at the next table was obviously drunk, talking to himself while sitting alone in a bar. Second, his claim to being the son of the town's emir is boastful, outlandish and childish, and shows a lack of respect for the emir, for even if he *were* his son, his mere presence in the bar – not to mention his drunken behavior – would be a royal disgrace. Third, the fact that my friend Idris got visibly and audibly angry and condescended to respond to the man's insinuation reflects a lack of equanimity and self-restraint, which Hausa men are supposed to cultivate. Although he had clearly triumphed rhetorically, Idris remained agitated for some time afterwards, and was embarrassed when I brought it up with him several days later.

Gidley's observation that habaici "is a very useful practice in Hausa society at all levels"[12] fails to take into account the ways in which ideologies of gender, rank, and social respectability affect normative ideas about the appropriateness of this particular form of 'indirect' communication for different types of people. That 'yan kama make use of a 'modified' form of habaici in order not to offend their audiences is a case in point. Consequently, while I argue, along with Gidley, that the skillful use of both habaici and proverbs by (some) 'yan daudu involves a high degree of social and linguistic skill and creativity, I do not concur with his observation that habaici is simply a 'useful' way of mocking someone without directly insulting him, or that the use of habaici is equally sanctioned 'at all levels' of Hausa society. Rather, 'yan daudu's cultivated proficiency in the use of such a stigmatized linguistic form reflects a defiant response to their own marginalization and stigmatization. Whereas other men, such as Idris, might feel they disgrace themselves through a public exchange of innuendo, 'yan daudu who use habaici do so as a way of proclaiming their rejection of behavioral norms.

Performing Proverbs and Habaici

As a doctoral student of sociolinguistics, I was anxious to record concrete instances of 'yan daudu's 'womanlike' talk. Examples of 'yan daudu using feminine names, pronouns and *shewa* were easy to find, and proverbs could be easily elicited, but their famously skillful use of habaici eluded me. In part, this was because my command of Hausa grammar and vocabulary was simply not up to the task of recognizing and understanding such artful kinds of language. But formal linguistic proficiency was not my only problem. I was also hampered by the fact that habaici is not a discrete linguistic form that can be isolated from the ongoing flow of conversation. Rather, it is a mode of speaking that by its nature is hard to detect. The elusive quality of habaici became a bit more understandable to me when Mai Kwabo and I sat down in Lami's restaurant to make a tape-recording with him, Mansur, Barbado and Haruna.

At one point, Audu, a young man from the neighborhood who had been watching from the sidelines, tried to help me explain what I meant when I asked Haruna and the others to provide specific examples of habaici. Haruna at first resisted this request, insisting that to comply would be 'useless work' [*aikin banza*]. He buttressed this claim by citing a number of proverbs, which are underlined.

Audu: Akwai habaici wanda za ka ji, an yi shi kamar karin magana=
Haruna: =Aikin banza! To, ai [(xx)
Audu: [Akwai habaici wanda za'a yi cikin magana=
Haruna: =Aikin banza! <u>Agwagwa tura ta cikin ruwa.</u>
Audu: Wannan karin magana ce.=
Haruna: =To, wane irin habaici? Habaici. Haba Allah. Ai tun kahin a daɗe ana yi. Billahillazi, <u>tun

A: There's habaici that you'll hear, it was done like a proverb=
H: =Useless work! OK, well [(xx)
A: [There's habaici that'll be done while speaking=
H: =Useless work! <u>A duck, push it in water.</u>
A: That is a proverb.=
H: =OK, what kind of habaici? Habaici. For God's sake. Since before a long time ago people

kahin a yi, duniya, Allah ya riga ya yi Manzon Allah. (xx) shi na duniya. Kuma tun kahin, a h[aih]i uwar mai sabulu, balbela ta[ke da farinta.

Barbado: [take da farinta ba? (.)
((slap)) Tun kahin a haihi uwar mai sabulu balbela (take da farinta)

have been doing it. By God, since before the world was made, God had already made the Prophet of God. (xx) him of the world. And since before the mother of the one with soap was born, the buff-backed heron had her whiteness.

B: had her whiteness, no? (.)
((slap)) Since before the mother of the one with soap was born the buff-backed heron (had her whiteness)

Audu attempted to elicit examples of habaici by comparing its use in conversation to the way people use proverbs. He elicited instead Haruna's disdainful remark characterizing Audu's request as 'useless work' [*aikin banza*]. (*Banza*, an abstract noun, is commonly used as an epithet denoting meaninglessness and worthlessness; it appears frequently in proverbs.[13]) Haruna emphasized this negative evaluation by citing a proverb which is most familiar to Hausa speakers as *Tura agwagwa cikin ruwa* ['Push a duck in water'], epitomizing useless action in a manner similar to the English idiom, "Carry coals to Newcastle." Audu ignored the intent of Haruna's statement and instead focuses on its formal status as a proverb, treating it as an interactional mistake; he thus implied that Haruna had confused the two genres, though Audu's own initial statement also obscured the differences between proverbs and habaici. Audu thus failed to acknowledge the cleverness Haruna had displayed in making use of a proverb at the same as he was criticizing Audu's request for a proverb-like example of habaici.

Haruna defended his resistance to producing examples of habaici with the claim that people have been doing habaici "since before a long time ago." Such an age-old phenomenon, he implied, needs no comment or elaboration. He then cited two proverbs which speak to the theme of ancient truths. The first recounts the doctrine that God created the Prophet Muhammad before creating the physical world – a belief derived from the Sufi (Islamic mystical) veneration of the Prophet.[14] The second proverb refers to one of God's more mundane creations, *balbela*, the buff-backed heron (also called the cattle egret), a bird renowned for its whiteness. 'The one with soap' [*mai sabulu*] refers to the individual who first brought or invented soap. That the buff-backed heron was white not just before the advent of soap, but even before the birth of the mother of the one who brought or invented soap, emphasizes the intrinsic nature of the bird's color. Both proverbs serve to buttress Haruna's critique of the business at hand, which is, broadly, to explain the phenomenon of habaici for the sake of a foreign researcher. By appealing to long-standing aspects of God's creation, Haruna implies that habaici, like the primordial existence of Muhammad and the buff-backed heron's whiteness, is an immanent reality that does not lend itself to rational explanation.

Barbado's echo of Haruna's statement reflects the call-and-response format that frequently characterizes the use of proverbs; it also reflects the fact that the *balbela* proverb in particular forms part of the linguistic repertoire of many 'yan daudu. On several occasions I was told by Hausa speakers – 'yan daudu and non-'yan daudu alike – that using this proverb typically marked a male speaker as woman-like; the thigh-slap which punctuated Barbado's statement is a stereotypically feminine gesture that reinforces the proverb's femin-izing effect. Men who are not 'yan daudu (or do not wish to be seen as 'yan daudu) are not likely to cite this proverb, lest they leave themselves open to accusations that they are "talking like a woman" or, even worse, "talking like a ɗan daudu." At various points in the conversation excerpted here, Haruna made several other seemingly incongruous references to *balbela*. For example, having offered up a toast and led the other 'yan daudu in a burst of *shewa*, Haruna invoked the buff-backed heron in the context of praising God's name: "*Wallahi tallahi*, by God who there is no god but Him. God we thank you. Between the buff-backed heron and the Lord- do- do more shewa please so the cassette will be good." At another point, after failing to lure another ɗan daudu inside the shop to participate in the tape-recording session, Haruna decided not to pursue the matter any further: "OK, by God, that's all. Between the buff-backed heron and the Lord, there's only thanks."

The mention of the buff-backed heron in these examples, where one might expect a more conventional, first-person expression of thanks to God, suggests a metaphorical association between *balbela* and 'yan daudu. In fact, the cultural image of the buff-backed heron, which, as a grammatically feminine noun, is always referred to as 'she' or 'her,' reflects the self-image of many 'yan daudu in interesting ways. Whiteness, the bird's primary distinguishing characteristic, typically connotes goodness and beauty in Hausa. For example, *farin ciki* ['white stomach'] signifies happiness, while the phrase *ya yi fari* ['he has become white'] indicates that the person referred to looks better and healthier than he did previously. The equation of whiteness with beauty is not just metaphorical; many Hausa people consider a light complexion to be more attractive and desirable than dark skin. Physical beauty is a matter of particular concern to many 'yan daudu, whose efforts at enhancing their looks, like those of many independent women, sometimes include using chemicals to straighten their hair and lotions to bleach their skin. The intrinsically white *balbela*, however, does not even need soap to maintain her beauty. Yet the image of the buff-backed heron has a less flattering side, as well. The expression *balbela ci da motsin wani* ['the buff-backed heron [which] eat[s] with the movement of someone else'] refers to the bird's practice of eating the insects which rise from the grass when other animals walk through it, and connotes a person who sponges off others.[15] *Balbela*, therefore, combines a beautiful appearance with an objectionable occupation, a striking parallel to the image of the ɗan daudu in Hausa culture: a feminized figure whom many find attractive and entertaining, at the same time as they criticize him for the ways he lives and works.

Habaici as Sexual Put-down

Despite Haruna's initial resistance to the idea of reciting habaici, he quickly warmed to the task, providing a number of examples, three of which are featured here. The elaborate structure of these examples illustrates Audu's contention that habaici is done *cikin magana*, 'in the course of speaking.' Indeed, although Audu speaks of a similarity between habaici and *karin magana*, Haruna's examples demonstrate that, at least in the idealized form in which he presents it, meaningful habaici is much more embedded in an ongoing discourse than proverbs typically need to be. Because proverbs constitute a canonized, albeit loosely defined, class of utterances, speakers can often recite and recognize them in isolation: one finds them written, for example, on the rear windows of public buses. In contrast, speakers typically describe habaici, which is a relatively undefined and stig-matized speech genre, as more context-dependent. This sense of habaici's greater embeddedness in discourse may have been one of the factors contributing to Haruna's initial unwillingness to provide examples of it.

Haruna: Habaici kuma **ke banza!** **Dinkin kasuwa. Yaushe ne? Ake ba ki takarda muke d- d- d- dariya muka ta- ta hana ki tafiya.** Habai[ci (xx)

H: And habaici, **you[f], useless! Market sewing! When is it?! Youf were being given papers, we were l- l- l- laughing we kept stopping you[f] from going.** Habai[ci (xx)

Barbado: [Yo wai, ba ka ma [[sani ba!
Haruna: [[Tsaya. **Kai don Allah, haba wawa. Zauna kurum. Zance ka zo, ba ni da ruwa in cika ka. Wallahi tallahi sori ɗinka.** Shi ne habaici.

B: [Hey, you[m] don't even [[know!
H: [[Stop. **You[m] please, come on, clown. Just sit down. You've[m] come to talk? I don't have any water for you[m]. By God by God sorry for you[m].** That's habaici.

Kai don Allah, in ka ga akuya ta zo, **ke! Banza ce, na- (na kiwon ruwa). Tsinanna 'yar iska. Allah haka yake son ganinki. Billahillazi, sai dai ki yiwo [titi ki yi kallo kuma ki ɗauki abinmu jama'a.** Shi ne habaici. . . .

You[m] please, if you[m] see a goat has come, **you[f]! Useless, (animal grazing in water).**[16] **Damned[f] good-for-nothing[f]. That's how God wants to see you[f]. By God, just cross over the street, look around and take a thing of ours, the people.** That's habaici. . . .

Haruna's opening remark ("And habaici . . .") and the coda ("That's habaici") frame his utterances as mini-performances executed at my, Mai Kwabo's and Audu's request. In the absence of any 'real' moti-vation, expressions of abuse such as 'market sewing' and 'clown' serve to set the stage for each habaici by identifying a (changing) imaginary recipient of Haruna's 'innuendoes.' Because of their arti-ficial nature, therefore, Haruna's examples represent a kind of ideal type of habaici rather than spontaneous instances of the genre. The three habaici he provides here display a common syntactic structure consisting of: (1) a vocative ('hey!' or 'you!'); (2) one or more abu-sive epithets; (3) a mild put-down in the form of a short rhetorical question or command, and (4) a series of clauses that constitutes the core of the habaici.

The first habaici represents an attempt to embarrass an imaginary female addressee, whom Haruna mocks by referring to the time her husband allegedly served her with divorce papers. Locating himself in a group of onlookers, presumably the co-wife and/or female neighbors of the addressee, Haruna says that, although her husband had just banished her, "our" laughter so humiliated her that she could not leave the house. Divorce is a very common phenomenon in Hausa society, and jealousy and competition among co-wives with respect to men are frequent themes of popular discourse. These themes are also strongly associated with an archetypal notion of habaici as a speech genre through which co-wives and other women articulate their rivalries and mutual hostilities. However, the overtly mocking tone of this first example, and the brusque reference it makes to the addressee's alleged divorce, show that the veil of 'indirectness' under which speakers are said to 'hide' their hostility can be quite transparent. Because 'yan daudu frequently use feminine pronouns to refer to each other, the addressee of Haruna's first habaici is likely to be another ɗan daudu rather than a woman. As a result, this habaici could serve to mock a fellow ɗan daudu's humiliation at being dismissed (served 'divorce papers') by a boyfriend (or 'husband'). Yet the habaici need not refer to an actual event. Because the mere utterance of such an insinuation in front of other people gives the speaker a rhetorical advantage vis-à-vis the addressee, the disparaging intent of the statement holds up even if it turns out that such a break-up never took place, or the alleged relationship never existed at all.

The disadvantaged position that 'yan daudu occupy in Hausa society provides a basis for them to create and maintain bonds of group solidarity, at the same time as it compels them to compete with each other over seemingly limited material and symbolic resources, including both the admiration of other 'yan daudu and the attention of potential boyfriends and husbands. Because linguistic prowess is seen to provide access to these social goods, language serves as an important site of such competition. This is evident in Barbardo's interruption, where he disparages Haruna's knowledge of habaici. Haruna, however, fends off the challenge to his verbal dominance by quickly producing another example showing off his rhetorical skills.

The second habaici, directed at a masculine recipient, exploits the vagueness of certain words and expressions in order to forestall other listeners' understanding of potentially inflammatory information. The vague import of this example derives largely from the indeterminacy of the word *zance*, whose generic meanings include 'talk, conversation' and 'subject, matter.' *Zance* also has the additional, specific meaning of 'courting,' the Hausa cultural ritual whereby a man visits a woman he wishes to marry (normatively, at her father's home), and attempts to win her affection by engaging her in conversation. Just as they use terms such as *aure* ['marriage'] to describe their relationships with men, 'yan daudu sometimes use *zance* to describe the ways *'yan aras* pursue their sexual companionship. Yet the term's inherent vagueness obscures its sexual implications when used between a dan daudu and another man. As a result, the rhetorical question *Zance ka zo?* ['You've come to talk?'] does not specify what it is the addressee has come to talk about, or even whether he has come to talk about anything in particular at all. In any event, Haruna's disdainful response, *Ba ni da ruwa in cika ka*, literally 'I don't have any water to fill you [with],' makes plain his unwillingness to try to impress or satisfy his putative interlocutor. (*Ba da ruwa* ['give water, make wet'] is an in-group expression meaning 'do something noteworthy, make an impression.') The vagueness of this and other terms allows 'yan daudu to spar with other men over the taboo subject of homosexuality while maintaining a veneer of discretion.

The final habaici example also employs a term from the 'harka dialect.' *Akuya* ['goat'] is used by 'yan daudu as a pejorative term applied to an outsider, such as another dan daudu whom one wants to make feel unwelcome, or a person who is not known to be homosexual. In the latter case, *akuya* is not used as an epithet directed at the person, but typically serves as a warning for others to guard their speech in the outsider's presence. In this habaici, the verbal abuse heaped on the newly arrived 'goat' (*akuya* is a feminine noun) suggests that the speaker's putative addressee is another dan daudu. By issuing a command for the 'goat' to come have a look where the speaker is standing in a group of people (*jama'a*), and to take *abinmu* ['a thing of ours'], the speaker of this habaici thus attempts to assert his social superiority by implying possession of some unspecified resource, whether material or symbolic, which the addressee ostensibly lacks.

Learning about Indirect Speech Indirectly

A couple of months after I started visiting Madari – I'd drive or take a bus or 'bush-taxi' (a hired car that takes 4–7 passengers to points outside the city) every two or three weeks, and usually stay for two or three days at a time; sometimes with Mai Kwabo or another friend, sometimes by myself – I was sitting with Alhaji Tasidi near his food-stand. Alhaji Tasidi (curiously, though the name Tasidi is feminine, he was always addressed with the masculine title *alhaji*), was the first person I'd met in Madari, at forty-something then the oldest 'ɗan daudu in the town. Though it was Sunday – market day – Alhaji Tasidi was taking a break from serving customers and came to sit with me on a nearby bench.

"When will you go back to Kano?" he asked me. When I told him I'd be leaving the next day, he pressed me to stay longer.

"I can't," I explained, "a friend of mine is getting married, and I have to go to the *ɗauren aure*." A *ɗauren aure* [literally, 'tying the marriage'] is a ceremony where a marriage is contractually sealed by male representatives of the bride's and groom's parents. It is brief – lasting no more than thirty minutes – but male friends and kinfolk are invited to attend and attendance is symbolically important. As a white-skinned foreigner, my presence would be especially notable and appreciated.

"Is he a 'ɗan daudu?" Alhaji Tasidi asked me, referring to the prospective groom.

"Yes," I answered. In fact, it was my friend Alhaji Damina from Rijiyar Kuka, but I kept his name to myself.

Alhaji Tasidi was quiet for a few moments, then informed me that he wanted to go back to Kano with me. Would I take him? Confused by this sudden request, I hesitated to answer. Alhaji Tasidi went on: he wanted to go to the Pilgrims' Camp, an area near Kano's international airport where travelers to Saudi Arabia are processed en masse by immigrations and customs officials before leaving for the annual *hajj*. Because many pilgrims engage in trade on their journey, the Pilgrims' Camp is also a year-round marketplace. Alhaji Tasidi explained that he wanted to go the camp to get a 'Mecca tooth' [*haƙorin Makkah*], a metal cap for an incisor tooth that was a popular fashion among returning pilgrims and anyone who wanted to look like one. 'Real' Mecca teeth are gold or silver, but cheaper metal caps are sold to people of lesser means. The Mecca tooth would cost 50 naira (then equivalent to about US$2); did I have 50 naira?

I didn't know what to make of Alhaji Tasidi's requests. They seemed so arbitrary, so out-of-the-blue. I also could not understand why he seemed impervious to the fact that my schedule was tight and that I simply wouldn't have time to escort him to the Pilgrims' Camp when I had my friend's wedding ceremony to go to. I offered Alhaji Tasidi 50 naira and told him I'd be happy to drop him off at the Pilgrims' Camp but we'd have to leave early so I could make it to the wedding ceremony. He refused both the money and the ride.

Later, I told Mai Kwabo what had happened and how perplexed I was. He explained that Alhaji Tasidi must have been jealous of my friendship with Alhaji Damina, and that Alhaji Tasidi must have assumed Alhaji Damina was my 'wife.' Though it now seems naive, I had not previously imagined that my friendship with Alhaji Tasidi might have an erotic dimension. His efforts at indirect communication had not worked with me! Though I had a decent command of Hausa vocabulary and grammar, my communicative competence[17] was still quite limited.

Fighting among 'Girlfriends': Argument as Sociability[18]

My road to communicative competence in the ways of 'yan daudu was sometimes quite rocky.[19] One day I got so frustrated with my 'girlfriend' Hajiya Asabe that I made a scene at City Club. I'd gone to visit him on two consecutive days – once with a 'shirted' ɗan daudu friend of mine, then with Mai Kwabo – and on both occasions Hajiya Asabe ignored us. After giving us a place to sit in his courtyard, he walked out without telling us where he was going or when he'd be back. On the first day we got tired of waiting and left. On the second day, Hajiya Asabe returned to find me and Mai Kwabo sitting outside the compound (we'd gotten tired of sitting inside). Without apologizing for having made us wait, Hajiya Asabe simply smiled and said, "Sani, get ready so we can go to the club."

"I'm coming," I said, using a common Nigerian expression that really means 'not now.' I figured it was my turn to make Hajiya Asabe wait.

So instead of following him straight to the club, I went with Mai Kwabo to Alhaji Yaro Faransa's place. Alhaji Yaro was a ɗan daudu who ran a restaurant and women's house a few blocks away; he'd gotten the nickname Faransa ['France'] because he had lived in Côte d'Ivoire, a former French colony, and spoke some French. At Alhaji Yaro's house we ate a dinner of scrambled eggs and french fries and chatted for a while with Alhaji Yaro and the other 'yan daudu who lived there. After about 45 minutes, Mai Kwabo decided to stay so I went on to City Club by myself. When I got there I approached the table where Hajiya Asabe was sitting with some other 'yan daudu and independent women, and proceeded, as is customary, to greet each person with a handshake. When I extended my hand to Hajiya Asabe, he turned away from me. For me this was the last straw.

"You refuse my hand?!" I barked, and proceeded to pour out a stream of complaints and accusations about how insulted I felt; how rude Hajiya Asabe had been to me and my friends; how it wasn't right to treat a ƙawa this way. He got a look of surprise and suppressed amusement on his face, but still did not return my gaze or respond to my words. I made to leave the club, loudly describing my intentions, only to be pursued by some of the women at the table, one of whom pleaded me with to exercise patience, not to leave, and offered to be my ƙawa. "Sani, I am your^m girlfriend" [Ni ce ƙawarka]. I eventually did calm down and took a seat next to Hajiya Asabe. We didn't speak, but some time later he bought a round of drinks for the table and put two bottles of Gulder in front of me – his peace offering.

The next day I called on Hajiya Asabe at his room in the morning. He saw me in and had me take a seat on his bed while he arranged things. We exchanged greetings back and forth a few times, then I brought up the 'fight' [faɗa] we'd had the night before.

"Is that what we did?" he asked. I initially interpreted his response as disingenuous, but later I realized that it was only I who had 'fought'; Hajiya Asabe hadn't said a word or done anything overtly hostile. And that was the problem, from my point of view. In any event, now he seemed similarly unwilling to do any overt reconciling. He resisted my attempts to explain my behavior.

"Hajiya Asabe," I addressed him earnestly. Assuming we could have a conversation about our miscommunication, I began: "I am a stranger here."

"Welcome, stranger!" Hajiya Asabe nearly cut me off.

"I don't speak Hausa very well," I explained.

"Oh no, you speak it very well!" he insisted.

"Sometimes I don't understand your customs," I tried to continue.

"But you've gotten quite used to us," he countered.

We were at an impasse. In the pop-psych terms of Anglo-American relationship counseling, I insisted on 'processing' what I could only see as our misunderstanding, while Hajiya Asabe insisted on acting as if nothing unusual had happened – even, it seemed to me, to the point of sarcasm.

But then, for some reason, he relented. " 'Yan daudu say," he instructed me, using a tone of voice and a sentence structure that reminded me of the way people cited proverbs: " 'We fought, now we can stay together' " [*Mun yi fada, yanzu ma iya zaman tare*].

It was a gracious gesture on his part. It put me at ease, and allowed us to go on more or less as we had before. But the problem that had led to our 'fight' was not resolved once and for all. For the remainder of my stay, I periodically found myself confronting the same cold disdain that I'd experienced that night at City Club, implicitly but strongly suggesting that, by maintaining close friendships with other 'yan daudu and 'civilians' like Mai Kwabo, I had failed to show Hajiya Asabe the kind of attention and respect he was due as my 'girlfriend.'

The Social Construction of Sexual 'Secrets'

One morning after our 'fight' I was sitting in the courtyard outside Hajiya Asabe's room while he was combing his hair and brushing his teeth. At some point Mama Ayo, the Yoruba woman who managed the compound, approached us with a look of consternation on her face. She told Hajiya Asabe that the previous night, when he was still at City Club, one of his friends from the club, a ɗan daudu named Hussein, had stumbled into the compound, obviously drunk, and made a commotion that woke everyone up. Hussein was a round-faced Chadian with expressive eyes who always greeted me in French (*Bonsoir, Sani! Ça va?*); like other immigrants living in Sabon Gari, he spoke passable Hausa and a small amount of Nigerian Pidgin

English. As if his drunken rantings weren't bad enough, Mama Ayo continued, Hussein started coming on to the young Igbo men whose room was next door to Hajiya Asabe's, saying he loved them, that he wanted them to be his husbands, touching them inappropriately. When the compound residents tried to get Hussein to quiet down, he only got louder and more belligerent. They eventually forced him to leave, but the Igbo guys were upset and so was Mama Ayo. She reminded Hajiya Asabe that she never meddled in his business, but if his friends disrupted things like that she would have to tell the landlord; if not, the Igbo guys or someone else might complain, and she would be blamed for not keeping order. Hajiya Asabe assured her it wouldn't happen again and that he'd take care of things. At first he didn't seem angry, just concerned. He got dressed quickly and asked me if I'd brought my car. I had.

Hajiya asked me to drive him to a house in a different part of Sabon Gari where a number of Chadian and Sudanese immigrants rented rooms, including Fadil, a good friend of Hajiya Asabe's who was also a kind of ringleader among the Arabic-speaking 'yan daudu and independent women in Kano. We went into Fadil's room and Hajiya Asabe told him and a few other 'yan daudu what Mama Ayo had said about Hussein. As he usually did with these friends, Hajiya Asabe spoke in a mix of Hausa and Arabic, but on a few occasions he turned to me to ask, "Right, Sani?" [*Ko, Sani?*]. At one point he even asked me to repeat what I'd heard Mama Ayo say, as if to verify his account. As he recounted the story, Hajiya Asabe got progressively more upset; his voice got louder, his speech got faster, and he stuttered more than usual. But he still didn't lose his cool. He just kept repeating, "My secret's been exposed!" [*An tona min asiri*] and "I'm going to be evicted" [*Za'a ba ni notis*].

Hajiya Asabe then had me drive him, Fadil and another ɗan daudu to a hotel a few blocks away. We all got out and marched up a few flights of stairs to a room where we found Hussein sitting on a mattress on the floor, wearing nothing but some loose drawstring trousers; another ɗan daudu was sitting on a mat against the wall. Hussein barely had time to greet us before Hajiya Asabe descended on him in a rage, yelling and crying as he pushed Hussein onto the mattress while punching him and pulling his hair. Hussein fought back weakly, and Fadil and the other 'yan daudu went to pull Hajiya Asabe off him, but Hajiya Asabe had the tenacious strength that comes with rage and refused to let Hussein go. He bit Hussein in the arm, drawing blood, before the others managed to pull him up. Fadil did what he could to mediate, alternately trying to calm Hajiya Asabe down while chastising Hussein. At first, Hussein looked confused and tried to defend himself by denying Mama Ayo's story, but that only agitated Hajiya Asabe, so he changed his tune and said he didn't remember what had happened. Hajiya Asabe kept crying and sniffling, uttering over and over, "My secret's been exposed. Today I've been evicted." Eventually we left and I drove Hajiya Asabe home. When I came back to visit him a few days later, his relations with the other residents in the compound seemed normal.

At first Hajiya Asabe's concern with 'secrecy' was a mystery to me. His occupation was no secret to anyone, after all, except perhaps his landlord (whom I never met). He was known to everyone by his feminine name, had independent women and 'yan daudu visiting him day and night, and he regularly entertained boyfriends in his room for the night. Yet neither he nor his guests ever displayed or discussed sexual matters explicitly in public. Hussein, however, had gone beyond the pale. When Hajiya Asabe spoke of his 'secret,' therefore, he was not referring literally to what his neighbors did or did not know about him. Rather, he was referring to his reputation as someone who minded his own business. Hussein's indiscretion threatened that reputation, exposing Hajiya Asabe to the negative judgments of others.

'Civilian' Uses of the 'Harka Dialect'

Because discretion is so highly valued throughout Hausa society, and because I was shy to ask people about sensitive topics, it was only after I had spent several months hanging out in places like City Club that I found out that there were conventionally masculine Hausa men who self-identified as 'men who seek men' [maza masu neman maza] or, more colloquially, as masu harka ['people who do the deed'] or homos. Some of these men frequented Sabon Gari and other bariki areas, but many avoided such places because they did not want to be associated with the immorality that was said to go on there. For these men, the fear of having their sexual secrets exposed was quite real. The importance of secrecy was indexed by some of the terms they used to distinguish themselves from non-homos. In addition to *masu harka*, for example, they called themselves *mai ido* ['one who has eyes'] and referred to heterosexuals as *makaho* ['blind']. Another common term for heterosexuals was *garwa* ['tin-can']. When I asked how this word had entered the 'harka dialect,' I was told it was because heterosexuals are likely to *yi garwa* ['bang the tin-can'], that is, to expose the fact that someone is a homo. (This image recalled the way public announcements were made in olden times, with the beating of a drum.) The acoustic metaphor highlights the spatial and linguistic practices of 'civilian' masu harka, who until the adoption of Shari'a often socialized in publicly accessible locations, but kept their homo identities secret in part by using the 'harka dialect.'

While the 'civilians' I met were all afraid of being exposed (or '*garwa*-ed'), this did not prevent them from getting together and enjoying each other's company socially. (I did meet some Hausa men who pursued sex with men without participating in the social world of masu harka, but my contact with such men was very limited.) They were able to do so because the cultural emphasis on discretion prevented outsiders from 'banging the tin-can' unless they had solid evidence of sexual misbehavior, and because of the spatial freedoms they enjoyed as men. Unlike women, who are required by local interpretations of Islamic law to restrict their movements outside the home, adult Hausa men have traditionally been free to interact socially in public places such as markets, storefronts, and outside their homes, and in the private space of the *zaure*, or front room of a traditional Hausa home, where men receive their guests. Many men have a group of friends that they hang out with regularly at a particular location. Popularly known as *majalisai* ['parliaments'], these meeting places include a range of architectural venues – from zaures to storefronts to mats spread out under trees – each of which affords a different level of protection against unwanted intrusion by either heterosexual outsiders or overt 'yan daudu who might blow their cover.

Since it was in the context of my social interactions with masu harka that I first heard the term 'parliament,' I initially thought it referred solely to a group of homos who habitually gather in a particular place. I later found out that the term was not unique to homos, but was used by Hausa men generally. The thing that makes certain 'parliamentary' spaces specifically 'homo' is the fact that when these men come together – they perform a particular type of talk; they flirt and gossip about homo-social affairs, and they use the 'harka dialect' to prevent outsiders from understanding them. Despite this precaution, no parliament is entirely impermeable, as male visitors can potentially stop by at any time. Inevitably, some visitors to homo parliaments will be outsiders, in which case someone is likely to utter a 'dialect' term like *makaho* ['blind man'] to discreetly alert the others that the conversation needs to turn to non-homo themes. Although such conversational shifts were a regular part of social life, many masu harka described them as intrusive, and complained about 'blind' visitors who stayed too long and impeded the discussion of homo-social topics. More than once I witnessed a homo host say good-bye to a 'blind' friend and thank him for visiting, only to return to his fellow homos and say, "Thank God, he's gone. Now we can enjoy our conversation again." Such statements demonstrate that homo parliaments do not exist as neat bounded spaces, either physically or socially. Rather, they are contingently constructed by the interplay between masu harka's linguistic and bodily practices and the communicative constraints imposed by architecture and social norms.

It is important to emphasize that different men have different kinds of access to homo parliamentary spaces. Not all men, for example, live in traditional-style houses with zaures. Many families in contemporary Kano live in crowded apartments where discreet gatherings of any kind are impossible. Younger, unmarried men are especially unlikely to have access to private space; they typically live in their fathers' homes and must go elsewhere if they want to socialize with their friends without being observed. Those who live in rented studio apartments are luckier in this regard, as these are an ideal site for masu harka's parliaments, though in some densely populated urban areas people still feel constrained to take care of what they say – even when using the harka dialect – lest a neighbor or passer-by overhear something incriminating. People who rent their homes are also vulnerable to being evicted if a landlord disapproves of their guests or the way they're using the rented space. This is one reason why many 'civilians' – whatever their living arrangements – are unwelcoming towards 'yan daudu, whose overtly 'feminine' behaviors call unwanted attention to their own gender and sexual nonconformity.

With the advent of Shari'a, homos throughout Kano became nervous about socializing in public, and began conducting the overwhelming majority of their parliamentary interactions indoors. The effects of Shari'a can be clearly spelled out in terms of gender, class and sexuality. While it has never been easy to be poor, female and unmarried, the few social, sexual and economic freedoms that some independent women had managed to claim for themselves became increasingly endangered, if not criminalized. The same was true for 'yan daudu, especially if they were not married. By contrast, conventionally masculine men were not threatened directly, though they did face limits on their social movements – commensurate with wealth, marital status, and to some extent age. Whether homo or hetero, to be wealthy, male, and married is to have greater access to private space in the form of a living room, an extra home away from one's family, or an exclusive club in the leafier upscale parts of town – which means more possibilities for indulging in social behaviors that became increasingly difficult to find in public. By this, I do not only mean drinking alcohol and having extramarital sex with women or with men; I also mean the simple pleasure of socializing with one's friends without having to worry about who is watching or listening. One friend of mine described the unequal effects of Islamic law this way: "*Wanda yake da daki, shi zai ci riba*" ['Whoever has a room, that's who will benefit'].

Notes

1 Rufa'i (1986: 90–91). Muslim men are legally allowed to marry up to four wives, and can divorce a wife at any time without reason. A woman who wants a divorce must argue her case in court with evidence that her husband has failed to live up to his moral and ethical obligations. Custody of children is usually granted to the father.
2 Rufa'i (1986: 93).
3 Linguists call pronouns and other person-referring forms social *deictics* [from Latin *dicere* 'to point'] because they point to, or index, the social context of speech. Such forms are also called *shifters* because their meanings shift depending on who is speaking to whom (Jakobson 1990 [1957]; Silverstein 1976). For a comparative discussion of the use of gendered social deictics by speakers with unconventional gender identities, see Rudes and Healy (1979); Hall and O'Donovan (1996); Kulick (1998); Besnier (2004); Valentine (2007).

4   Gidley (1967: 75).

5   P. Hill (1972).

6   Skinner (1969: 157).

7   Skinner (1980); Yahaya and Dangambo (1986); and Gidley (1974).

8   C. Hill (1971).

9   Yahaya and Dangambo (1986: 169).

10 Rufa'i (1986: 90)

11 Gidley (1967: 79–80).

12 Gidley (1967: 79).

13 Skinner (1980: 17).

14 Baldick (1989: 38).

15 Bargery (1934: 69).

16 In an earlier version of this chapter I transcribed this expression as *nakiyan ruwa* 'gravel under water' (Gaudio 1997: 422). However, subsequent hearings by me and native Hausa speakers have led me to change the transcription to *na kiwon ruwa*, which can be translated as '[animal] which grazes in water' or possibly 'afraid of water' (Bargery 1934: 615).

17 *Communicative competence* is a term coined by linguistic anthropologist Dell Hymes (1974) to describe speakers' implicit awareness of the norms governing speech and social interaction in a particular community or setting.

18 This section heading is a homage to Schiffrin (1984).

19 For a detailed account of why the process of acquiring communicative competence is often rocky, see Briggs (1986).

5

PLAYING WITH FAITH

In the mid-1990s a story circulated in bariki circles about an exchange that supposedly took place when one ɗan daudu saw another sitting in a bar, drinking a beer, in the middle of the day during Ramadan. "Girlfriend!" the first ɗan daudu exclaimed, "Aren't you^f fasting?" [*Kawata! Ba kya azumi?*]. "No," replied the other, "I'm menstruating" [*A'a, jini nake yi*]. In my experience and the experience of others who heard this story,[1] this punch line never failed to generate laughter – or at least a surprised smile – among anyone familiar with Ramadan, the holiest month in the Islamic calendar, when adult, able-bodied Muslims are supposed to abstain from food, drink, smoking and sex during daylight hours. Children and the infirm are exempt from fasting, as are travelers and menstruating women, who are also exempt from daily prayers. Drinking alcohol is forbidden at all times, of course, but even Muslims who do drink often make a special effort during Ramadan to abstain from it, along with other illicit activities like gambling and adultery. As a result, in the bars and women's houses of Sabon Gari, Zakawa and other bariki areas, business drops dramatically during Ramadan and picks up just as quickly when the month of fasting ends. The story is thus irreverent on many levels, and epitomizes 'yan daudu's brazen reputation for defying Islamic norms. This reputation is summarized in a proverb, *Sai yadda ta yiwu, ɗan daudu a kabari* ['Whatever happens, happens, [says] the ɗan daudu at the grave'], in which the proverbial ɗan daudu greets death, and the possibility that he will be condemned to eternal hellfire, with resigned indifference.

Like most stereotypes, popular representations of 'yan daudu's irreverence have a limited factual basis. The following exchange, for example, could be seen as 'proof' of this stereotype, were it not for the exchange that followed it. As mentioned in previous chapters, one evening when I was visiting Lami and Mansur in Katsina, I asked them and some friends of theirs if I could make a tape-recording while they were relaxing after a hard day's work of cooking and serving food. Knowing that I was interested in 'yan daudu's use of 'women's talk,' in exchange for letting me audiotape them, they asked me for money to buy some whisky. By the time I started up the tape, the four 'yan daudu and four other men who assembled in Lami's shop (including myself) were in a festive mood. With all the 'yan daudu except Lami holding glasses of whisky, Haruna, a ɗan daudu of about 30, offered a toast. "All right, *bismilla!*" he exclaimed, using a shortened version of the classic Islamic invocation ('in the name of God') which Hausa Muslims use as an invitation to food or drink. After clinking their glasses, the 'yan daudu exploded into the kind of jeering laughter (*shewa*) that they, like women, are known for.

Although Haruna and his friends seemed to take pleasure in his sacrilege, it would be a mistake to assume they were unconcerned with observing Islamic norms. A short while after Haruna's toast, Mansur decided he'd had enough to drink. Haruna tried to entice him, however, by playing down the consequences of breaking the rules of Islamic behavior.

Mansur: . . . (ko) kaɗan ce, ba zan kara sha ba.
Haruna: To ai ba komai ke! Ranar fati ne! Ki fata Ubangiji huwallazi arrahaman² shi ma shi ba ki ikon wannan. Don billahillazi la ilaha illa huwa, 'yar Mansuriya, haba. Ki daina salla za ki ga Annabi.
Mansur: Insha'allahu. In daina salla, zan ga Annabi?
Haruna: Billahillazi za ki ga (xx)
Barbado: Daina salla, za ki ga Annabi.
Haruna: Ka ji. ((snaps))

M: . . . (even if) it's a little, I won't have any more to drink.
H: All right, no problem, you[f]! It's a party day! You[f] should hope that the Lord who is the Merciful also gives you[f] the ability to do this. Because by God who there is no god but Him, little Mansuriya, come on. Stop praying, you[f] will see the Prophet.
M: If God wills. I should stop praying, and I'll see the Prophet?
H: By God (who) you[f] will see (xx)
B: Stop praying, you[f] will see the Prophet.
H: You[m] hear. ((snaps))

| *Mansur.* To ba- ni ban sha ('yar oba) ba. Ban sha komai ba. | *M*: Well, not- I haven't drunk (too much). I haven't drunk anything. |

In spite of the fact that he had been drinking alcohol not to mention uttering profanities elsewhere in the conversation, Mansur refused to accept Haruna's (and Barbado's) assertion that *salla*, daily prayer, is a dispensable part of religious practice. Apparently, for Mansur, an explicit commitment to basic Islamic values can outweigh one's sins when it comes time for God to decide whether one will be permitted to "see the Prophet" in heaven. Even Haruna, for all his irreverence, was committed to observing Islamic norms. On the day following the 'party' in Lami's shop, we were all invited to Haruna's house to celebrate the naming of his newborn son. In keeping with Islamic custom, he and his wife gave the boy a Muslim name and recited passages from the Qur'an; they also slaughtered a goat and shared the meat with family, friends and the beggar boys (*almajirai*) in their neighborhood.

As the conversation grew more lively in the food shop, some of the 'yan daudu started to sing. Barbado, a ɗan daudu in his late teens, spontaneously performed a song. Note that the refrain (*iye nanaye ayyareyiye*) is typical of songs sung by Hausa girls (Gidley 1967: 75).

Barbado's song

Allah ka bar mani Halima,	God, leave Halima for me,
Ba da rashin kunya ba,	Not for lack of shame.
Iye nanaye ayyareyiye	Iye nanaye ayyareyiye
Za'a yi so ko ba za'a yi ba?	Is one going to do love, or is one not?
Za'a yi auren budurwa.	One is going to marry a maiden.
Aure da ciwo, mutuwa	Marriage is painful, death
Tana da yankan ƙauna.	cuts love short.
Iye nanaye ayyareyiye	Iye nanaye ayyareyiye
Allah ka ba ni Sagiru,	God give me Sagiru,
Allah ka ba ni Basiru,	God give me Basiru,
Allah ka ba ni fa Audu,	God give me Audu too,
Ba da rashin kunya ba.	Not for lack of shame.
Iye nanaye ayyareyiye	Iye nanaye ayyareyiye

The first two-thirds of this song represent a kind of prayer which is consistent with the values of mainstream Hausa society: a young man asks God to let him marry the girl he loves. But in the last section Barbado satirizes mainstream norms by asking God for three different men: Sagiru, Basiru and Audu. Despite Barbado's repeated disavowals of shamelessness ("Not for lack of shame," i.e., it's not out of shamelessness that I ask this), his requests epitomize a brazen lack of shame, on account of both his implied homosexuality and his greediness in asking God for three men.

A few months after I heard Barbado's song, I was treated to another impromptu performance in which a ɗan daudu friend of mine used poetic, prayerful language for humorous effect. The performance occurred at Alhaji Yaro Faransa's house in Sabon Gari a few days prior to my departure from Nigeria. When I got up to say my good-byes, one of Alhaji Yaro's 'daughters,' Dan Zaria, asked me where I was going. He had just taken a bath, and was sitting on the floor wearing a towel around his waist as he applied lotion to his face, legs, arms and torso. I told him I was leaving for America, but hoped to come back to Nigeria the following year. Dan Zaria then performed a series of prayers that are customary when bidding someone farewell.

"Well then," Dan Zaria said, "may God deliver you [home] safely."
"Amen," I replied.
"And may God bring you back [to Nigeria] safely."
"Amen."
"May God cause you to find your parents in good health."
"Amen."
"May God cause you to make progress in your work."
"Amen."
"And may God make it that, when you come back, my breasts have come out fully."
"Amen."

Because Dan Zaria's was talking so fast, I made my response to his last 'prayer' before I realized how funny it was. At that point, everyone in the room broke out laughing, in part because of 'Dan Zaria's campy humor, but also because of my momentary naïveté. People laughed because Dan Zaria cleverly subverted the routine nature of the exchange; his prayer for God to make his breasts come out contradicted the norms associated with such supplications, and, coming after a series of more conventional prayers, allowed him to catch his audience offguard.

Not all examples of irreverence were so poetic. One time, when I was visiting Madari, a group of 'yan daudu asked me to drive them to a neighboring town where a ɗan daudu was having a biki. On the way there, as my friends talked about who they were hoping to see at the biki, one of them exclaimed, "May God bring us 'yan aras!" – that is, 'boyfriends.' Unsurprisingly, stories about sex involved the most graphic combinations of sacred and lewd imagery. A day after the 'party' at Lami's shop, Mansur, whose travel stories were discussed in Chapter 3, went on to tell his friends about the sexual escapades he'd had in the course of those travels. Much of this talk amounted to bragging – how he stole the attention of one man from another ɗan daudu, or how attractive his suitors were in terms of wealth or physical attributes. About one man's endowment, for example, Mansur declared, "Promise of God! Despite the size of that dick, I grabbed that dick with my hand. . . . The dick went in, whoosh! I invoked blessings on the Prophet Muhammad and informed God [of my faith] in my heart." This statement may sound shockingly irreverent, but no one commented on it at the time. Mansur's earlier refusal to accept Haruna's discounting of prayer showed that irreverence has its limits, but this example shows that those limits are not fixed.

The image of Haruna pouring whisky while talking about God and the Prophet may epitomize cocky irreverence, but in that same conversation Haruna explicitly acknowledged God as the creator of all, including 'yan daudu. His statement came in response to a question I posed about 'yan daudu's expertise in the use of proverbs and *habaici*, verbal genres stereotypically associated with women's speech (see Chapter 4).

"And why is it," I asked, in rather stilted Hausa, "that you[pl] 'yan daudu are more surpassing in this aspect of language?"

"The reason is," Haruna replied. "Because we, God made us. Our customs are those of women, however, it is claimed, 'There's one[m] who put [it] on himself.' Women's customs should not be for you[m], damn! This thing that you[pl] do. Unbelief has caused you[m] to do [it]."

The reason Haruna gave as to why 'yan daudu distinguish themselves in the use of women's language is simple: "God made us [this way]." This comment reveals a conviction, widespread among 'yan daudu as well as many other Hausa Muslims, that womanlike behavior in men is a personality trait bestowed by God; it is not uncommon, for example, for non-'yan daudu to explain a ɗan daudu's woman-like behavior by saying, *Haka Allah ya yi shi* ['That's how God made him']. Haruna's subsequent comments paraphrase the argument of a hypothetical adversary who would dispute the idea that 'yan daudu's effeminacy is part of God's design and accuse 'yan daudu of "putting it on" themselves out of *kafara* ['unbelief'] or a lack of commitment to Islamic norms. It is the uneasy coexistence of these conflicting perspectives that makes 'yan daudu's social situation such an embattled one.

On Muslim 'Humorlessness'

Humor is an important part of 'yan daudu's lives and social ident-ities, and a lot of their humorous banter plays with the boundaries of what most Hausa Muslims consider decent and proper – for men, for women, and for people in general. This chapter considers the cultural implications of such talk. Some of this talk consists of fre-quent, mundane swears whose literal meaning is largely bleached or – at least at the time of the utterance – irrelevant to the speaker. But my primary focus is on statements, where, judging from the sociocultural context and others' responses (e.g., laughter), people are likely to be aware of the apparent contradiction between religiosity and profanity. My analysis suggests that 'yan daudu's often humor-ous and ironic juxtaposition of religious and profane references articulates an approach to religion and to life which acknowledges human fallibility, and which allows for and even celebrates apparent contradictions in God's will, all in a manner which more literal-minded followers of many faiths might find outrageous or even blasphemous.

Some readers may read what I've written about Hausa and other Muslims' distrust of humor and be reminded of cultural stereotypes of Muslims as humorless. These stereotypes are widespread. In 2005, for example, Warner Brothers Studios released the film *Looking for Comedy in the Muslim World*. This title could only make sense to audiences who believe that humor is harder to find in the so-called 'Muslim world' than in other human societies. (Note that, despite its title, the film takes place in just two countries: India and Pakistan.) The idea that Muslims are fundamentally, psychologically different from Westerners has a long history. In *Orientalism*, Edward Said describes how European writers and artists have for centuries used emotionally charged imagery of Middle Eastern people and cultures, especially Muslims, in order to portray them as less civilized than Europeans. In recent decades, certain of these stereotypes, such as the image of Muslims as decadent and oversexed (think of harems and belly-dancers), seem to have become less prominent; but others, such as the image of Muslim men as violent, misogynistic fanatics, have arguably grown stronger. Humorlessness is a key component of this image. In 2006, when certain groups of Muslims protested a Danish newspaper's publication of satirical cartoons depicting the Prophet Muhammad, a number of Western media pundits criticized the protesters by saying they couldn't take a joke. Images of Muslim rioters burning the Danish flag, destroying Danish and other Western-owned businesses, and even killing Christians reinforced the idea that Muslims are inherently, even pathologically, humorless.

To say that Western media coverage of the violence triggered by the Danish cartoons reinforced anti-Muslim stereotypes is not to discount the suffering caused by that violence. The fact that in retribution for the offensive cartoons a small minority of Northern Nigerian Muslims attacked and killed scores of Nigerian Christians (not Danes or other Europeans) cannot be denied. In other parts of Nigeria, Christians retaliated by killing Muslims. In the end, the Nigerian death toll from the cartoon riots was over 100 – higher than in any other country in the world. Such violence is horrifying, and the people who instigated it deserve to be condemned. But it is unhelpful to attribute the actions of a few Muslim rioters to an inherent tendency towards violence or humorlessness among Muslims in general. The problem with the stereotype is not simply that it is false. The problem is also that – like all stereotypes – it prevents us from recognizing the social and historical factors that have led some Muslims to embrace a profoundly humorless interpretation of their faith. The stereotype also prevents us from asking about the factors that lead Muslim and non-Muslim observers alike to grant authority to such orthodox interpretations of Islam and to discount other, less rigid forms of Islamic religiosity.

'Yan daudu's irreverent talk achieves various effects – delighting some, offending others – in large part because it indexes the political and ideological contests that are currently raging in Northern Nigeria among Islamic revivalist movements, Sufi (Islamic mystical) orders, and practitioners of Bori, as well as the various participants in the Nigerian state and the global capitalist economy. The ways 'yan daudu have been treated recently in Hausa Muslim society differs from the relative tolerance they seem to have enjoyed in the late nineteenth and early twentieth centuries (see Chapter 2); that tolerance reflects the flexible notions of morality that scholars have described as typical both of rural West African Islam and of some forms of Sufism.[3] While mystical and syncretic forms of Islamic practice had long coexisted in an uneasy tension with more orthodox interpretations of Islamic doctrine, in the late twentieth century this tension was aggravated by the vigorous polemics of Islamic reformists. The Islamists' growing popularity among rich and poor alike put Sufi orders on the defensive in Northern Nigeria as well as other Muslim societies throughout the world.[4] While most Hausa Sufis emphatically condemn homosexuality and cross-gender behavior as un-Islamic, the recent convergence of anti-Sufism and other forms of social intolerance on the part of Islamic revivalists – including their intolerance of Bori – is no mere coincidence. On the contrary, as we saw in Chapter 2, it has important historical precedents.

'Yan daudu's performances of humor and what I call 'faithful irreverence' can be seen as forms of Islamic cultural citizenship – forms of participation in the Northern Nigerian and transnational Islamic publics. These performances are not designed to circulate widely; they take place in relatively private or protected settings, and are almost never transcribed or recorded. (This chapter is an unusual exception.) But they do circulate within the social networks of 'yan daudu, independent women and other people of the bariki, for as individuals visit or move from one location to another, they bring with them stories, jokes and modes of performance, along with clothing, photographs and other objects. All these practices can be seen as forming what Michael Warner calls a counterpublic – a set of collective responses to the inequalities of gender, sexuality and class that 'yan daudu face in Northern Nigeria and (along with inequalities of nation and race) in the transnational Islamic community.[5]

Swearing to God

In Northern Nigeria, as in other parts of the country, people remind each other of God's presence and power at every turn. Mosques and churches are a ubiquitous feature of the urban landscape, and expressions of faith are painted or plastered onto walls, trucks, buses, and hand-held amulets. In their everyday speech Hausa Muslims invoke the name of Allah, the Prophet Muhammad and the Qur'an in a variety of ways and contexts. In the course of a telling a story, for example, people often utter swears like *wallahi tallahi* [Arabic: 'by God by God'] or *Alkurani!* ['the Qur'an'] to affirm the truth of what they're saying. Wishes and predictions are qualified by the Arabic expression *insha'allah* ['if God wills'] or its Hausa equivalent *in Allah ya yarda* ['if God agrees']. References to God's power are also embedded in conversational routines. If I happened to see my landlord while leaving my house, for example, I'd always greet him and tell him I was going out. "May God bring you back safely," he'd say, to which I replied, "Amen." If I saw him again upon returning home, he'd ask, "Have you come back?," to which I learned to answer, "Yes, God has brought me back safely." Such statements reflect a general tendency among Hausa Muslims to acknowledge God's hand in all things, and not to attribute everyday events simply to chance or coincidence, or even to human effort. In a study of Islamic references in colloquial Arabic, Michael Piamenta argues that by using such expressions speakers acknowledge their human "contingency," that is, their dependence on God and their acceptance of divine will.[6]

But how do we know that, when people refer to God, they are actually aware of the religious content of their words? In fact, we can't know for sure. In her discussion of English expressions such as "God knows" and "Christ knows," for example, Deborah Hill suggests that, like greetings and farewells, such phrases are conversational routines or "prefabricated linguistic units," whose function is primarily phatic – serving to establish or maintain social connectedness – rather than informational.[7] Yet the semantic content of such expressions cannot be dismissed out of hand. Their religious significance may be effectively 'bleached' or irrelevant for secularized individuals, but the same cannot be assumed for speakers or communities of faith. In the Catholic catechism I learned as a child, for example, I was taught to follow the Commandment, "Thou shalt not take the Lord's name in vain." Although my parents and other elders were far less vigilant in enforcing this commandment than they were about regulating my use of words like *fuck,* I took care to observe it in the presence of our parish priest, and sometimes invoked it myself in order to chastise – and exercise a kind of power over – my brothers, my parents or my babysitter ("Oooh, you took the Lord's name in vain. That's a sin!"). For quite different reasons, similar language policies were promulgated in Soviet Russia, where the officially atheistic Communist Party discouraged the use of religious expressions such as *Bozhe moi* ['Oh my God'] and *slava Bogu* ['Thank God'] because these supposedly reinforced 'superstitious' ways of thinking and impeded the masses' embrace of scientific socialism. The effect of these policies was not automatic, of course, but varied according to the formality of the social interaction and the ideological convictions of the participants.

Criticisms and policy statements about the use of oaths and swear words are evidence that speakers do pay attention to the religious content of such speech. But the degree of such attentiveness varies within and across religious communities. In contrast to observant Christians and Jews, for example, Piamenta claims, "[t]he Arab does not consider it a lack of respect to swear by Allah, provided he does not perjure himself."[8] But Piamenta also identifies a tension between speakers' widespread acceptance of swearing and Islamic injunctions against it. He notes, for example, a Qur'anic admonition that believers should not let swear words substitute for serving God. Casual oath-taking was also condemned by the eighteenth-century Arabian scholar Shaikh Muhammad Ibn 'Abd al-Wahhāb, whose writings formed the ideological basis of the modern Saudi state and continue to inspire Islamist movements throughout the world. Shaikh 'Abd al-Wahhāb cited the Qur'an as well as *hadith* (sayings of the Prophet) to condemn frequent swearing, and took a decidedly ill-humored stance against the joking use of such language.[9]

An ideology of language similar to Shaikh 'Abd al-Wahhāb's holds sway to some extent in Northern Nigeria. Hausa speakers who pepper their everyday speech with swear words like *Wallahi!* often refrain from doing so in the presence of an imam, lest they come across as irreverent. If someone says *Wallahi!* to punctuate a claim that you find questionable, you might warn them, "Don't swear to

God" [*Kada ka rantse da Allah*], in other words, don't risk God's wrath by invoking His name to cover your lies. As a metapragmatic statement (that is, a statement about language use), this kind of warning doesn't just index the speaker's individual awareness of the religious meaning of *Wallahi!*[10] It also indexes an ideology of language that calls on all people to be mindful of the religious implications of their words at all times. This lesson was driven home for me one day when I and a neighbor of mine, a German (non-Muslim) student of Hausa, were making plans to get together with some friends of ours the next evening. In the presence of our landlord, my friend told me (in Hausa) that he would be leaving the next morning for a trip out of town, but assured me he would be back before nightfall. After he walked off, our landlord turned to me and said, "He didn't say *insha'allah*. He's taking a risk!" According to our landlord, it was naive and even arrogant of our friend to assert he would return from his trip without acknowledging the contingency of his plans on God's will. This was 'risky' because it left him vulnerable; if you don't ask for God's protection, He might not protect you.

Laughing about Arabs and Hausa Muslim 'Big Men'

At another point in our conversation, Haruna offered an even more graphic representation of the contradictory pressures 'yan daudu face in Hausa Muslim society. After a playful display of his knowledge of certain colloquial Arabic expressions, he turned to me to compliment me on the interest I had taken in Hausa language and culture. He then went on to describe his own ambivalent relationship with mainstream Hausa society by referring to the hypocrisy of Hausa men who have sexual relations with 'yan daudu but who denigrate them at the same time.

Haruna: "**Marhaba buka (ashara)**" wallahi tallahi (xxx) in ji Larabawa.
Kullum "**sauwa-sauwa**" wallahi, ƙawata ta je Saudiya- <. . .>

H: "*Greetings to you*^m *(ten times)*" *by God by God (xxx)* *so say the Arabs.* *Every day "**just right**," by God, my girlfriend went to Saudi Arabia-* <. . .>

Wallahi ta tafi.

"Shwoye-shwoye. Marhaba buka"

kuma ma "**shwoye**,"
wallahi tallahi Mohammed Sani.
Tsakaninka da jama'a sai godiya ga Allah.
Wallahi tun da har ka shigo cikin Hausa,
ka ji Hausa kuma
ka saurara abin da Hausa ke so=
Mansur. =Ni ai [an doke ni.]

H: [(Tun da) ƙaunar Hausa] nake, [(ka doke ni,)]=
M: [Billahilazi.]=
H: =ka ba ni ruwa wal[lahi].

M: [Alka]walin Allah, [saboda haka billahilazi la ilaha illa huwa (xxxx)
H: [Wallahi sori ɗin wasu (xxx).
<...>
Sabo da mu wallahi tallahi.
Mu a ce musulma ne masu arna masu yaro masu kwana a soro, maci yaro. Wallahi tallahi mu 'yan daudu sh- dankali sha kushe ne. Wall[ah]i ana cinmu ana kushenmu=
M:　　[A'!]　　=E wallahi.

By God she's gone away.

"A very little bit. Greetings to you^m"

and "a little," by God by God,
Mohammed Sani. Between you^m and the people,
<there is> only thanks to God.
By God for you^m have even entered into Hausa <clothes or culture>,
you^m have understood Hausa and
you^m have listened to what Hausa likes=
M: =Me, oh, I'm impressed. <'I've been beaten.'>
H: (Because) I love Hausa, (you^m have impressed <'beaten'> me),
M: *By God who.*
H: you've^m impressed me <'given me water'>, *by God.*
M: *Swear to God, therefore, by God who there is no God but him (xxx)*
H: *By God,* sorry for others (xxx).
<...>
Because we by God by God. We, one could say, are Muslims^f who have pagans, who have boys, who sleep in entry-rooms, who fuck boys. By God by God we 'yan daudu- are slandered sweet-potatoes. By God we get fucked, we get slandered.
M: *Oh!　　Yes, by God.*

The opening section of this exchange involves a different sort of Hausa-Arabic codeswitching from the kind Haruna produced earlier, insofar as the Arabic phrases he uses here have no religious implications. Thus, while the expression, *huwallazi arrahaman* ['He who is the Merciful], is clearly Islamic in nature, the phrase *marhaba buka* ['greetings to you^m'] is simply an Arabic greeting. Haruna's use of this expression echoes that of another ɗan daudu, possibly Mansur, just prior to this section of the transcript (the noisy nature of the tape-recording makes the speech difficult to discern). It is possible, however, that by repeating this greeting and producing further examples of colloquial Arabic, Haruna was attempting to demonstrate his own familiarity with the language, which has a high prestige value among Hausa Muslims. His subsequent utterance, *Kullum sauwa-sauwa* ['Every day [they say] *sauwa-sauwa*'], suggests that Haruna may be parodying the way Arabs talk, an interpretation supported by the fact that he pronounced the term *sauwa-sauwa* with a slight constriction of the pharynx (in the back of the throat), a distinctive feature of spoken Arabic that is often employed by Hausa speakers as a way of making their pronunciation of Arabic words and borrowings sound more authentic. It is also possible, in light of Haruna's lament about his 'girlfriend' in Saudi Arabia, that he was parodying the speech of Hausa Muslims who, after returning from the pilgrimage to Mecca, put on airs by peppering their speech with Arabisms. These affectations are especially pronounced among those people known as *'yan Kano-Jiddah* who have made repeated trips to Saudi Arabia; as discussed below, this social category includes a significant number of 'yan daudu.

As he repeated the Arabic greeting *marhaba buka*, Haruna turned and addressed me as "Mohammed Sani" – the full, more formal version of the name Sani, which evokes a more explicitly Muslim identity (Figure 5.1).[11] Haruna's use of the more complete, Islamic version of my name accompanies the praise he heaps on me for my presumably peaceful relations with other people. Although the term he uses – *jama'a* ['people, society'] – is nonspecific with regard to which people Haruna is talking about, his subsequent remarks, in which he declares his appreciation of the fact that I have "entered into Hausa," "understood Hausa," and "listened to what Hausa likes," indicate that he is referring to my status as a visitor in Hausa society. The sequence of clauses describing my involvement with Hausa society merges the territorial, linguistic and sociocultural aspects of Hausaness, and seems to conflate my interest in Hausa with my interest in the speech of 'yan daudu. (I often made this conflation myself in order: (1) to emphasize to 'yan daudu that I was not interested in spying on them for nefarious reasons; and (2) to mitigate the suspicions provoked by my telling other Hausa people that my research focused on such a disreputable class of people.)

The phrase *cikin Hausa* ['inside Hausa'] indexes a complex of ideologies of language and social space, some of which are gendered.

Fig. 5.1   Rudolf Gaudio (a.k.a. Sani) in Rijiyar Kuka, 1994. (Photo by Alhaji Damina.)

Haruna uses the idea of 'inside Hausa' to imply that I have made friends with Hausa people and that I have a good understanding of Hausa language and culture.[12] My interest in proverbs and habaici – one of the chief reasons I gave for wanting to make this tape-recording – is particularly strong evidence of the extent to which I have 'entered inside Hausa,' insofar as the ability to appreciate these verbal genres is seen to require an especially intimate acquaintance with Hausa language and culture. Moreover, as discussed earlier, proverbs and innuendo are often associated with speech that occurs among women *cikin gida* ['inside the home']. That which is 'inside Hausa' thus indexes a spatial conception of Hausa identity, which, because of its association with domesticity, is implicitly gendered. As feminine men who are stereotypically believed (and who proudly claim) to have a special, esoteric knowledge of the Hausa language, 'yan daudu can also claim to be more 'inside' Hausa culture than other men. Yet having the status of linguistic and cultural insiders does not afford 'yan daudu social respect or power. Indeed, as noted earlier with respect to the notion of *wasa* ['play'], that which can be deemed 'inside Hausa' – women who live their lives inside the home, Maguzawa and Bori practitioners who are said to preserve pre-Islamic

Hausa traditions, or 'yan daudu who display expertise in the use of proverbs and innuendo – is typically excluded from the dominant channels of power in Hausa Muslim society. In the case of 'yan daudu, insider status contradicts their marginalization as *mutanen banza* ['worthless people'] who are relegated to the 'outside,' *bariki* areas of Hausa cities and towns.

Notwithstanding the social and moral ostracism that he and other 'yan daudu face in Hausa society, Haruna explicitly aligns himself with abstract notions of Hausaness. Emphasizing that he "loves Hausa," he echoes Mansur in declaring that I have "impressed" him. Note that both 'yan daudu use in-group terms – *doke* ['beat, strike'] and *ba da ruwa* ['give water'] – in place of the standard Hausa *birge* ['impress']. The use of these in-group terms (both of which have possible sexual connotations) is further indication that Haruna and Mansur are impressed not only by my proficiency in Hausa, but by my specific interest in the linguistic practices of 'yan daudu. Because the in-group meanings of these terms are generally unknown to non-'yan daudu, their use here highlights a contradiction between Haruna's declared affinity for 'Hausa' and the social, cultural and linguistic differences that separate 'yan daudu from the rest of Hausa society. Social differences of a less explicit kind are also indexed by Haruna's use of the English loanword *sori* ['sorry'] as a put-down of unnamed 'others'; this recalls the *habaici* examples discussed in Chapter 4, in which Haruna uses *sori* as a kind of rhetorical weapon in the context of verbal sparring. Although it is not possible in this case to identify with certainty the 'others' for whom he feels condescendingly 'sorry,' with this put-down, Haruna represents himself as someone authorized to distinguish between those who 'impress' him and those who do not. This representation, like that of 'yan daudu as cultural insiders, stands in contrast to 'yan daudu's defining status as a culturally and religiously suspect and subordinate class.

Haruna uses extremely graphic language to focus on the hostility and contradictions that characterize 'yan daudu's relations with the dominant society, especially with regard to sexuality. His use of the feminine noun *musulma* ['Muslim^f'] in the sentence, "We, one could say, are Muslims,"[13] conveys the irony of 'yan daudu's status as Muslims and gender-deviants, followed by a list of epithets representing the speech of hypothetical opponents who accuse 'yan daudu of having sex with infidels, children and 'big men.' The construction *masu* + [noun] literally translates as 'ones who have [noun],' though its use here with the nouns *arna* ['pagan'] and *yaro* ['boy'] clearly connotes a sexual relationship, especially in light of Haruna's use of the explicit phrase *maci yaro* ['one who fucks boys']. This latter construction highlights the ambiguity of 'yan daudu's gender and sexual identities, insofar as it casts them in the masculine role of the sexually active partner vis-à-vis young boys, in contrast to the feminine role 'yan daudu typically assume in relationships with older men. The sexual implication of the phrase *masu kwana a soro* ['ones who sleep in entry-rooms'] is more indirect. A *soro*, like a *zaure,* is a small room near the entrance of a house in which a man receives and entertains his guests. (Recall that *cikin gida*, the inside of the home, is reserved for women and children.) Among 'yan daudu and other masu harka the soro is also known as a place where a male patron puts up those guests with whom he wants to have illicit sex; because it is set apart from the other rooms the patron can go to the soro late at night and have sex with his guest without attracting the attention of the other members of his household.

Rumors abound in Hausaland about homosexual *manya*, 'big men' who, under cover of darkness, secretly indulge their appetite for sex with 'yan daudu or young boys. Yet such men are rarely if ever singled out and harassed for their sexual behavior. Rather, it is 'yan daudu who bear the brunt of Hausa society's moral indignation. 'Yan daudu, who know perhaps more than anyone else the extent to which these rumors are true, are highly aware of the hypocrisy of this situation, which Haruna indexes by use of the idiom *dankali sha kushe*, literally, 'sweet-potatoes [that] drink slander.'[14] Bargery defines *dankali sha kushe* as an epithet meaning, "A person whom others get advantages from, yet belittle and speak against."[15] Haruna's next comment spells out the advantages people get from 'yan daudu: *ana cinmu ana kushenmu* ['we get fucked [and] we get slandered']. This graphic complaint, affirmed by Mansur, summarizes the hypocrisy which many 'yan daudu perceive in the treatment they endure at the hands of the dominant Hausa Muslim society.

As Hausa Muslims accused of deviance and 'unbelief' – often by the very 'big men' who seek them out sexually, in whose soros 'yan daudu sleep – 'yan daudu's relationship to dominant cultural and religious ideals is characterized by a fundamental ambivalence.

Yet, as Haruna, Hajiya Bilki and others made clear to me, many 'yan daudu remain committed to the beliefs and practices with which they were raised. And some, such as Haruna's 'girlfriend,' join the ranks of their fellow Muslims in fulfilling the Islamic duty to travel to Mecca to pay homage to the site where God first spoke through the Prophet Muhammad. The idea of the journey to Arabia as both spiritually and materially rewarding has a long history in Hausaland, for the hajj has long provided Hausa Muslims with opportunities for trade along the various routes that pilgrims have followed between West Africa and Arabia. John Works, for example, notes that the historically close and mutually reinforcing relationship between trade and the pilgrimage makes it difficult to distinguish – as colonial administrators sometimes tried to do – between those who travel for religious reasons and those who migrate for economic ones.[16] Although both the Nigerian and Saudi governments have tried in recent years to discourage pilgrims from exploiting the hajj as a commercial opportunity,[17] the traditional Hausa Muslim association of travel and trade lives on. Indeed, the widespread availability of plane travel from northern Nigeria to Saudi Arabia, fueled largely by government subsidies for Muslim pilgrims, has given rise to a loosely defined category of individuals known as 'yan Kano-Jiddah, literally ['children of, or ones who do, Kano-Jiddah'], so called because most Northern Nigerian travelers to Saudi Arabia fly out of Kano's international airport and land in the Saudi port city of Jiddah.

As participants in a latter-day trans-Saharan trade, 'yan Kano-Jiddah bring back to Hausaland material and cultural goods in a way that complicates traditional understandings of what is often discussed as the impact of Islamic Arab culture on Hausa society. This is particularly true for Kano-Jiddah 'yan daudu and independent women, for while they are frequently subject to arrest, extortion and abuse in both Nigeria and Saudi Arabia, some of them are nevertheless able during their sojourns abroad to acquire an impressive amount of material wealth and religious and cultural *savoir-faire*.[18] These accomplishments enable 'yan Kano-Jiddah to construct identities as sophisticated actors on a transnational Islamic stage without ever shedding the stigma associated with what is seen as their culturally and religiously deviant behavior. As men who are seen to degrade themselves by acting like women, and as relatively well-to-do pilgrims accused of promoting immorality, the contradictory positions that Kano-Jiddah 'yan daudu assume in Hausa society confound the rigid ideologies of conservative religious and political leaders. Similarly, the alternative identities that 'yan Kano-Jiddah construct for themselves as observant but unconventional Muslims expose the inadequacy of Western observers' attempts to characterize Islamic identity and practice as monolithic and inflexible.

Along with Hajiya Asabe, who had been to Saudi Arabia several times before I met him in 1993, another dan Kano-Jiddah whom I got to know well was Alhaji Damina, a dan daudu whom I initially met at Alhaji Lawan's restaurant in the Rijiyar Kuka section of Kano when he returned after having spent several months in Saudi Arabia (see Chapter 1). Through Alhaji Damina, I met Alhaji Zinari, whom Damina called his kawa ['girlfriend'], and whom he sometimes addressed by the feminine nickname Zinariya. Shortly after I met them Alhaji Damina and Alhaji Zinari moved their wives and families into a house together in Rijiyar Kuka. Damina told me he also owned another house in the area that he was planning to fix up when he saved up some more money.

Previously, Damina and Zinari had lived in the nearby home of an older dan daudu named Alhaji Balarabe. Alhaji Balarabe was a well-to-do dan Kano-Jiddah of about 50 who supported a wife and several children and various other clients, including some younger 'yan daudu, in his two-story house, which featured an Arabian-style architecture that is popular among Kano's big-men and was one of the fanciest in his neighborhood. Inside, a parlor and dining area on the second floor showcased the wealth Alhaji Balarabe had amassed over the years: an overstuffed sofa and chairs, plush carpeting, a large television on a chrome-and-glass shelf unit, a stained wood dining set, and an air-conditioner. When Damina and Zinari were younger and had only recently left their family homes, Alhaji Balarabe had taken them in to live with him. With his guidance Damina and Zinari had learned how to dress and act in ways that would attract men of means, and his social connections had enabled them to meet such men. Alhaji Balarabe had assisted them financially and logistically in making their first trips to Saudi Arabia. In Jiddah, they stayed in a house that Alhaji Balarabe had leased. Alhaji Balarabe sometimes called Damina and Zinari his 'daughters' ['ya], and they in turn sometimes referred to him as uwa ['mother'], though in my presence they almost always called him alhaji.

Although Alhaji Damina and Alhaji Zinari had not yet attained the status of their 'mother' Alhaji Balarabe, they had acquired on their many trips to Saudi Arabia a degree of wealth and worldly knowledge that greatly enhanced their social position back home. They wore exotic perfumes and well-tailored clothing from Jiddah. Zinari had gold caps – 'Mecca teeth' – on three of his incisors. They peppered their speech with words and phrases from colloquial Saudi Arabic, and could mimic the accents of Egyptians and Iraqis. They were experts at dealing with immigration authorities and had the right connections to obtain passports and visas. They knew the departure and arrival schedules of the international flights that served Kano airport, and debated the quality of service provided by the various airlines. And they raved about the creature comforts that Saudi Arabia had to offer: telephones, air conditioning, a constant supply of electricity and running water. "*Ba abin da babu,*" they would say, 'There's nothing that isn't there.' In the year following Alhaji Damina's wedding, he and Alhaji Zinari made two more trips to Saudi Arabia: a month-long visit at the end of Ramadan, and, less than two months later, a six-week visit during which they performed the hajj. In that same year, Alhaji Balarabe stayed in Jiddah for over six months.

After Damina and Zinari's return from one of these trips, I accompanied them on a visit to Alhaji Damina's home village. When I came with my car to pick them up, Damina had prepared several bags full of gifts, including cloth for women's and men's garments, plastic-wrapped packages of soap, and facial creams and lotions. The village consisted of several clusters of mud-and-thatch compounds along a bumpy dirt road about two hours from Kano. Our arrival was greeted with considerable excitement. Damina's relations, including two daughters by his first marriage, eagerly showed us into his senior brother's compound, where a large straw mat was spread out for us under a tree. Before sitting down, Damina casually handed his gifts to the women and girls, who immediately put them away inside their rooms. (It is generally considered impolite to open gifts in front of the giver.) For most of our two-hour stay, Damina's senior brother and some other men sat and talked with us on the mat, though occasionally someone would take Damina aside to one of the rooms to talk with him privately. It is likely that Damina gave his relatives money on this trip as well. Alhaji Damina's visit to his home village reflects a cultural phenomenon that is prevalent throughout Africa and in traditional rural communities all over the world: a son goes off to seek his fortune in the big city and takes on the role of provider for his family of origin. While many Hausa people look down on 'yan daudu as low-class and disreputable, Damina's poor, rural family could probably overlook his stigmatized occupation because of the material and social benefits he provided them. As frequent fliers to the land of Mecca, 'yan Kano-Jiddah like Alhaji Damina and Alhaji Zinari took pride in their ability to perform important Islamic rituals, and in knowing that they are part of a global community of Muslims. They expressed support for Muslim causes in cases of conflict with non-Muslims, whether this be in Kano, Bosnia or the Persian Gulf. But this heightened sense of Muslimness did not necessarily translate into support for any particular Islamic political movement or leader. For 'yan Kano-Jiddah's experiences in both Nigeria and Saudi Arabia make them highly aware of the gap that exists between the pronouncements of Islamic moralists and the actual practices of real-life Muslims. They tell highly entertaining and provocative stories about the peccadilloes of men from a variety of backgrounds, from traditional Qur'anic scholars to wealthy Saudi businessmen and followers of Islamic reform movements such as Izala and the Muslim Brothers.

One day, when I was hosting, Alhaji Damina and Alhaji Zinari had come over to my house with a friend of theirs. At one point, Alhaji Salisu, who was also a ɗan Kano-Jiddah, recounted a story about one of the most prominent imams in Kano who had supposedly delivered a sermon exposing the existence of a covert homosexual community after receiving a suggestive letter from a local ɗan aras or 'civilian.' Although Alhaji Salisu did not depict the imam as a fellow *mai harka*, his story suggests that the imam's sexuality was perhaps not as orthodox as one might assume.

Salisu: Malam Halifa Tukur wani ko ya aika mar leta ya ce ((buga cinya)) yana sonsa. (.)	S: Malam Halifa Tukur, someone wrote him a letter saying ((slaps thigh)) he liked/wanted him (.)
Damina: To!	D: Well!
Zinari: Yana so-	Z: He liked/wanted-
S: Yana son ara- (.) e, [yana son aral-	S: He wanted to do ara- (.), yeah, he wanted to do aral- <= have homo sex>

D: [Bai faɗi sunansa ba?
S: Bai faɗi sunansa ba. Sai dai (xx). Ya ce, "Malam ina son ka ga- a je gun wurin da duk za'a haɗu. Ka fito. A shanka ɓe. In ba ka iya ba a koya maka." ((buga cinya))
Z: ? ((dariya))
S: "In kuma ka iya ka ci gaba da yi." Ya ma karanta a baina jama'a, ya ce, "a'a! duniya." Wai "tsofai tsofai da ni wai aka rubuta min leta ana sona." ((group laughter, *shewa*))
S: A! Mutane, akwai tsinannu.

D: He didn't say his name?
S: He didn't say his name. Just (xx). He said, "Malam, I want you[m] to see-to go where everyone will get together. Come out. Get all wet. If you[m] don't know how, let someone teach you[m]." ((slaps thigh))
Z: ? ((laughs))
S: "And if you[m] do know, keep on doing it." He read it in public, he said, "uh-oh, this world!" He said, "old and tired as I am, someone wrote me a letter saying he likes me."
S: Oh! Some people are really damned. <'People, there are accursed ones.'>

Although, according to Salisu, Halifa Tukur's sermon included an exposé of the secret code that 'yan daudu and other masu harka use to discuss sexual matters, and revealed that there are particular sites where they "get together," Salisu did not appear to consider it a threatening attack. Rather, his rendition of the sermon, featuring the imam's tantalizing translations of terms from the 'harka dialect' like *lemo* ['penis, dick'] and *birni* ['anus,' literally 'large city'], seems as suggestive as the letter he allegedly received from a male admirer. In addition, Salisu depicted Halifa Tukur's response to the letter-writer's erotic invitation as one of wistful amusement rather than righteous indignation; the imam suggests that he faults the letter-writer for focusing his affection on a man who is past his prime rather than on a man *per se*. Salisu also begged the question as to what Halifa Tukur's response to the letter would have been if he had been a bit younger. The group's laughter signaled their appreciation of the humor in Salisu's portrayal, while their subsequent outburst of shewa laughter emphasized the story's irreverence. Another source of humor in Salisu's story is the ironic way he focused on the "accursed" behavior of non-'yan daudu, though we all knew it is 'yan daudu rather than their 'civilian' counterparts who form the usual targets of religious leaders' moral diatribes.

As speakers of the language of the Qur'an, Arabs have a collective position of honor in Hausa Muslim society, where knowledge of Arabic and familiarity with Arab culture are indices of religious knowledge, moral respectability, and social sophistication. With the advent of air travel and Nigerian government subsidies for the hajj, access to these symbolic resources is now more widely available. Thousands of Nigerians travel to Saudi Arabia every year for religious purposes as well as for the opportunity to earn money, often extra-legally, through petty trade or the performance of menial labor. These travelers, who inevitably include some 'yan daudu, return to Nigeria with an awareness not only of the material and spiritual splendor of Saudi society, but also of the quirks and shortcomings of individual Arabs and people of other nationalities who participate in this highly multicultural event. References to these shortcomings sometimes form part of the public performance of a returning pilgrim's cosmopolitanism. When I visited Kano in 1997, for example, Alhaji Zinari had recently returned from Saudi Arabia. (Alhaji Damina was still there, while Alhaji Balarabe had passed away in 1995, apparently from diabetes.) One afternoon I stopped by the roadside food-shop where Alhaji Zinari usually spent his daytime hours and took a seat beside him on a bench just outside the shop's front door, where we could lean against a wall in the shade of a corrugated tin overhang. Gazing out at the hustle and bustle of the street, Alhaji Zinari regaled me with stories about 'Saudiyya' that painted a picture of Saudi social life far different from what I'd imagined while reading the *New York Times*.

I was especially intrigued by his descriptions of the sexual excesses of Arab men, whom he characterized as *jarababbu* ['horny, oversexed']. In response to my curiosity, Alhaji Zinari seemed to take relish in providing examples of Arab men's *jaraba* ['lasciviousness']. One of these seemed designed to demonstrate not only his cultural knowledge about Arab men's sexuality, but also his own alluring qualities as a ɗan daudu. "If they see a ɗan daudu in the street, they'll get an erection and follow you all the way home." Zinari then underscored his powers of ethnographic observation by adding, "Especially Egyptians."

Alhaji Zinari went on to describe other 'Arab' sexual practices that he claimed to find strange or even repulsive. Implicit in these examples was a comparison of Arab men's sexual predilections with that of Hausas. Regarding oral sex, for instance, Alhaji Zinari said,

"Some of them insist on putting their penis in your mouth. But me, I don't do that. Don't let any filth get into my mouth."

Struck by Alhaji Zinari's rejection of a practice that I considered mundane, I replied, "Me, I do that."

"Of course, it's your[pl] work!" Alhaji Zinari exclaimed, which I understood to mean, "You [white homos/white folks] have been doing it all along; it's your[pl] thing!"[19]

Another practice Alhaji Zinari found unusual was Arab men's recent adoption of condom use. "And nowadays, some of them won't do the deed unless they put a piece of rubber on their penis. Like this." He hoisted his bare foot onto the bench and unrolled an imaginary condom onto his big toe.

"Yeah, because of disease, right?" I said, nodding with recognition.

"Yeah, because of disease."

I then sought to inform Alhaji Zinari that condom use – and by implication, an awareness of how HIV/AIDS could be sexually transmitted – was not limited to Arabs. "Us too, we use that," I told him.

As it turned out, I needn't have doubted Alhaji Zinari's cultural awareness. "Yeah, they learned it from you[pl]. You're[pl] the ones who teach them!"

While Alhaji Zinari had a particular gift for story-telling, the details of his accounts were hardly unique, for the subject of Arab men's sexual peccadilloes was a popular topic of conversation not only among the Hausa homos I knew, but among many heterosexuals too. The ways in which these stories subverted the normative image of Arab Muslim piety and respectability reminded me of Western Apaches' joking portrayals of 'the Whiteman' as described by Keith Basso.[20]

In addition to portraying the sexual life of 'Arabs,' my exchange with Alhaji Zinari yielded two generalizations about white men's (homo)sexual practices on the basis of the self-reported behavior of a single white man – me. First, Alhaji Zinari transformed my first-person singular statement about oral sex ("I do that") into a report about whites generally. After that, it was I who chose to speak for white/Western people as a class. Whether I intended to represent Western homos specifically or all sexually active Westerners, I still cannot say. In any event, the ambiguity of my intention clearly did not stop Alhaji Zinari from appropriating my generalization in order to elaborate on his descriptions of Arab men. Apparently accepting my ability to represent white (homo) society as a whole, Alhaji Zinari constructed an implicit narrative of sociocultural change. Whites were figured as the originators and primary practitioners of 'filthy' and technologized sex (oral sex and condom use, respectively), while Arabs were positioned as having acquired these practices later, ostensibly through contact with whites. This conforms to a general sense shared by many Hausa people that Arabs are closer to Europeans than Africans are, not only geographically, but racially, culturally and technologically as well. While this racial cosmology undoubtedly reproduces colonialist modes of thinking, it can also be used – as in Alhaji Zinari's statements – to criticize Arabs and especially whites as morally inferior to Hausas.

'Yan Kano-Jiddah's experiences in both Nigeria and Saudi Arabia make them highly aware of the gap that exists between the pronouncements of Islamic moralists and the actual practices of real-life Muslims. Stories like Alhaji Zinari's and Alhaji Salisu's recall other entertaining and provocative accounts of the shortcomings of men from a variety of backgrounds, from Qur'anic scholars to wealthy businessmen and followers of Islamist movements such as Izala and the Muslim Brothers. These stories depict a worldwide community that includes men of all nations and races who enjoy sex with both women and men, men who drink alcohol and take other drugs, and even men like 'yan daudu, who talk and act like women. 'Yan daudu also know that the *malamai*, the Islamic teachers and scholars among whom Malam Halifa Tukur is a leading figure, constitute a highly diverse and fractious community that is riven along lines of ideology, education, rank and socioeconomic class. Although many malamai, especially those associated with the Islamic revivalist movements and the traditional Sufi orders, condemn 'yan daudu for their woman-like behavior and their association with illicit sexuality, there are some who have 'yan daudu as clients. Like Bori practitioners, these malamai are typically less well-educated and serve rural communities and the urban poor, using their skills and powers as mediators of supernatural forces to assist 'yan daudu and others in dealing with problems related to health, finances, family and social relations. As they do for all their clients, these malamai make use of Islamic symbols, charms, prayers and incantations which more orthodox Muslims consider un-Islamic. Equally unorthodox are those malamai who are known in certain circles as *masu harka*, men who 'do the deed,' and who are sought out (discreetly) by other such men, including 'yan daudu. These malamai provide their clients many of the same services that other malamai provide, as well as some that relate specifically to 'the deed,' such as the making of charms and incantations to elicit someone's affection or to defeat a rival.

The work of these malamai, like the faithful irreverence displayed in the humorous exchanges examined here, suggests that apparent contradictions between Islamic doctrine and homosexuality, gender-nonconformity, and even the sacrilegious speech examined here, need not be seen, following Shaikh 'Abd al-Wahhāb, as a threat to divine order. Rather, these contradictions can be seen as reflective of a human affinity for diversity, humor, and play which is itself, as Haruna insisted, part of God's creation. Although 'yan daudu understand that their unconventional gender and sexual practices make them imperfect Muslims, they also know that such imperfection exists throughout the Muslim world, even among those who revile them. Despite these shortcomings, many 'yan daudu remain devoted to their Islamic faith. The patience, tolerance, and good humor they exhibit in the face of the suffering they endure at the hands of state authorities and their fellow Muslims reveal a strong and tenacious faith in the power and mercy of Allah and the message of peace and justice delivered by His Prophet.

Notes

1 Pierce (2007) relates the same anecdote.
2 **Boldface and underlining** are used in this chapter to transcribe Arabic codeswitches (expressions that are not integral to the colloquial Hausa lexicon) and their English translations.
3 Levtzion and Fisher (1986).
4 Umar (1993); Sirriyeh (1999); Soares (2005).
5 Warner (2002).
6 Piamenta (1979).
7 D. Hill (1992: 211, citing Coulmas 1981: 2).
8 Piamenta (1979: 41).
9 'Abd al-Wahhāb (n.d.: 154–156).
10 Silverstein (1993).
11 While I never identified myself as anything but "Sani" – the name given me by my first Hausa-language instructor – the presumption

that my full name was Mohammed Sani occasionally caused tensions in northern Nigeria when people asked whether I was a Muslim, and, more rarely, suggested that it was improper for a non-Muslim to carry a Muslim name.

12 The verb *shiga* ['enter'] can also refer to putting on the clothes of a particular group of people, e.g. *ya shiga mata* ['he has put on women's clothes.'] I rarely wore Hausa clothes, and was not wearing them at the time this recording was made.

13 It is not uncommon for Hausa speakers to use singular nouns with plural referents.

14 The verb *sha* ['drink'] is commonly used to mean 'do a lot of' or 'undergo an unpleasant experience,' e.g. *ya sha duka* ['he drank beating, he got a lot of beatings'].

15 Bargery (1934: 25).

16 Works (1976: 172).

17 Clarke and Linden (1984: 62).

18 Although in mainstream spoken Hausa *'yan Kano-Jiddah* refers to wealthy businessmen (and some women) who shuttle between northern Nigeria and Saudi Arabia, in this chapter I use the term to refer specifically to 'yan daudu who travel between the two countries. During my stay in Nigeria, I did meet independent women who were known as *'yan Kano-Jiddah*, but I never got to know them as well as their 'yan daudu counterparts.

19 Although Alhaji Zinari's reference to oral sex as 'your[pl] work' [*aikinku*] could imply that 'we' – white homos – perform oral sex for money, my interpretation is based on the fact that *aiki* ['work'] can also be translated as 'function' or 'activity.'

20 Basso (1979). See also Mendoza-Denton's (2008: Ch. 4) discussion of the ways Chicana and Chicano youth gang members in California appropriated and reconfigured hegemonic notions of race and nation in their talk about *Norteños* and *Sureños* ('northerners' and 'southerners').

6

MEN ON FILM

In 2002, Sarauniya Studios, a Kano-based production company, released *Ibro ɗan Daudu* (*IDD*), a Hausa-language video-film in which popular actors perform humorous impersonations of 'yan daudu (Figure 6.1). The title role is played by Rabilu Musa ɗanlasan, the Hausa film industry's most popular actor, whose chameleon-like screen persona 'Ibro' has starred in dozens of comedies, such as *Mijin Hajiya* ['Hajiya's Husband'], about a man who is dominated by his wealthy wife, and *Ibro Niga* (from 'nigga'), about African American youth styles and the young Nigerians who imitate them. In his role as a ɗan daudu, Ibro is the 'mother' of a group of 'yan daudu who operate a restaurant and women's house where well-heeled 'big men' come to visit their unmarried girlfriends. These 'people of the bariki' are all portrayed as unscrupulous hedonists who take advantage of their families and neighbors, and occasionally each other. The film's other characters are portrayed as obedient to Hausa Muslim social norms, and it is this ethical integrity, bordering on naïveté, that makes them vulnerable to being exploited by 'yan daudu. The most glaring – and entertaining – sign of 'yan daudu's disregard for social norms is their outrageous 'womanlike' behavior. No matter where they are or who they're talking to, Ibro and his 'daughters' wear head-ties and waist-wrappers, swing their hips, speak in high-pitched voices, and refer to each other as 'she,' 'mother' [*bábà*] and 'girl' [*yarinya*]. These behaviors persist in the most unlikely and inappropriate contexts, such as when the fictional 'yan daudu are interacting with their parents, wives and children, and even with the local imam.

Fig. 6.1   Videocassette packaging for the film *Ibro Ɗan Daudu*.
Source: Courtesy of Yoko Productions, Inc.

The film's popular success derives from Danlasan's clever interpretation of the well-known stereotype of 'yan daudu as 'shameless.'
As we have seen in previous chapters, real-world 'yan daudu
sometimes act in accordance with this stereotype, but never, as far
as I know, in such an exaggerated fashion as is depicted in *IDD*.
Indeed, despite their many differences, all the 'yan daudu I met were
concerned to maintain an image of respectability and discretion, even
when they seemed to be flouting social norms. This was especially
the case when it came to recording their words and images on
audio- or videotape. With respect to the research I did for my
dissertation, for example, my friends were happy to include me in
conversations where they playfully engaged in 'women's talk,' but they

were generally reluctant to let me tape-record their speech. Over the course of a year and a half in 1993–94, I was able to make only eight audiotapes, and on my shorter visits since then I have not wanted to push the issue. Similarly, though I was usually encouraged to take posed photographs (with the expectation that I would give copies to each person photographed), I did not feel welcome to take candid photographs at restaurants, nightclubs or markets.

The only partial exception was at the large outdoor parties known as *bikis,* which in Kano and other large urban areas were usually taped by hired videographers. At these events I was generally welcome to take candid photographs of the performers – musicians, praise-shouters, and younger 'yan daudu and independent women while they danced – but not of the audience members. On the one occasion when I brought my own video-camera to a biki, I was permitted to use it from the seat I'd been given next to the musicians, but I was discouraged from roving around as the hired videographer did. In addition to the videotape I made at that party, two 'yan daudu – Alhaji Balarabe and his 'daughter' Alhaji Damina – gave me copies of the 'official' videotapes of their bikis. Unlike the fictional 'yan daudu in *IDD,* whose clothing, gestures and speech are consistently loud and often disagreeable, in their biki videos Alhaji Balarabe, Alhaji Damina and their older associates sit silently in expensive masculine attire, which befits their relative status and aspirations as 'big men.' This is the public image sought by many 'yan daudu as they grow older, and it crucially relies on their ability (financial and sexual) to marry, procreate and support a family. Bikis play an important role in that process, for in addition to enhancing the host's social prestige, they yield financial capital in the form of monetary gifts from guests.

Although 'yan daudu can be seen talking with each other in the biki videos, their speech is not audible. The only voices that can be heard clearly are those of the professional singers [*mawaƙa*] and praise-shouters [*maroƙa*] who used microphones and public-address systems. As a linguist interested in 'yan daudu's talk, I initially treated biki videos as largely irrelevant to my research. For several years, I used them mainly to supplement my lectures with entertaining images of the 'womanlike' clothing, gestures and dances that some 'yan daudu, especially younger ones, perform at bikis. Seeing and hearing *Ibro Dan Daudu,* however, helped changed my perspective, for it made me realize that the ways 'yan daudu represented themselves in their biki videos was not something I could take for granted. In particular, comparing the ways in which *IDD* and the biki videos represent talk vs. silence helped me understand why many of my friends and acquaintances were unwilling to let me tape-record their 'feminine' speech. It was one thing to play with language and gender in face-to-face interactions, but quite another to let those performances be captured (or 'entextualized') on audiotapes that could be circulated (or 'recontextualized') in ways that could do them harm.[1]

This chapter treats *Ibro 'Dan Daudu* and Alhaji Damina's biki video as audiovisual texts, comparing their vocal, linguistic and visual content along with the contexts in which each video was produced and received (i.e., watched and listened to). The differences between them highlight some of the social tensions that have emerged in Northern Nigeria since the late 1990s, a period in which Islamic reform movements and the Hausa video-film industry have grown increasingly powerful. Both of these social forces have helped to reinforce the image of an Islamic, Hausa-speaking, Northern Nigerian public, yet the unity of that public is challenged by a number of tensions, many of which revolve around gender and sexuality. The film industry, for example, often uses emotionally and erotically charged imagery to attract mass audiences, and these images (though exceedingly tame by Hollywood standards) are seen to contradict Islamic values of modesty and self-restraint. For their part, Hausa filmmakers insist that they are committed to promoting Islamic values. In *IDD*, for example, the local imam is portrayed as a straightforward, peace-loving intellectual, while the 'yan daudu are depicted as devious purveyors of immorality. The meanings of these images are not set in stone, however, for the 'yan daudu's entertaining, 'womanlike' performances have the potential to stimulate responses that challenge prevailing interpretations of Islamic morality.

An even more complicated challenge to Islamic reformists' image of Northern Nigeria is presented by 'yan daudu's biki videos. With a format modeled after the 'traditional' celebrations hosted by married Hausa women, biki videos highlight the fact that some 'yan daudu have been able to use their 'feminine' linguistic and bodily practices to attain wealth, social connections and 'masculine' respectability. The videos circulate within bariki social networks where they are eventually viewed, compared and gossiped about by hundreds, if not thousands, of people. The circulation of these videos (like the biki photographs that circulated into the 1980s) has arguably helped to reinforce and reshape an image of the *bariki* as a 'counterpublic,' or alternative social space, that welcomes and nurtures (some) people with 'deviant' desires, identities and practices.[2] Yet, as we have seen, bariki life is not entirely 'counter' to, or distinct from, the larger society in which it is embedded; it is riven with conflicts and hierarchies of gender, age, class and other categories of difference. Some of these hierarchies are represented in 'yan daudu's and independent women's biki videos. The conflicts, in general, are not. In this regard, Alhaji Damina's biki video is only slightly less fictional than *Ibro Dan Daudu*.

Ibro Dan Daudu

The film opens with a shot of four middle-aged men, one of them an imam, sitting in the shade of a wooden canopy by the side of a narrow dirt road. The men are debating the connection between the way a child is raised and the way he turns out. One man expresses the opinion that when a child behaves badly, the fault lies with the parents who failed to raise him properly. The other men generally disagree, especially the imam, who in Arabic and Hausa counsels the first man to pray, be patient, and leave fate in God's hands. As the men continue their discussion, the camera pans left to show Ibro (Rabilu Musa Danlasan) walking down the road dressed in a woman's head-tie and waist-wrapper over a loose man's gown. With his arms bent at the elbows and wrists, Ibro swings his hips and sings to himself quietly as he slowly approaches the men. Without stopping to bend or crouch down – as a younger man ought to do when greeting his elders, and as lay people should do before an imam – Ibro greets them in a voice that is distinctively breathy and high-pitched. His appearance and voice are matched by the feminine implications of his opening lines. "Sons of men!" he calls out, as if he were an older woman addressing a group of younger men, "*Salamu alaikum. Sannunku.*" The first of these greetings (an Arabic phrase meaning 'peace unto you[pl]') is considered somewhat formal and is typically associated with men, while the second (a Hausa greeting meaning roughly 'Hello, everyone') is relatively informal and more commonly used between women.[3] The men's reactions differ in ways that reflect their earlier discussion: the first man voices surprise and contempt ("God damn him!"), while his companions respond with smiles and laughter; the imam displays virtually no affect at all.

Another scene takes place in Ibro's home, a typical Hausa domestic compound, where he announces his intention to give his daughter away in marriage. As the scene opens, the daughter is complaining to her mother (played by Lubabatu Madaki) about the teasing she endures because of her father's deviant behavior. Ibro's wife is sympathetic but advises her daughter to exercise 'patience' [*hakuri*]. At that moment Ibro walks in, displaying the very behaviors his daughter has been complaining about: wearing a head-tie and waist-wrapper, he swings his hips and throws his head from side to side as he calls out greetings in the same high-pitched voice we heard in the first scene. Despite this performance of exaggerated femininity, Ibro's wife defers to his patriarchal authority, as good Hausa wives are supposed to do, by giving him her stool, sitting down on the mat below him, and addressing him as *maigida* ['head of house']. At the same time, however, she shows contempt for her husband by rolling her eyes, pursing her lips, and by verbally challenging him. Ibro's daughter, meanwhile, dutifully greets him as *bàbá* ['father'] but otherwise remains sullen and quiet throughout the scene.

Although Ibro's wife says nothing about his feminine clothing, gestures or voice, she does comment critically on both the form and content of his speech, faulting him for failing to remember their daughter's name, and interrupting him to criticize the playful way he tries to summon the girl's attention. These commands – "*Saurayeni. Ki nutsu. Ki sakaci kunnenki. Ki raraki kunnenki*" ['Listen to me. Be attentive. Clean out your[f] ears. Empty out your[f] ears.'] – have a simple poetic structure that epitomizes 'yan daudu's supposed penchant for artful banter, and prompt Ibro's wife to admonish him to "leave the daudu at the door," that is, to stop act liking a woman when he comes home. Her criticism of this behavior as a 'shameful thing' [*abin kunya*] precipitates a tense exchange that recalls the stereotypical bickering of Hausa co-wives.

In her role as Ibro's wife, Lubabatu Madaki delivers a number of classic examples of *habaici*, the practice of exchanging insulting innuendo that is commonly associated with women, especially co-wives. As we saw in Chapter 4, proverbs [*karin magana*] are a prototypical feature of such exchanges. 'Yan daudu are widely reputed to be skillful performers of proverbs and habaici, and they often claim to be even more skilled than women at the use of these genres. In this scene, however, Ibro's verbal abilities are no match for his wife's. His speech may be artfully 'feminine' in some ways, but it is not clever. On the contrary, many of his statements constitute blunt exercises of patriarchal authority. Thus, when his wife calls on God to grant Ibro 'patience' [*hakuri*], he responds with a momentary silence – effectively ignoring her – before announcing his decision to give their daughter away in marriage.

Ibro:	Na yi miki miji.	I've found you[f] a husband. ((Fixes head-tie, rolls eyes.))
Wife:	Ka yi mata miji?	You've[m] found her a husband?
Ibro:	Na yi.	Yes.
Wife:	Ka yi me?	You[m] did what?
Ibro:	Miji.	\<Found her\> a husband.
Wife:	Wane irin miji?	What kind of husband?
Ibro:	Ba ki san shi ba fa.	You[f] don't know him.
Wife:	Shi nake tambaya, wane irin miji. A ina yake=	That's what I'm asking, what kind of husband? Where=
Ibro:	=Miji wannan. Wannan 'yar- 'yar yarinyar nan wacce muka aika:, wata 'yar kuta tsiyar nan.	=This husband. This little[f]- little[f] girl that we se:nt, a girl who gives a lot of lip.
Wife:	Me?	What?
Ibro:	Wata 'yar kuta tsiya ai, doguwa doguwa, ba ita ba du-	A girl who gives a lot of lip, really tall[f], isn't she-
Wife:	A'a tsaya.	No, stop.
Ibro:	Wata 'yar yarin- yarinya. 'Yar shina na yi mat.	A little[f] gir-, a girl. A knowledgeable girl I've found for her.
Wife:	To dakata min. Ai ka ce miji.	Now hold on. You[m] said husband.
Ibro:	Hn.	M-hm.
Wife:	Kuma ka gaya mace. A garin nan ba haka ba maigida! Ina ka taɓa ganin an yi aure da mace da mace?	And you[m] said woman. In this town it's not like that, sir! Where have you[m] ever seen a marriage between a woman and a woman?

Ibro:	In kin gama magana,	If you're[f] done talking,
	ki- ki- ki yi min magana,	you[f]- you[f]- you[f] finish talking to
	zan ci gaba magana [(xxx)	me, I'll continue talking [(xxx)
Wife:	[A'a yo ai tambaya ce na yi maka,	[Hey I asked you[m] a question,
	sai ka ba ni amsa ko?	you[m] should give me an answer,
		right?
Ibro:	Na yi miki mji!	I've found you[f] a husband!
Wife:	Gaskiya, (da safe	Truly, (in the morning
	an maimaita ƙadaga.)	the refusal is repeated.)
Ibro:	To.	So be it.
Wife:	Babu yanda da za'a yi ,yata,	There's no way my daughter
	ta auri ɗan daudu.	will be made to marry a ɗan
		daudu.

By rejecting the idea of having a ɗan daudu as her son-in-law, Ibro's wife implicitly voices unhappiness with her own marriage and a desire to spare her daughter a similar fate. The plot of *Ibro Dan Daudu* is highly conventional in this regard, for the politics of arranged marriages are standard fare in Hausa video-films as well as in the popular genre of novels known as 'love stories' [*labarun soyayya*].[4] The film's appeal lies in the way it takes this conventional plot line and spices it up with the hint of sexual transgression. In this scene that goal is accomplished in part through Ibro's use of both masculine and feminine forms to refer to his daughter's fiancé: the labels 'husband' [*miji*] and 'girl' [*yarinya*], and morphologically gendered adjectives like 'tall[f]' [*doguwa*]. Although Ibro's wife would presumably be accustomed to such gender switches, here she responds with a naive confusion, as if she believes Ibro were arranging a same-sex marriage for their daughter. She soon 'realizes,' however, that the 'husband/girl' is in fact a ɗan daudu. Because she comes to this realization with no explicit guidance from Ibro, her initial misinterpretation can thus be read as disingenuous – a way for the filmmakers to invoke the taboo subject of homosexuality and thus to allude to 'yan daudu's reputation for promoting sexual immorality.

Her exclamation – "In this town it's not like that, *maigida*!" – implicitly accuses Ibro of eschewing the sexual norms of Hausa Muslim society and adopting the values of other places where same-sex marriage is presumably tolerated. (*Gari* ['town'] is a common metonym for society or country.) In the early 2000s, Hausa-speaking audiences were likely to have heard of such places thanks to news reports in both the Nigerian and international media, including Hausa sections of the BBC and the Voice of America. Audiences were also likely to be familiar with the discourses of Northern Nigerian nationalists which, like the discourses of African and Islamic nationalists generally, often characterize homosexuals as a fifth column of Western cultural hegemony. By invoking these discourses under the guise of Ibro's wife's apparent confusion, the filmmakers effectively perform a kind of habaici of their own: they reinforce an image of 'yan daudu as sexual outlaws – and cultural traitors – without directly accusing them of homosexuality or any other sexual infraction.

For his part, although Ibro does describe the 'husband' in feminine terms, he does not call him a ɗan daudu. Indeed, neither Ibro nor any of the film's other 'yan daudu characters ever utters the term. His wife's eventual and only use of it ("There's no way my daughter will be made to marry a ɗan daudu") marks the moment of her apparent realization of the fiancé's gender identity and simultaneously highlights the stigma it conveys. By using the generic label *ɗan daudu* in such a negative context, Ibro's wife expresses contempt not only for the 'girl/husband' he has picked out for their daughter, but for 'yan daudu as a class, including Ibro himself.

Spitefulness is also a stereotypical feature of ɗan daudu identity. This trait is illustrated in a subsequent scene, when, after having spent three months under Ibro's tutelage, the fiancé (Dan Bàbá) returns to his parents' home to tell them about his upcoming marriage. Dan Bàbá's quarrelsomeness is performed with none of the verbal artistry exhibited by Ibro's wife; rather, like Ibro, Dan Bàbá incites quarrels simply by acting 'like a woman' and by making unreasonable demands of his kinfolk. The scene opens with a shot of Dan Bàbá (whose name literally means 'Father's son') walking alone into the open area of his parents' compound and calling out greetings at the door of his mother's room. Wearing a head-tie and waist-wrapper over a man's gown and calling himself 'Yar Bàbá ['Father's daughter'], he shocks his parents not only with his feminized appearance but also with the disrespectful way he greets them. He announces his presence crudely, shouting "Hey there! I'm home!" instead of the conventional Arabic greeting *salamu alaikum* or a Hausa equivalent; he fails to crouch down and avert his gaze; and he continues to smile even when his parents become visibly (and audibly) upset.[5]

Ɗan Bàbá's mother expresses surprise at his feminine self-presentation with a series of questions that can be read as naive or rhetorical, or both. At one point she addresses him using both masculine and feminine forms in a way that seems purposefully designed to generate laughs: "When I was talking, were you^m saying it was you^f calling out greetings?!" [*Ina magana, kana cewa ke ce kike sallama?*]. Here Ɗan Bàbá's mother performs a kind of 'confusion' that is similar to what Ibro's wife pretended to experience when he construed their daughter's fiancé as both 'husband' and 'girl.' Although Ɗan Bàbá's mother has never seen or heard her son act 'like a woman' before, she is quick to display her awareness of the way he uses gendered pronouns to perform his new ambiguous social gender identity. The humor in both scenes derives from the way the filmmakers exploit this awareness to highlight the supposed incongruity of a man speaking as a woman.

Ɗan Bàbá is reluctant to acknowledge the gender ambiguities in his own discourse. The closest he comes to doing so is when he refers first to 'Father Ibro' [*Bàbá Ibro*], but stops himself abruptly and repairs this to 'Mother Ibro' [*Bábà Ibro*]. This self-repair reflects the transformation Ɗan Bàbá recently underwent in shifting his public self-presentation from masculine to feminine, a process that required him to train himself to address Ibro and other senior 'yan daudu as 'mother.' Curiously, this self-repair occurs while Ɗan Bàbá is declaring his intention to marry Ibro's daughter – one of the only ways that both he and Ibro remain conventionally masculine.

Another way in which Ɗan Bàbá construes himself as socially (if not grammatically) masculine is through his request for money; this implicitly reproduces the Hausa custom of bridewealth whereby the groom and his kin are supposed to give money and other presents to the bride's family. His affiliation with conventional masculinity is immediately contradicted, however, when Ɗan Bàbá reports that the money will be used to pay for his biki. The fact that Ɗan Bàbá refers to 'my celebration' [*bikina*], as opposed to his bride's, puts him in a conventionally feminine subject position. The fact that Ɗan Bàbá has come home to ask for money, rather than simply to greet his parents, and the emphasis he places on the cost of his biki reproduce commonly held stereotypes of 'yan daudu as greedy and selfish. A similar stereotype of 'yan daudu recurs throughout the film. One minor subplot, for example, concerns one of Ibro's 'daughters' who, while ostensibly running errands for Ibro, dupes a shopkeeper into giving him a sack full of merchandise that he has no intention of paying for. When the shopkeeper comes seeking payment, the 'yan daudu reject the man's claim and gang up on him verbally and physically. In another scene, Ibro catches his foot on a man's rake and loudly accuses the man, a humble worker, of intentionally trying to hurt him. Despite the man's earnest apologies, Ibro continues making a fuss until the imam comes by and attempts to pacify him. Though he verbally accepts the imam's appeals, Ibro's bodily demeanor and vocal prosody convey a stubborn, childlike petulance.

That Dan Bàbá's shortcomings are intended to represent those of 'yan daudu in general becomes especially apparent when Dan Bàbá's father enters the scene. In an ironic twist of fate, the father turns out to be the man in the film's opening scene who expressed contempt for Ibro and who so vehemently insisted on blaming parents when children act badly. As the only man in the film whose son becomes a ɗan daudu, Dan Bàbá's father can be seen as a negative example of the suffering and indignity that come from 'lack of patience' [rashin haƙuri], that is, not leaving fate in God's hands. This trait is manifest in the father's apparent inability to control his emotions. Whereas the mother responds to Dan Bàbá's feminine self-presentation with incredulity and even sarcasm, the father reacts with explosive anger and sadness. With Dan Bàbá standing in front of him wearing a head-tie and waist-wrapper, he is compelled to blame himself by asserting that "I've got a spoiled ɗan daudu in my house" [nake da ɗan daudu gata a cikin gidana ke nan]. This is remarkably similar to the sentiment expressed in the poem "Dan daudu" where, as we saw in Chapter 2, Aƙilu Aliyu describes his hypothetical son as "spoiled from not being punished."

But there is a crucial difference between Dan Bàbá's father and the hypothetical father conjured by Aƙilu Aliyu. Both men experience the same lamentable fate, but only Dan Bàbá's father loses his cool. His angry outbursts alternate with tearful sorrow and self-pity, and his emotions escalate to the point where he throws a plastic watering-can at Dan Bàbá and chases him out of the house under a torrent of verbal abuse. By contrast, Aƙilu Aliyu imagines no such direct confrontation. Instead, he criticizes 'yan daudu in a general fashion and even, indirectly, calls on God to take his hypothetical son's life ("Better he should die"). By channeling his hostility to 'yan daudu through the canonical literary genre of the *waƙa*, Aƙilu Aliyu thus transforms a personal emotional response into an edifying public text. A similar claim can be made about *Ibro Dan Daudu* as a whole, which stages a series of emotionally intense social interactions that model the kinds of behavior deemed proper and improper for women and men, especially in the context of marital and familial relationships. Indeed, Hausa video-film producers and artists consistently make such claims about their films. *IDD*'s moral significance is less straightforward than the poem's because *IDD* makes greater use of indirect and nonverbal forms of communication, such as gesture, parody and humor.

When Dan Bàbá says "Amen" in response to his father's curse, he reproduces a popular perception of 'yan daudu as irreverent and lacking 'shame' [*kunya*]. That Dan Bàbá's shameless behavior is meant to reflect that of 'yan daudu generally is apparent in the parallels between this scene and the one involving Ibro and his family. Thus, his mother's questions accusing Dan Bàbá of shamelessness echo the words of Ibro's wife when she asks him, "don't you^m feel shame?" Another parallel is manifest in Dan Bàbá's father's lament about having "a spoiled ɗan daudu in my house"; this recalls Ibro's wife's declaration that she will not let her daughter marry a ɗan daudu. Each use of the label *ɗan daudu* indexes contempt for 'yan daudu as a class and the speaker's unhappiness about being personally – and publicly – associated with one. Seen in this light, the title *Ibro Dan Daudu* stands out as a negative judgment in its own right, an iconic preview of the film's portrayal of 'yan daudu as social deviants. It is thus not surprising that many real-world 'yan daudu were suspicious of the film before they ever saw it.

Receptions of *Ibro Dan Daudu*

In this section I explore the different ways *Ibro Dan Daudu* was received by certain Hausa audiences in the months following its release. The receptions I analyze include male viewers' reactions that I observed in the course of watching the film or that were reported to me in informal conversations; I also analyze responses to the film that were published on the internet and in a popular magazine. Some of the viewers I spoke to were 'yan daudu, while others were conventionally masculine *masu harka* ['people who do the deed']. The writers of the published texts did not identify their gender or sexual orientations but were presumably masculine and heterosexual.

Abdalla Uba Adamu, a prominent Kano-based scholar of Hausa popular culture, described the film's appeal in a post to the internet listserv Finafinan_Hausa ['Hausa Films'], as follows:[6]

> Ibro Dan Daudu is a study of the Hausa transvestite society, and as such focuses attention on the transvestite community. Transvestites, while tolerated, were never really fully accepted in Hausa society, and even in this era of increasing tolerance to deviancy. [. . .]
>
> The film was definitely well-conceived, and although deals with a very serious matter, yet approaches the theme from a more relaxed, and laid-back perspective, and I think that is the magic of the success of the film. There were no pretensions: just clean fun. The actors have also done extremely well in their acting – indeed it is this type of plot element that gives them a chance to over-act. One cannot help but simply laugh at the exaggerated swishy walks, the adoption of the female speech patterns, the body rhythm and movements and the feminine mannerisms. It was really funny. [. . .]
>
> All told, the film is well executed, light-hearted but dealing with gender ambiguity in a serious manner. There are the usual song and dance, but not irritating enough to take away the main story. I like it![7]

To the extent that Adamu's responses represent Hausa society at large, it seems *IDD* was commercially successful because of the way the film-makers managed to strike a balance between the need to treat the subject of 'yan daudu "in a serious manner" and audiences' desire for "just clean fun." By this, Adamu seems to mean that the film offered humorous portrayals of 'yan daudu while upholding the dominant view of them as contemptible. Yet not all audiences found this combination so appealing. In particular, most of the 'yan daudu ('shirted' and overt) with whom I watched the film or talked about it found *IDD* inaccurate and insulting, even while they appreciated the comedic abilities of Ibro and his fellow actors.

I watched *IDD* twice in Kano in June 2002 – first with a friend who self-identified as *mai harka*, and then with a group of nine *masu harka*, two of whom also self-identified covertly as 'yan daudu. The latter occasion took place at the home of my friend Mahmud, an unmarried man in his late twenties whose apartment was the regular gathering-spot for over a dozen masu harka, any number of whom might show up on a given night. In addition to Mahmud's friendly personality, his friends were attracted by the amenities his place had to offer. Although he lived in a large family compound belonging to his father, his apartment had a separate entrance so he could social-ize with his guests without having to worry about sudden intrusions from relatives or unannounced passers-by. It consisted of two small bedrooms and a sitting room that featured a carpeted floor, pillows, a mounted wall-fan, a radio/audiocassette-player, television and VCR. (During Kano's frequent power outages, Mahmud and his guests chatted by candlelight and listened to music on battery power.)

I had not planned to watch *IDD* with Mahmud and his friends; I happened to visit him one evening just as they were getting ready to watch it. I could tell Mahmud had visitors when I arrived at the vestibule outside his sitting-room and saw a cluster of shoes on the floor. Two of Mahmud's guests were 'shirted' 'yan daudu: outwardly masculine in appearance, they held conventional jobs (not cooking or 'prostitution') and only acted 'like women' in the company of other masu harka. Mahmud's remaining guests were conventionally masculine. As far as I could tell, everyone was between 20 and 40 years old and middle-class by Nigerian standards. Mahmud, for example, had attended (but not finished) secondary school, spoke limited English, and worked as a salesman for a small company that sold linoleum flooring. His social network was almost exclusively Hausa-speaking, and he was an avid consumer of Hausa, Arabic and American videos and music.

As Mahmud inserted the tape into the VCR, we repositioned ourselves to face the TV screen. Some people sat with their backs against the wall, others leaned on pillows or each other, or reclined with one man's head in another's man lap. The mood in the room was one of wary excitement. After having heard of the film for sev-eral months, people seemed eager to see it for themselves, especially in the (exclusive) company of other masu harka where they could voice their reactions without restraint. Like Abdalla Uba Adamu, Mahmud and his friends agreed that the actors in *IDD* "overacted," but they did not all share Adamu's favorable critique. At the film's opening scene, in which Ibro sashays across the screen and calls out "Sons of men," a number of people laughed. "Hey, he can do the thing!" someone shouted, and others agreed. "Bastard Ibro!" [*Shege Ibro*] someone else said, conveying an ambiguous mix of admiration and condemnation. Indeed, the group's reception of the film was profoundly ambivalent overall. The burlesque qualities of the fictional 'yan daudu's 'feminine' performances generated considerable laughter, but they also evoked indignation and hostility, particularly among the two self-described 'yan daudu, who harumphed and sucked their teeth repeatedly throughout the video.[8] About Ibro's limp-wrist gesture, for example, one of them complained, "He's overacting" ['*Yana overaction* (ova'akshin)']. The other turned his admiration of Ibro's acting into a kind of accusation, saying, "This is no imitation. One has to have the thing in one's body [to be capable of that]."

The same two critics issued a number of other complaints as well: "One has exposed ['yan daudu's behaviors], what a calamity" and "What's the use of this slander?" It is notable that such complaints came primarily from the covert 'yan daudu in the group, for while virtually all masu harka – including 'yan daudu – fear being 'exposed' [*yi garwa*; see Chapter 4], and 'slandered' [*yi sharri*] as homosexuals, 'shirted' 'yan daudu also fear exposure of their hidden gender identity. This fear often leads them to avoid interacting with overt 'yan daudu in public.

The behavioral excesses of Ibro and his fellow actors were not the only thing that attracted commentary from Mahmud and his friends. A number of individuals made a point of identifying the geographical locations depicted in the film, such as the river that runs through the town of Wudil (Rabilu Musa 'Danlasan's hometown) and the bridge that runs over it on the road to Kano. People also seemed to take pleasure in naming the actors, commenting on their looks and comparing their performances in *IDD* with the same actors' performances in other films. One actor who attracted particular attention was the teenage boy who plays Ibro's daughter's boyfriend – the boy she loves and wants to marry instead of 'Dan Bàbá. "He's good-looking," someone said, using an in-group term, *fili* [literally, 'open space, opportunity'], to describe attractiveness. "Yes, he is good-looking," someone else replied, "and he has eyes" – meaning he too likes sex with men. The latter claim generated laughter, but turned out to be unverified wishful thinking.

The responses of Mahmud and his friends were more boisterous than those I heard from Nasiru, the friend with whom I first watched *I'DD*. Nasiru was in his thirties, owned his own home, and ran a small business with his brother. He was engaged to marry a woman but self-identified as a mai harka, and he was generally even more discreet about his sexuality than Mahmud and his friends. Nasiru also had more cosmopolitan class aspirations. He'd attended university and spoke English fluently, his social networks included many non-Hausa-speakers, and he generally consumed non-Hausa and non-Nigerian entertainments. He had heard of *I'DD* but he might never have seen it if I hadn't asked him to drive me to the video store one day so I could buy a copy of it. From there we went back to his house to watch it. Nasiru laughed and chuckled modestly throughout the movie. He seemed to enjoy the actors' 'feminine' performances and was not inclined to criticize their accuracy, though he recognized that the film's portrayal of 'yan daudu was exaggerated and acknowledged that some 'yan daudu would probably not like it.

By contrast, when I spoke with overt 'yan daudu who had either seen *I'DD* or had heard about it, their responses echoed the largely negative reactions of the covert 'yan daudu I'd met at Mahmud's. In Madari, for example, I spoke with Jamilu, the ɗan daudu known as 'Boxer,' who had seen the film at a local video parlor some weeks earlier. He told me that "all" the 'yan daudu in Madari had gone to see *I'DD*, but "we" didn't like it because it was insulting (*wulaƙanta*) and unpleasant (*ba daɗi*). Similar judgments were reported to me by other 'yan daudu, including Alhaji Damina. After spending much of the period between 1994 and 2001 in Saudi Arabia (I did not see him on my trips to Nigeria in 1997 and 2000), Alhaji Damina was again living with his wife and children in Rijiyar Kuka where he now ran a small restaurant. One day I was sitting with him outside his shop and mentioned that I'd just seen *Ibro Dan Daudu*. "Ibro ɗan iska!" he shouted, artfully replacing the term *ɗan daudu* with *ɗan iska*, an epithet whose literal meaning is 'son of a spirit' (or 'son of wind') but was equivalent here to the English expression *son of a bitch*. Although he had not seen *I'DD* himself, Alhaji Damina did not like what he'd heard about it. Regarding the film's depiction of 'yan daudu wearing women's clothes, for example, Alhaji Damina said that it was only 'children' [*yara*] who put on head-ties or waist-wrappers, not 'adults' [*manya*].

By distinguishing the social practices of younger 'yan daudu from those of older ones, Alhaji Damina provides a more subtle sociological analysis than we see in *IDD*, which depicts 'yan daudu as uniformly 'feminine' and therefore contemptible. My own ethnographic observations largely confirm Alhaji Damina's claims. In the real world 'yan daudu rarely present themselves in such an exaggeratedly feminine manner, especially to outsiders, and they almost never do so in the presence of their heterosexual kin. Even away from their families, the appearance and actions of many 'yan daudu are often quite 'masculine' by conventional Hausa standards. Except at *bikis*, I rarely saw 'yan daudu wearing a head-tie or waist-wrapper, and I never saw any dan daudu wearing both items at the same time. The use of stereotypically feminine gestures and speech was more frequent, but this too varied considerably across individuals and social contexts. Indeed, some 'yan daudu displayed few if any stereotypically 'feminine' traits and would have been virtually indistinguishable from other men were it not for the 'women's work' they did as cooks or as men's companions. It is also notable that, whereas real-world 'yan daudu are known and admired (at least by some) for their biting wit, the speech of 'yan daudu as represented in *IDD* is largely devoid of the 'feminine' verbal genres associated with that wit, such as proverbs and innuendo. Their absence in the speech of the fictional 'yan daudu in *IDD* reinforces the film's representation of them as disconnected from Hausa cultural norms.

'Yan daudu were not the only people offended by *Ibro Dan Daudu*. The actor and the film also drew criticism from people with Islamist sympathies. In a letter to the editor published in July 2002, a reader of the magazine *Fim* complained about the recent releases of both *Ibro Dan Daudu* and *Ibro Usama*, a video-film in which Rabilu Musa Danlasan impersonates Osama bin Laden. (The name Osama is frequently rendered in Hausa as Usama.)

ALL THAT'S LEFT IS IBRO DAN FODIO, RIGHT?!
DEAR FIM MAGAZINE,
Please give me the opportunity in this popular magazine of ours to say something about Rabilu Musa (Ibro).

Ibro, truly everyone who watches your shows these days knows *the skunk lost its stink* a long time ago. Now for God's sake, if Hausa shows are supposed to morally instructive, what kind of message is there in the film Ibro Chinaman and Ibro Shehu Jaha? Now it appears you've done Ibro Dan Daudu and Ibro Usama too. So next we should expect the film Ibro Dan Iska, Ibro Drunkard, and Ibro Usman Dan Fodio,

right? Yet Sheikh Usman Dan Fodio (God's mercy be upon him) and Osama bin Laden are both saints of God, jihadists on the path of God. Ibro! No strumming . . . !
Danladi Zakariyya Haruna
Kano

Using a Hausa idiom, *tusa ta kare wa bodari*, that translates roughly as 'the skunk lost its stink,' Danladi Zakariyya Haruna insults Ibro in two ways: he suggests that Ibro's talents are no longer as strong as they once were, and he implies that those talents were never very appealing to begin with. Haruna seems particularly vexed by the recent, nearly simultaneous release of *Ibro Dan Daudu* and *Ibro Usama*. By comparing the former to such hypothetical titles as *Ibro Dan Giya* ('Ibro Drunkard') and *Ibro Dan Iska* (a curious echo of Alhaji Damina's retort discussed above), Haruna puts 'yan daudu in the same immoral league as drunkards and rogues. By contrast, Haruna compares Osama bin Laden to Usman Dan Fodio, the Islamic revolutionary who founded the Sokoto Caliphate two hundred years ago (see Chapter 2). Both men are widely revered in Northern Nigeria today as Muslim heroes. Accordingly, for Ibro to impersonate such a heroic figure using (supposedly) the same comedic conventions that he uses to impersonate a dan daudu would be morally transgressive. Haruna's final comment is a shortened form of the saying, "No strumming, make butter," which is idiomatically used to mean 'Actions are needed, not words.'[9] In other words, if Ibro and his defenders want to claim that his movies have positive social value, they need to prove it by making films that clearly conform to orthodox Islamic values.

Although *Ibro Usama* was the object of complaints and protests before its release, these died down once it became clear that Rabilu Musa Danlasan's impersonation of Osama bin Laden is far more respectful than the parodic roles he plays in *IDD* and other video-films. Nevertheless, Danlasan and his collaborators take pains to defend themselves against the charge that his films, and video-films generally, contravene Islamic morality. Magazines like *Fim* regularly feature articles with titles like "Hausa films provide good moral training" and 'Ibro' and other film stars have repeatedly gone on record to affirm their commitment to Islam and Shari'a.[10] Additionally, as is the case with many Hausa video-films, after a Hausa version of the standard copyright warning, the film opens with a written Hausa translation of the *fatiha*, the first line of the Qur'an: "DA SUNAN ALLAH MAI RAHAMA MAI JIN KAI" ('In the name of God, the Compassionate, the Merciful'). This is complemented by the imam's declaration at the end of the film when he says to Ibro's friends, "God rejects you[pl] ['yan daudu]. And I reject you[pl]." These statements frame *IDD* as a 'serious' text, instructing viewers to interpret its humorous portrayal of 'yan daudu as a cautionary example of how respectable Hausa Muslims should not behave. Not all viewers shared Abdalla Uba Adamu's appreciative uptake of this framing, however. For some viewers, the film's portrayal of 'yan daudu was not morally critical enough. Others, including nearly all the 'yan daudu I spoke to, enjoyed the film for reasons that neither he nor the filmmakers were likely to consider (at least not openly), such as the physical beauty and questionable sexuality of its male actors, or the forbidden pleasure of watching (and hearing) 'yan daudu flout cultural norms. Ultimately, however, the film's moralistic framing led many of these viewers to condemn it as insulting and slanderous. In particular, they rejected its implication that being a ɗan daudu is incompatible with being a respectable Hausa Muslim man.

Alhaji Damina's Biki Video

Several weeks after I first starting visiting Alhaji Lawan's restaurant in Rijiyar Kuka, Alhaji Damina, a solidly built ɗan daudu in his late twenties, returned from Saudi Arabia where he had recently performed the hajj. Alhaji Damina's appearance and demeanor set him noticeably apart from the other 'yan daudu at the shop. While Alhaji Lawan and the others usually wore the same work clothes every day, Alhaji Damina's clothes were always clean and pressed, and he often wore a different outfit every day, drawn from a large wardrobe that included Hausa, Arab, southern Nigerian and Western fashions (Figure 6.2). He chatted freely with customers and merchants and strolled around the market area with a poise and self-confidence that contrasted with the relative reticence of the other 'yan daudu. Also unlike the others, Alhaji Damina prayed regularly at the nearby mosque. Although he was the youngest ɗan daudu at the shop, his relative

Fig. 6.2   Alhaji Damina outside his own restaurant in Rijiyar Kuka, 2002.
Source: Photo by R. Gaudio.

wealth and his status as an *alhaji* conferred on him a degree of social prestige disproportionate to his youth. Though he spent many hours a day at the shop, Damina normally did none of the cooking or serving. Instead, he served as a kind of host who engaged Alhaji Lawan's customers in friendly conversations which were often humorous and even flirtatious. Occasionally he would prepare a plate of food for particular friends and visitors, especially 'big men,' who would sit and chat with him inside the shop or on benches outside the front door.

Alhaji Damina had accumulated enough wealth on his travels to Saudi Arabia to be able to marry shortly after I met him. This was his second marriage; he had divorced his first wife, who had borne him two daughters, a few years earlier. Within a few weeks of his return to Nigeria, Alhaji Damina was married in a traditional ceremony that took place in his home village outside Kano. He then hosted a *bikin aure*, or wedding celebration, in Kano about a week and a half later. Because Hausa men are not supposed to have bikis of their own, Alhaji Damina's biki highlighted the feminine aspect of his *dan daudu* identity. At the same time, his biki was held to celebrate his masculine accomplishment in having taken a new wife, who presumably had her own, traditional wedding biki in her home village.

Alhaji Damina's biki took place over the course of two days in August 1993 on the gated grounds of a state-owned hotel in a commercial area of Kano. The biki video, filmed over the course of both days, lasts about three hours, and the camera's field of vision remains within the play space for its entire duration. The camera focuses most frequently on the singer and his musicians, who sit on benches and mats in two parallel rows with their backs to a wall. In the 'play space' [*filin wasa*] in front of the musicians, young 'yan daudu and a few young independent women gather intermittently to dance, and praise-shouters stand to announce the monetary gifts offered by various guests to the musicians, to Alhaji Damina, and to the praise-shouters themselves. The play space is also where the activities associated with Bori begin, though practitioners tend to roam once they are possessed by spirits, and the camera follows them when they do. Opposite the musicians is a cluster of plastic chairs where Alhaji Damina, his 'parents' and other 'big men' sit in expensive men's attire, usually a *babbar riga* [literally, 'large gown'] and a cap [*hula*]. Further away from the musicians, benches mark the perimeter of the play space. One set of benches is occupied by older independent women; the others are occupied by 'yan daudu and other men of different ages. In addition, numerous men and boys stand or crouch nearby. Every so often one of the older men or women approaches the musicians to offer some money.

Because I had only recently met Alhaji Damina, I was invited to his biki by word of mouth (not with a printed invitation; Figure 6.3 is to Hajiya Asabe's biki) and mostly stayed on or near the outer benches; a white American female friend accompanied me part of the time. I approached the musicians – and am briefly visible on the

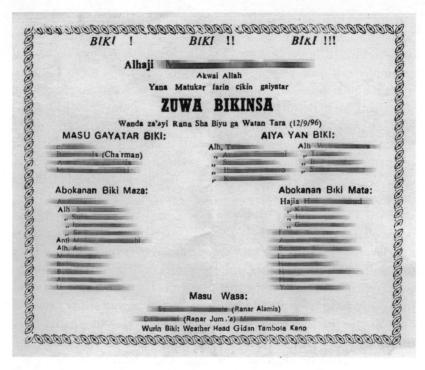

Fig. 6.3   Invitation to a biki hosted by Hajiya Asabe in Sabon Gari, 1996. The text reads as follows: 'Allah Exists / Alhaji Dan Asabe is extremely happy to invite [you] to his biki.' It then gives the date and location, and lists the names of the 'Inviters' (including the 'Chairman'), 'Parents,' 'Male Friends,' 'Female Friends,' and 'Players' (i.e., musical performers).

videotape – on one occasion when I offered a monetary gift that was announced by a praise-shouter. Alhaji Damina gave me a copy of the video several weeks later, with the understanding that it would help in my research and that I would show it in that context.

Prior to the adoption of Shari'a, bikis usually took place in publicly accessible venues, such as the courtyards of commercial buildings or undeveloped plots of land, where they attracted scores of onlookers – boys and men who were conventionally masculine (some of whom might be 'civilian' masu harka), and perhaps a few young girls who were not yet subject to Islamic norms of gender segregation and who were sent to sell homemade snacks on behalf of their mothers. Permission to use the space was obtained, often for a fee, from the owner or recognized neighborhood leader or 'ward head' [mai unguwa], as appropriate. Guests were notified of the date and place by word of mouth and by printed invitations that listed the names of the host, the singer, and the 'parents' [*iyaye*] who helped plan and pay for the biki; these invitations were written in Hausa or English and were considered important even though most of the participants – overt 'yan daudu and independent women – were unable to read in either language. Chairs and benches were borrowed or rented for the occasion, and were usually arranged in a large circle that delineated the play space; at some bikis this space was kept clear by uniformed guards who were hired to push back the crowds of onlookers using words and small sticks.

Most bikis had a flexible schedule. Singers and musicians would typically begin playing in the afternoon or evening and would continue late into the night as long as the weather and the electric supply held out. (Urban bikis tended to rely on generators, while bikis in smaller towns usually did without electricity altogether.) Dancing, informal gift-giving and Bori happened in no particular order, though spirit-possession mostly took place late at night. Guests and onlookers would come and go, sit or stand, chat or remain silent, more or less at will. There were regular breaks at Muslim prayer times, and meals were usually served to the host's honored guests at a location away from the play space. The most formal event of a biki was a gift-giving ritual known as *ajo* that always took place on the final day.

As they do for married women, the bikis hosted by 'yan daudu and independent women gave them and their guests the opportunity to listen to live music, perform or observe women's dances, receive visits from spirits, and socialize with friends, some of whom might have come from far away for the occasion. Bikis also served an important economic function, requiring considerable expenditures by the host, who expected to receive generous financial gifts from certain of his guests in return. In larger urban areas, the host of a biki would hire a professional cameraman to record it on videotape. He would then have a small number of copies made and give these to a few of his friends, so that they could show them to other people in the wider bariki networks.

The spatial arrangement of the biki's participants and their respective involvement in the activities of singing, making music, dancing, praise-shouting, and spirit-possession – all commonly described as 'play' – index a social hierarchy of gender, age, wealth and respectability.[11]

For the most part, this hierarchy conforms to dominant Hausa cultural norms. To outside observers the main indication that this was a 'deviant' biki would be the sight of men performing 'women's dances' [*rawar mata*]: individual dances, where people wait in line to approach the musicians and dance for about a minute at a time; and circular dances, where people stand front to back in a circle, following one another as they dance and walk. (Line dances were also popular, but were not performed at this biki.) The 'yan daudu who perform these dances are mostly in their teens or twenties, presumably unmarried, and they are all dressed in basic masculine attire – Hausa men's trousers [*wando*] and long shirt [*doguwar riga*], or an Arab-style robe [*jallabiya*], or Western-style shirt and trousers. In addition, many (but not all) of the 'yan daudu dancers wear a woman's waist-wrapper or a head-tie (Figure 6.4); the few young women dancers wear both. Sometimes the same piece of cloth is passed from one ɗan daudu to another as they take turns dancing. Like women's dances, a waist-wrapper or head-tie immediately indexes the wearer's status as 'feminine.' It also indicates youth. At all the bikis I attended, I rarely saw a ɗan daudu over 30 dance or wear a waist-wrapper, and when I did, the performer was usually unmarried and therefore classifiable as a 'young man' [*saurayi*] regardless of his actual age; or he was obviously drunk.

With their visual and acoustic images of Hausa music, dancing, gift-giving, praise-shouting and Bori, biki videos represent 'yan daudu as participants in what is often called 'traditional Hausa culture' [*al'adun Hausa na gargajiya*].[12] Much of this culture is derogated by orthodox Muslims, but it is widely admired nevertheless, both as distinctive of 'Hausaness' [*zaman Hausa*] and as a popular space of social belonging for those who feel excluded or alienated from the orthodox Hausa Muslim mainstream (see Chapter 2). Biki videos can thus be viewed as claims to public space and status on behalf of 'yan daudu, independent women and other subordinate groups, such as Bori practitioners and musicians. In Alhaji Damina's case, this claim was initially asserted when he and his associates rented the space and distributed the invitation cards; it was asserted more forcefully by the staging of the event itself. As the biki video circulated through the networks of 'yan daudu and independent women, it served to remind viewers that 'yan daudu have enjoyed access to public space and may inspire them to make similar claims in the future.

Fig. 6.4 Dancing at a biki in Zakawa, 1993. Dancers are wearing 'women's' waist-wrappers over conventional men's attire.
Source: Photo by R. Gaudio.

Yet the alternative public imagined by this video and others like it is not a space of radical democratic citizenship. Rather, it is a public in which material and symbolic resources are distributed unequally by virtue of age, sex, gender, occupation, marital status, and personal qualities such as 'shame' [*kunya*] and 'popularity' [*farin jini*, literally, 'white blood'], which are themselves highly gendered. It is thus similar in many ways to the publics imagined through such 'old' Hausa genres such as song-poems [*wak'a*] and Friday sermons [*hotuba*] as well as 'new' media like newspapers and video-films. Bikis and biki videos can thus be seen as a form of 'yan daudu's participation in the Northern Nigerian public sphere. Such exercises in cultural citizenship have been repressed, but not eliminated, in recent years. After the adoption of Shari'a, it became more difficult for 'yan daudu to secure the use of public space, and they feared assaults at the hands of the police and hisbas. As a result, their bikis have become less frequent, but they have not disappeared.

The Sound of Silence

The most notable semiotic contrast between our two main video texts is auditory: the 'yan daudu's loud, obnoxious voices in *IDD* vs. their near-total silence in Alhaji Damina's biki video. Both representations can be explained by a Hausa ideology of language that values silence among respectable, high-ranking people, and treats public speech as a specialized craft. Historically, this ideology was hegemonic not only in Hausaland but also in other hierarchical West African societies, where wordsmiths known as praise-shouter, praise-singer or griot (Hausa *maroki*, Mande *jali*, Wolof *gewel*) constituted a distinct caste and were bound by custom to perform their services for the benefit of noble lineages to which they were officially affiliated.[13] When the Hausa (Habe) monarchs began to embrace Islam in the fifteenth century C.E., Muslim scholars emerged as another class of wordsmiths whose ability to read, write and interpret sacred texts could be put to important political use. These scholars' influence increased dramatically as a result of Usman Dan Fodio's jihad and remains strong to this day. It is represented in *Ibro Dan Daudu*, where the imam, played by Auwalu Idris, is a voice for reason, patience and faith. Popularly known as Malam Dare, Auwalu Idris is widely admired for reciting quotes from Islamic scripture in his films.[14]

The status of praise-shouters fell with the overthrow of the Habe dynasties, and it eroded still further under European colonial rule, when many were forced to look for patrons among new elites who would pay them to perform. Alhaji Damina's biki was one such performance venue. Though only modestly elite relative to Hausa society at large, Alhaji Damina had enough financial and social capital (money and friends) to host his biki, and thus to act and be treated as a patron or 'big man' vis-à-vis people of lesser status, including the singer, musicians and praise-shouters who were paid to speak and perform on his behalf. The biki video itself is the product of such patronage, for the videographer was hired to 'speak' on behalf of Alhaji Damina by creating an audiovisual document that would represent him in the most respectable light possible. It is thus no coincidence that the camera and microphone ignore the informal conversations Alhaji Damina had with his guests and focus instead on the music, song and praise epithets. Alhaji Damina's silence is an index of his (aspired-to) social status. By contrast, the fictional 'yan daudu's 'womanlike' quarrelsomeness and volubility in *IDD* index a profound lack of shame, disqualifying them from Hausa Muslim cultural citizenship.

Another important semiotic contrast between *IDD* and Alhaji Damina's biki video is visual and kinetic. Whereas *IDD* depicts all 'yan daudu as equally (and outrageously) 'feminine' in terms of dress and bodily comportment, the biki video distinguishes older 'yan daudu, who wear men's clothes and remain relatively still, from younger 'yan daudu who dance while wearing waist-wrappers or head-ties. A similar distinction is evident between older and younger independent women with respect to dancing (but not clothing). This pattern is indicative of the patron–client relationship described above, for the younger 'yan daudu and independent women who dance at Alhaji Damina's biki are potential clients who might need his help, just as he was helped by the 'parents' who occupy seats of honor at the center of the play space. Indeed, the only times when older 'yan daudu or independent women are shown moving is when they rise to approach the musicians with a monetary gift. As is common throughout Africa, these donations (or 'dashes' in Nigerian English) are performed with great flourish: holding a wad of cash in her or his hand, the donor places bill after bill on the forehead of the individual being honored by the gift.[15] As represented in the biki video, then, 'yan daudu are both mindful of the same social hierarchies of age, gender and wealth that prevail within Hausa Muslim society at large.

'Yan daudu's 'feminine' linguistic performances – stereotypically characterized by humor, indirectness and emotional volatility – are widely perceived to violate an ideology of language and gender that privileges seriousness, restraint and literalism, and associates these with the public speech of 'respectable' Hausa men; women's talk, though appreciated as artful, is conventionally restricted to the domestic sphere. This ideology is reproduced in both *Ibro Dan Daudu* and Alhaji Damina's biki video, but in different ways. With the exception of Dan Baba's father, the male characters in *IDD* talk and act in a dignified, low-key fashion; married, 'respectable' women are seen and heard only at home. By contrast, 'yan daudu are depicted as frivolous, devious and argumentative, and they flaunt these 'feminine' behaviors in virtually every scene. In the biki video, on the other hand, older 'yan daudu epitomize the dignified self-restraint associated with Hausa Muslim 'big men' and they perform this exalted status through their silence, their stillness, and their generous patronage. Younger 'yan daudu can be seen performing women's dances and wearing items of women's attire, but their speech, too, is inaudible. Although the biki video challenges hegemonic norms that would exclude women and 'women's customs' from the public realm, 'women's talk' remains conspicuously off-screen and out of earshot.

As a mass-market commodity produced by Hausa Muslim capitalists concerned to preserve their connections with the Northern Nigerian religious and political establishments, *IDD* illustrates what Susan Philips calls the "multisitedness" of hegemonic power.[16] Philips describes how a particular ideology of gender and language is used in Tongan court-rooms to legitimate the Tongan nation-state. In a similar fashion, I have attempted to show how *IDD*'s negative (yet amusing) representations of 'yan daudu's performances of 'women's talk' help to construct an imagined Northern Nigerian public that is distinct from the rest of Nigeria and allied with other Islamic publics worldwide by virtue of its adherence to orthodox Islamic norms of gender and sexuality. The transnational parameters of this imagined public are indexed by a number of intertextual references within the film, such as the Hausa translation of the Qur'anic *fatiha*, the imam's recitations of Arab-Islamic scripture, and Ibro's wife's implicit reference to other 'towns' where women are allowed to marry women.

References to cultural boundaries within Nigeria are somewhat harder to discern, for the film makes virtually no reference to the country's ethnic, religious or linguistic diversity. The dialogue, for example, is almost entirely monolingual (save for occasional Arabic oaths or scriptural quotations) and is peppered with examples of 'traditional' Hausa verbal art (spoken by women, not 'yan daudu). The absence of English-Hausa codeswitching – a common urban linguistic practice known as *Ingausa* – is particularly striking. The only reference to the Nigerian political economy occurs when a wealthy politician gets arrested for corruption while visiting his girlfriend at the women's house adjacent to Ibro's food shop. Here state corruption is linked to the sexual immorality of prostitutes and 'yan daudu (in their role as prostitutes' agents), for it is the latter who are the ultimate beneficiaries of the money embezzled by the politician, leaving his wife and children unprovided for and thereby harming society at large. By showing the 'big man' being arrested inside the women's house, the film represents the state as flawed, but ultimately self-policing. By contrast, the 'yan daudu and karuwai remain morally unredeemed yet curiously, and unrealistically, beyond the reach of the police. If the integrity of the imagined Northern Nigerian public is threatened, therefore, it is 'yan daudu and karuwai who are to blame – not the state, nor the social inequalities that make prostitution so economically attractive, nor the ethnic and religious diversity that belie the idea of a unified North.

Yet the moral implications of this narrative are not absolute, for the image of a 'big man' driving in a Mercedes to pick his girlfriend up at a women's house is semiotically complex. Though framed as immoral, its glamour and erotic appeal may be attractive to many viewers. A similar contradiction between morality and aesthetics is evident in the film's portrayal of 'yan daudu's 'feminine' voices, clothing and bodily movements as both shameless and funny. It is such contradictions that fuel Islamists' complaints about the video-film industry, for they undermine the notion of a Northern Nigerian public unified by its strict adherence to Islamic norms of gender and sexuality.

Although the makers and defenders of *Ibro Dan Daudu* portray it as unambiguously supportive of Islam and Shari'a, their claims are belied by the diverse ways in which the film was received. This diversity was facilitated by the film's heteroglossia – the many voices and discourses it brings together, which speak to different audiences in different ways.[17] As noted by Charles Briggs, the heteroglossic nature of texts makes it possible to trace the ideological tensions that exist within the society in which the texts were produced. Drawing on the work of Raymond Williams, Briggs argues that it is unduly simplistic to posit the existence of a single dominant ideology for any given society because no domination ever rests unopposed.[18]

Ibro Dan Daudu and Alhaji Damina's biki video are similarly heteroglossic texts, produced by agents who seek to enshrine certain ideologies as authoritative, but who cannot avoid referring to discourses that undermine those ideologies. This is especially notable in the case of *IDD*, where an orthodox Islamic ideology of language and gender is constructed as morally superior by juxtaposing the speech of sympathetic characters, especially the imam, alongside the speech of 'yan daudu, who are represented as dishonest and disrespectful of social norms. The film thus illustrates Briggs' observation that dominant practices and ideologies are frequently asserted through 'intertextual' representations of subordinate others, while the ways in which some viewers recontextualized those representations reveals that such domination is always subject to resistance. The biki video is a more challenging text in this regard, for it features no overt conflicts and makes few explicit references to discourses external to it; its ideological dominance thus appears to be natural and uncontested within the social network of 'yan daudu in which it was designed to circulate.[19] Briggs calls such naturalized dominance into question, insisting that the absence of overt conflict within a text should not be read as reflecting a lack of conflict in the world outside it. Alhaji Damina's biki video, for example, makes no mention of the social and legal persecution to which all 'yan daudu are vulnerable, nor does it refer to the jealousy, competition and hostility that often characterize 'yan daudu's relationships with one another.

Both Briggs' and Michael Warner's arguments are illustrated by the textual contrasts between *Ibro Dan Daudu* and Alhaji Damina's biki video and by the participant structures of their production and reception. The material limits that Briggs writes about are manifest in the radical discrepancy between the limited circulation of 'yan daudu's biki videos, which became even more limited after Shari'a was adopted in 2000, and the successful proliferation of *IDD* and other commercial video-films in that same period. Yet the 'counterpublic' imagined by Alhaji Damina's biki video and others like it is limited not only by unequal access to space, media and other resources; it is also limited by (some) 'yan daudu's apparent embrace of hegemonic cultural norms with respect to age, gender and wealth. Paraphrasing Warner, these contradictions derive in part from the fact that the counterpublic imagined by 'yan daudu's biki videos is distorted – or at least influenced – by its subordinate relationship to the Northern Nigerian public imagined by more dominant texts, of which *IDD* is one example.

To the extent that texts like *IDD* are perceived to represent Northern Nigerian culture at large, they help to construct an Islamic Northern Nigerian public that is distinct from – and morally superior to – the rest of Nigeria and the Nigerian state. Such texts also install particular ideologies of gender and language as hegemonic norms regulating people's participation in the Northern Nigerian public sphere. This public might be an alternative or counterpublic with respect to the Nigerian nation-state, but it exerts considerable hegemony within Northern Nigeria. Although few if any 'yan daudu are so politically motivated, their biki videos arguably construct a similar 'counter-counterpublic' – an alternative vision of a Northern Nigerian public that is more inclusive (but no less hierarchical) than that imagined by the supporters of Shari'a. Another 'counter-counterpublic' can be glimpsed, if only provisionally, in the hostile and ironic ways in which some 'yan daudu responded to *Ibro Dan Daudu*. These responses, and the communal contexts in which they were articulated, challenge communication theorist Jürgen Habermas' claims about the 'individuated' nature of reception in an age of commercial mass media, and underscore the need for ethnographic research that pays close attention to entextualization, decontextualization and recontextualization, that is, the specific social processes whereby texts are made, circulated and interpreted.[20] The interactional nature of these practices allows for kinds of debate that, while not necessarily 'rational' in the ideal, Habermasian sense, do have the potential to be 'critical.'

Notes

1 Bauman and Briggs (1990).
2 Warner (2002).
3 Rufa'i (1986: 71).
4 See Furniss (2003); Larkin (2002b); A. Adamu (2006).
5 Thanks to Susan Philips for calling my attention to 'Dan Baba's persistent smiles.
6 Adamu began his post in Hausa, but switched to English in order to accommodate readers who might experience "difficulty understanding [it] in Hausa" [*wahalar fahimta da Hausa*].

7   A. Adamu (2002).
8   Sucking teeth is a gesture signifying annoyance and disdain; it is used throughout West Africa and the African diaspora (Rickford and Rickford 1976).
9   The full expression is *Ba giringirin ba dai, a yi mai*; see Bargery (1934: 390).
10 See, e.g., Gora (2002).
11 See Keating (1998) for a detailed account of how space, speech and movement are used to index social rank at official chieftancy meetings in Pohnpei, Micronesia.
12 The plural term *al'adu* 'customs' is frequently translated by the singular English term 'culture,' e.g., *Hukumar Tarihi da Al'adu ta Jihar Kano* ['Kano State History and Culture Bureau'].
13 On Hausa praise-shouters, see M. G. Smith (1957); Furniss (1995, 1996); Pellow (1997). On praise-singers elsewhere in West Africa, see Irvine (1989); Diawara (1997); Hale (1998); and Ebron (2002).
14 Gora (2002).
15 Askew (2002), for example, describes similar scenes at live performances of Swahili music in Tanzania.
16 Philips (2000).
17 Bakhtin (1981).
18 Briggs (1998).
19 Kroskrity (2000) describes a similarly monolithic ideological structure in Arizona Tewa ritual performances.
20 Bauman and Briggs (1990); Habermas (1989); Warner (2002).

LOST AND FOUND IN TRANSLATION

"MAN MARRIES MAN IN KANO" [*Namiji ya auri namiji a Kano*].

This provocative headline appeared on the front page of *Al-Mizan*, a Hausa-language weekly affiliated with the Muslim Brothers, on the fourth day of Zul-Hajji in the year 1414.[1] (Unlike most Hausa periodicals, *Al-Mizan* carries only the Islamic date, which corresponds to May 13, 1994, on the Christian calendar.) Presented as the findings of an undercover reporter, the article alleged that a same-sex wedding party had recently taken place at the same hotel where Alhaji Damina had hosted his biki several months earlier. "Let us continue intimating the enlightenment and development of the Europeans," it began, sarcastically implying that the 'wedding' was a sign of decadence imported from the West. In the style of an exposé, the article then listed the names of participants as these appeared on the invitation card: musicians, organizers, 'father' and 'mother' of the biki. Also exposed was the host, identified as 'the one[m] taken in marriage' [*wanda aka aura*], that is, the 'male bride,' though the name that was given, Madhuri Mairawa ['Madhuri the dancer'], was clearly a feminine nickname inspired by Madhuri Dixit, an Indian actress who had starred in numerous Bollywood films.[2]

In keeping with the political ideology of the Muslim Brothers ['*Yan'uwa Musulmi*], the article's primary target was the Nigerian state, whose local representatives were accused of facilitating the event. "Something many people do not know," it contended, "is that . . . a group of Muslims [i.e., affiliates of the Muslim Brothers] attempted to prevent the wedding from taking place. But alas, on that day the police were sent to shield the deviants." The article similarly alleged that a group of Muslim students were rebuffed when they tried to get CTV Kano, the state television station, to publicize the event. As evidence of the state's involvement, the *Al-Mizan* reporter claimed to have spotted at the event numerous "fancy cars" and "large gowns" (formal men's wear), an implicit reference to corrupt 'big men' who supposedly use their political influence to support 'yan daudu and protect them from punishment. Reinforcing the stereotype of 'yan daudu's shamelessness and impunity, the article quoted one of the party's alleged organizers: "Oh, this isn't the first time, we've done this a lot, it's just that people didn't know. This time we felt we ought to make it plain. And this time the groom has offered [as bridewealth] three suitcases with wheels, with all sorts of bridal gifts inside." The final line drove home the theme of civilizational decline: "Muslim community: where are we headed?"

News of the article spread quickly through Kano's networks of 'yan daudu and masu harka, as did copies of the newspaper itself. (Though I did not manage to buy that edition of *Al-Mizan*, a friend let me borrow it so I could make a photocopy.) As chance would have it, I had attended the party in question and took part in a number of conversations in which people read and commented on the article. Unsurprisingly, it incited both fear and outrage, especially among those who had attended the biki. "It's a lie!" many exclaimed in response to the headline, noting that the invitation card described the event as a "Sister Wedding Ceremony," that is, a party honoring the host's sister, who had recently gotten married (see Figure 7.1). The fact that the newspaper published the participants' names was especially offensive and led many readers to condemn the article as 'slander' [*sharri*]. Some worried that the Muslim Brothers might send more 'spies' [*masu leken asiri*, literally 'those who peek at secrets'] to other parties. Although many 'civilians' stayed away from 'yan daudu's bikis, some did go from time to time despite the risk this posed to their reputations. These partygoers often took simple precautions like avoiding bikis that took place near their relatives' homes and staying away from the videocameras. The *Al-Mizan* exposé made them afraid that such precautions might not be enough to avoid a scandal or potential arrest.

Though seemingly intended to incite public outrage, the *Al-Mizan* article had few practical consequences. No protests were mounted,

Cordially Invite

TO HIS

Sister Wedding Ceremony
Which will take place as follows :

VENUE :-
DATE :- 16th — 4 — 84
YINI :- 2:00 p.m. Malwasa
AJO :- 5:00 p.m. Malwasa
GUGAG GIDA :- 12:00 p.m. till dawn Malwasa

CO-ORDINATORS :-

ALH.   HAJIYA
UBAN BIKI   UWAR BIKI

Fig. 7.1   Invitation to Madhuri Mairawa's biki, 1994. The text gives times for particular segments of the biki and names the 'father', 'mother' and performers.

no bikis were shut down, and the police were no more abusive than they had ever been. Since the people whose names had been exposed were already known to be 'people of the bariki,' they were accustomed to living with a certain degree of stigma. The one person accused of homosexuality, the host known as Madhuri Mairawa, reportedly kept a low profile for a while, but he did not face additional punishments. An important reason for this, I was told, was that, unlike most 'yan daudu, Madhuri Mairawa still lived with his father, who was said to be unusually tolerant of his son's gender nonconformity.

Thirteen years later, similar accusations had more serious ramifications. In April 2007, the southern Nigerian newspaper *This Day* reported that state-sponsored hisbas destroyed a theater in Kano where a "polygamous lesbian wedding" had allegedly taken place. The host of the celebration, one Aunty Maiduguri, and her four 'brides' were reported to be in hiding. (The English-sounding name Aunty Maiduguri was presumably a nickname, Maiduguri being the largest city in northeastern Nigeria.) The story was quickly picked up by the Western news media and disseminated over the Internet by gay-rights organizations and bloggers. With a grainy image of her face circling the globe (supposedly from the poster commemorating her 'wedding'), Aunty Maiduguri was on her way to becoming an African Muslim lesbian icon whose brave attempt to assert her rights was being crushed by Islamist militants. A few days later, she publicly rejected that honor. In an audio interview broadcast on the BBC website, she told a reporter in clear, Nigerian-accented English, "It's a lie, it's unbelievable. I have never in my life seen where a lady can marry four ladies at one time. I have never practised – never heard the word 'lesbian' – truly."[3] The story quickly receded from public view. As far as I can tell, no follow-up stories were published on the real nature of the party or the fate of Aunty Maiduguri and her friends.

Another international media frenzy erupted in August 2007, when hisbas in the city of Bauchi (250 km southeast of Kano) arrested 18 men at a hotel party and charged them with being "dressed in female attire" and "organizing a gay wedding." According to a report issued by the International Gay and Lesbian Human Rights Commission (IGLHRC), the men spent 19 days in detention, where they were "beaten, caned, and cursed by their jailors and court officers." Local protesters demanded that the men be prosecuted for sodomy, prompting IGLHRC, a non-governmental organization (NGO) based in New York City, to send its African regional specialists to help in their defense. Once again, the men denied the allegations and insisted they were not homosexuals. In a curious echo of Madhuri Mairawa's invitation card, the men claimed to have organized "a combination birthday/graduation party for a local man . . . and the celebration of the marriage of his sister." They also objected to being called 'yan daudu, which the IGLHRC report glossed as "a Hausa term that is often derogatorily used to refer to any male who publicly exhibits gender non-conforming behavior." The sodomy charge was dismissed due to lack of evidence and the men were released on bail, though other charges, including "vagabondage" and "membership in an unlawful society," were still pending as of February 2008.[4]

In their coverage of the so-called "Bauchi 18" (including an interview I agreed to do on the BBC radio program, Focus on Africa),

Western news media and international gay-rights organizations emphasized the plight of homosexuals in Nigeria: homosexuality is outlawed under both Shari'a and federal law, and the national legislature had recently debated a bill known as the "Same Sex Marriage (Prohibition) Act," which would have banned not just weddings, but all gay organizing as well as public displays of same-sex affection. (Despite support from Christian and Muslim legislators alike, the bill was never brought before the full assembly for a vote.) What the international media did not discuss were the historical factors that led to this state of affairs. Without such a discussion, Western audiences might be inclined to believe hostility towards homosexuality is an intrinsic part of (Northern) Nigerian culture. Yet the different fates of Madhuri Mairawa and the Bauchi 18 suggest that Northern Nigerians' sexual attitudes have shifted in recent years, and cannot be attributed simply to their Islamic faith or to a timeless Hausa, Nigerian or African 'culture.'

What happened between 1994 and 2007 that made homosexuality, and the specific issue of same-sex weddings, the object of such intense public debate? The most obvious answer is the Northern state governments' adoption of Shari'a. This gave certain Islamist groups the power, by means of the newly created hisbas, to enforce their interpretation of Islamic law. The Muslim Brothers, formally known as the Islamic Movement, were not one of these groups, for while they believe in the primacy of Shari'a, they view the Federal Republic of Nigeria as an illegitimate creation of the Christian European colonizers.[5] Other groups, such as the Izala, take a more practical stance and have endeavored to work within the system gradually to spread their reformist ideas.[6] The Muslim Brothers are further marginalized because, whereas the Muslim population of Nigeria (and West Africa) is almost entirely Sunni, they are widely believed to be Shi'ites. Their leader, Malam Ibrahim al-Zakzaky, makes frequent trips to the Islamic Republic of Iran and has well-known ties with its ruling clerics. Al-Zakzaky and his followers neither acknowledge nor reject the Shi'ite label, preferring to describe themselves simply as "Muslims."[7] Their newspaper, *Al-Mizan*, is admired for its trenchant criticism of government leaders' corruption, but its polemical tone makes many reluctant to take its news reports at face value. A front-page story about an alleged same-sex 'wedding' could easily have been dismissed as yet another frivolous provocation.

In 1994, the Muslim Brothers had neither the popular support nor the access to state power that would have allowed them to follow through on their accusations against Madhuri Mairawa and his friends. By 2007, however, Islamic reformist ideas had been embraced by the Northern states (but not by the federal government) with the apparent approval of most of their constituents. But the adoption of Shari'a by itself does not explain why the issue of same-sex weddings had become so important. Hausa Muslims have been observing Shari'a for centuries without devoting much energy to policing what Islamic jurists call *liwāṭ*, or 'sodomy' [Hausa: *luwadî*]. The recent prominence of this issue is particularly mysterious given the virtually total absence of openly gay communities in Northern Nigeria and the weak presence of gay-rights organizations anywhere in the country.[8] In formulating their anti-homosexual agendas, therefore, Northern Nigeria's Islamists and the nation's federal officials must have taken their inspiration from elsewhere.

Do You Harka?

In the 13 years prior to the alleged same-sex weddings in Bauchi and Kano, gay rights also emerged as a controversial issue in other parts of Africa. In 1994, a newly liberated South Africa became the first nation in the world to enshrine gay rights in its constitution. Shortly thereafter the rulers of other African states, primarily in eastern and southern Africa, made public proclamations condemning homosexuality as 'un-African' and reviling homosexuals, sometimes in violent terms. President Daniel arap Moi of Kenya, for example, asserted that "words like lesbianism and homosexuality do not exist in African languages," while President Robert Mugabe of Zimbabwe compared homosexuals to pigs and dogs.[9] In his analysis of these statements, Neville Hoad suggests that for leaders of the so-called Frontline states that had supported the anti-apartheid struggle, the rise of a rich, powerful, black-ruled South Africa (still largely dominated by white capital), threatened their influence in the region and weakened their authority within their respective countries. According to Hoad, South Africa's embrace of gay rights gave these rulers a rhetorical weapon which they used to define themselves as 'authentically African' versus their racially hybrid neighbor to the south.[10]

Meanwhile, in Egypt, new telecommunications technologies were contributing to the emergence of urban gay subcultures that became the target of public condemnation by Islamic leaders, especially those with reformist sympathies. Ever mindful of the challenge Islamist groups posed to their leadership, Egypt's secular authorities in the early 2000s staged a series of police raids on homosexual establishments in which scores of men were arrested and jailed. Joseph Massad traces the Islamist anti-gay discourses that helped trigger these raids to the human-rights rhetoric of the 'Gay International,' a term he coined to refer to the loose alliance of gay-rights organizations such as IGLHRC and ILGA (the International Lesbian and Gay Association) and their supposed allies in academia, journalism and commerce.[11] Building on the work of Edward Said, Massad contends that the 'Gay International' relies on Orientalist representations of the Arab world's exotically 'repressive' attitudes towards sex in order to justify the global pursuit of sexual 'liberation.'

Massad further contends that this 'liberation' is in fact a new form of Western imperial domination, for it imposes notions of sexual identity and human rights that do not conform to the cultural realities of the people and places the 'Gay International' insists on 'liberating.' In so doing, it "produces homosexuals, as well as gays and lesbians, where they do not exist, and represses same-sex desires and practices that refuse to be assimilated into its sexual epistemology."[12]

According to Massad, in postcolonial contexts characterized by widespread poverty and extreme inequalities of wealth and power, the imperialistic activities of the 'Gay International' generate popular resentment and end up 'inciting' the very homophobic violence that it claims to be fighting against. In Egypt, this is evident in the discourses of Islamist ideologues who have made the identification and punishment of homosexuals a cornerstone of their political project. Although the Islamists' stated goal is the restoration of an Islamic state along the lines of the earliest Muslim community, their obsession with sexuality is a contemporary innovation that draws on both liberal and conservative movements in the West. On one hand, the Islamist movement has adopted the basic premise of modern psychology that sexual practices can be categorized as either 'hetero' or 'homo,' as well as the gay-liberationist idea that social identities can and should be based on these categories. On the other hand, the Islamists mimic Christian conservatives when they use these same categories to vilify homosexuals and exclude them from the Egyptian body politic.

If some Egyptian men have embraced a 'gay' identity, Massad characterizes them as cosmopolitan elites whose desires and practices have little in common with those of ordinary folk. As evidence, he cites the fact that the homosexual establishments raided by the Egyptian police catered to the middle and upper classes, and that many of the men who were arrested had participated in online chat-rooms.[13] He also describes how some gay-rights activists in the Arab diaspora supposedly tailored their rhetoric to satisfy the expectations of Western donors and funding agencies. Hoad describes a similar dynamic in Southern Africa, where the availability of funds from the global North spawned a number of gay-rights NGOs, the membership of which was suspiciously low. The passion of Massad's critique comes from his conviction that, when Islamist agitation leads Arab governments to scapegoat homosexuals, "[i]t is not the Gay International or its upper-class supporters in the Arab diaspora who will be persecuted but rather the poor and nonurban men who practice same-sex contact and who do not *necessarily* identify as homosexual or gay."[14] In a parallel argument, Hoad notes that in southern Africa the "unwitting conspiracy between homophobic regimes and local and international [gay-rights] activists"[15] results in the "foreclosing [of] the diversity of desires, practices, and possibly identities and communities on the ground."[16]

Who are these "poor and nonurban men"? These desires, practices, identities and communities "on the ground"? The ethnographic details implicit in Hoad's and Massad's claims are only hinted at. In part, this is because, as literary critics, they concentrate on published texts rather than other, less easily accessible discourses. But they also have principled suspicions about anthropological research on Arabs,' Muslims' and Africans' sexuality, which can be and has been deployed in ways that do not serve, and might even harm, the people it claims to represent. Nevertheless, their arguments offer an invitation for ethnographic research that documents how the "incitement to discourse about sexual identities and practices" has transpired at particular places and times.[17]

'Incitement to discourse' is a phrase coined by Michel Foucault to describe the obsession with sexuality that emerged in middle-class European society in the nineteenth century and has characterized Western popular culture ever since.[18] According to Foucault, the modern sciences of biology, psychology, sociology and anthropology sought to understand and control 'deviant' sexual behavior by documenting it in painstaking, often titillating, detail. This gave rise to notions of sexual identity that most Westerners today take for granted, including the idea that 'homosexuals' and 'heterosexuals' are distinct types of persons. In colonial settings the scientific obsession with sexuality produced graphic descriptions of the bodies and intimate practices of 'natives,' who became the objects of white Europeans' curiosity, revulsion and desire.[19] As Said and others have detailed, the same racial voyeurism was evident in fiction, travel writing and other literary genres,[20] and it lives on in such contexts as sex tourism and 'exotic' pornography, as well as *National Geographic* and even, one might argue, ethnographies like this one.[21]

The experiences of Aunty Maiduguri and the Bauchi 18 lend qualified support to Hoad's and Massad's arguments. None of the targeted individuals self-identified as gay or lesbian (at least not publicly), yet local Islamists and international gay-rights organizations colluded (temporarily) to label them as such. Even after they were released from police custody, this 'unwitting conspiracy' had certainly produced a social environment in which it would be difficult if not impossible for them to engage in any same-sex social or erotic practices they might desire. With its opening remark about 'imitating' Europeans, *Al-Mizan*'s 'outing' of Madhuri Mairawa seems like an even clearer example of the 'incitement to discourse.' Responding to this incitement, the indignant cries of "Slander!" and "It's a lie!" could be read as an example of 'same-sex desires and practices that refuse to be assimilated' into Western/Islamist sexual categories. Similar 'refusals' could also be attributed, albeit speculatively, to the public denials of the Bauchi 18 as well as that of Aunty Maiduguri. These hypothetical 'refusals' appear less definitive, however, when we consider that many of the men who cried "Slander!" privately self-identified as *homos*; that the Bauchi 18 (whose reason for throwing a party was surprisingly similar to Madhuri Mairawa's) may well have been hoping to engage in a bit of gender or sexual nonconformity;

and that Aunty Maiduguri's fluent command of English makes it hard to believe that she "never heard the word 'lesbian'."

Regardless of its truth or falsity, Aunty Maiduguri's claim highlights the questions of language raised by these controversies. One set of questions concerns the problems of categorization and translation. Simply put, international gay-rights activists presume that sexual categories like 'gay' and 'straight' can be translated with relative ease from one linguistic/cultural setting to another, while extreme cultural nationalists like former President Moi reject the universal translatability of sexual categories. Both discourses have roots in European colonialism. Almost a century before President Moi, for example, Sir Richard Burton declared that "the negro race is mostly untainted by sodomy and tribadism."[22] At other times, European colonialists enacted labor, educational and housing policies that presumed (and imposed) the translatability of European notions of gender and sexuality in African settings, such as the cultural ideal of the male breadwinner and female home-maker.[23]

Inspired by Foucault and Said, Hoad and Massad emphasize the ways in which categorization and translation can be used as tools of domination and 'discursive violence.' Their cautions are important, but it is also important to acknowledge that both practices are inherent features of human language and social interaction, performed by powerful and powerless alike. Accordingly, while it has become *de rigueur* for social theorists to describe categorization as a process that excludes, and translation as a practice whereby meaning is lost, it is also important to ask: what is *gained* by these processes, and by whom? In considering these questions, my aim is not simply to pass judgment about whether a particular gender or sexual category (or the very categories of 'gender' and 'sexuality') can or cannot be translated across linguistic and cultural lines. Rather, I seek to understand the use (or avoidance) of such categories as rhetorical acts that take place for different reasons and with varying effects – including the drawing and blurring of cultural boundaries themselves. What is at stake, for example, in using an English word like *lesbian* or *homosexual* to label African individuals, communities, and their social practices? Conversely, what is at stake in denying the validity of such labels?

While it has become commonplace among anthropologists of sexuality to refrain from using terms from a colonial language (English, French, Dutch, etc.) to describe the identities and practices of people who speak different (usually non-European) languages, scholars have paid little attention to translation that operates in the other direction. The Hausa-language newspaper *Kakaki*, for example, had no trouble reporting on President Clinton's ill-fated proposal to permit gay men and lesbians to serve openly in the US armed forces, though the term used for 'gay men,' *'yan ludu* [literally, 'sons of Lot'] conveys a negative moral judgment akin to English 'sodomites.' *'Yan madigo*, the term used for 'lesbians,' has more neutral connotations.[24]

Such translations occur in day-to-day conversations as well. In talking with Hausa friends I frequently found myself using terms like *harka* and *dan daudu* to describe gay life in the USA. I also heard such terms applied to me.

One day in 1993, Mai Kwabo took me to a bar in Sabon Gari that was known, by those who should know, as a meeting place for *masu harka*. A short while after we sat down and ordered our beers, we were joined by Alhaji Hamza, a well-dressed man whom I had never met, though he and Mai Kwabo clearly knew each other. After the requisite series of greetings, Mai Kwabo asked his friend: "How are the merchandises?" [*Yaya hajoji?*] *Haja* ['merchandise'] is a term from the 'harka dialect,' a grammatically feminine noun that refers to the lower-status (younger, poorer, feminized) partner in a typical homosexual relationship. In addition to revealing Alhaji Hamza's homosexuality, therefore, Mai Kwabo's question indexed his friend's status as older, wealthier, and 'masculine' vis-à-vis his sexual partners.

Alhaji Hamza was momentarily speechless. His eyes grew wide as he glanced nervously in my direction. Sensing his friend's discomfort, Mai Kwabo sought to reassure him. "Don't worry, he does it."

Alhaji Hamza responded to this information with apparent amazement and disbelief. Looking at me, he asked, "Huh? Is it true?"

"It's true," I replied.

My straightforward affirmation seemed only to heighten Alhaji Hamza's incredulity. "White men do it too?!" he exclaimed [*Turawa ma suna yi?!*].

Alhaji Hamza's surprise was not unique; the disclosure of my homosexuality in groups of *masu harka* frequently elicited comments like his. Yet such comments almost always met with patronizing rebukes from other, seemingly more cosmopolitan *masu harka* along the lines of, "Come on, fool, of course they do it; everyone does it." At the same time, relatively few of the 'yan daudu and masu harka I met had much if any awareness of Western gay life, and many reacted to the idea of gay rights as ridiculous and absurd.

A notion of homosexuality and gender nonconformity as frivolous forms of play was also evident in some of the 'harka dialect' terms that were used to refer to 'yan daudu. A number of these terms were borrowed from English, such as *anti* ['aunty'], *mandiya* (possibly from the British pronunciation of 'm'dear'), and my favorite: *ji-sebin* ['G-7'], which in the discourse of English-speaking political pundits is an abbreviation for 'Group of 7,' ostensibly the richest and most powerful nations on earth. 'Yan daudu's use of this term to refer to themselves – *Ji-sebin ce sosai* ['She's a real G-7!] – indexes a novel and playful engagement with the global political economy that is not directly related to international debates over sexual rights or to the global circulation of 'Gay English.'[25]

Another example of playful engagement with globalization is the use of *indiya* ['India'] to mean *ɗan daudu*. Among the 'yan daudu I knew, the actresses in Hindi-language Bollywood films (such as Madhuri Dixit) were camp icons of glamour and style, or what my friends called *indiyanci* ['Indianness'].[26] The following vignette recalls a performance of this style.

Zakaria, known to some of his friends as Fatima, was an unmarried civil servant in his mid-twenties. Though 'shirted' he had an unusual number of friends who were overt 'yan daudu, and was happy to accompany me when I went to visit people like Hajiya Asabe and Alhaji Damina. (Some of my other 'shirted' friends were afraid just to venture into Sabon Gari.) When I asked Zakaria how he knew so many 'yan daudu, he told me he had spent a lot of time with 'yan daudu when he was in his teens, and had seriously considered going into daudu himself. If his parents had been unable to send him to high school, he said, he would certainly have become a ɗan daudu. The lure of daudu had been strong. He had a vivacious personality and a wicked sense of humor that seemed wasted in his government office, but he was grateful for the steady, if modest salary and enjoyed an active social life.

One day Zakaria took me and a mutual friend, Aliyu, to visit another friend of theirs named Mato. All of us self-identified as 'shirted' 'yan daudu, though we more frequently used the term *ashoshi* [singular: *ashi*, possibly from Yoruba *ashawo*, or 'prostitute']. At some point in the conversation Mato mentioned that he had just purchased a cassette tape of Indian film music [*wakar Indiya*]. As he listed the song titles, in Hindi, Zakaria and Aliyu nodded in recognition. One title, which I heard as *Mé larké hu*, got them particularly excited.

"Put it on!" Zakaria shouted. "I want to dance!"

Without a word he and Aliyu jumped up and went to draw the curtains while Mato placed the tape in his boom-box. As Mato fast-forwarded the tape to the appropriate song, Zakaria struck the pose of what I took to be a classical Indian dancer: palms together, arms over head, right leg on the floor, left leg jutting out to the side, knees and ankles flexed. He smiled and glanced flirtatiously at each of us, as if to tell us we were in for a big treat.

As the music played, Zakaria flitted and jumped around the room, gracefully flexing his wrists, fingers and elbows in sync with the rhythm while mouthing the Hindi lyrics.

"*Shegiya*, Fatima!" Aliyu cried, using the Hausa word for 'female bastard' with a tone of affection that translated in this case as something like 'you silly bitch!'

"*'Yar iska!*" Mato chimed, using the feminine form of *dan iska*.

To our naughty delight, Zakaria continued dancing, smiling and lip-synching till the music ended. As he stood trying to catch his breath, I asked him if he really understood the song's words. I assumed he did not, and had simply memorized the syllables.

"Of course I do!" he replied. He enunciated the song's title: "*Mé larké hu*. It means 'I'm a girl' [*Ni yarinya ce*]." Admitting that he didn't know *all* the words, he went on to translate a few other short lines from Hindi into Hausa.

Later on, I asked a Hindi-speaking friend of mine, an Indian expatriate who'd lived in Kano for many years, if *Mé larké hu* was an actual Hindi expression. He didn't understand my pronunciation, so I repeated myself and explained, "It supposedly means 'I'm a girl'."

He smiled with recognition. "*Mēhn ladki hũ*," he corrected me. "Yeah, 'I'm a woman, I'm a girl' – that's what it means." He was amused to hear how I'd learned the expression, and said my description of Zakaria's performance reminded him of the *hijras* back in India. As far as I know, Zakaria had never heard of *hijras*.

Sexual Citizenship in Regional, National and Global Perspective

Massad and Hoad link recent debates about gay rights in Africa to the liberalization of international trade and finance, otherwise known as neoliberal globalization, that has taken place in the decades since most African nations won their independence. While the legal principle of 'human rights' was ostensibly developed to protect people's freedom, neoliberal policies award rights to corporations and have thus contributed, according to many economists, to increasing disparities between classes, nations and regions, often glossed as the global North and South. It is these inequalities that have made many people in the global South suspect that 'rights' talk is another strategy for rich folk in the global North to enhance their power.

These suspicions erupted in the worldwide Anglican Communion when liberal bishops, most of them from the USA and the UK, submitted a proposal in the late 1990s to allow individual dioceses to ordain gay and lesbian bishops and to recognize same-sex marriages.[27] With the exception of six South Africans, most of the African bishops sided with conservatives from the global North in opposing the measure, claiming that the issue of gay rights distracted the Church's attention from other, more pressing issues such as poverty and globalization. They also criticized their liberal Western colleagues for attempting to impose 'modern,' secular notions of morality on 'traditional' Christian and African cultures. The African bishops thus took a classic anticolonial argument and merged it with a discourse – the defense of the heterosexual Christian family – that had its roots in colonialism. Hoad describes this homophobic reconstruction of African tradition as 'phantasmatic' and 'historical amnesia' because it ignored the Church's history of repressing Africans' 'traditional,' non-Christian kinship and sexual practices. That legacy of colonial domination was also ignored by the liberal bishops, whom Hoad accuses of 'inciting' the African bishops' anti-gay activism: "Had that first [pro-gay] resolution not been put forward, no such condemnatory resolutions would have been passed."[28]

As the controversy persisted into the next decade, it resonated loudly in Nigeria, home to the largest Anglican province in the world. Archbishop Peter Akinola became a leading spokesman for the antigay position, which he frequently framed in cultural terms. In a speech to a gathering of African bishops, he complained about the liberal sexual values that prevailed at many seminaries in the global North: "You now have on campus men and men cohabiting, which is against the African way of life." His comments were echoed by Nigerian President Obasanjo, an evangelical Christian who addressed the bishops to commend "your principled stand against the totally unacceptable tendency towards same-sex marriage and homosexual practice. Such a tendency is clearly un-Biblical, unnatural and definitely un-African."[29]

Like Presidents Moi and Mugabe, who used homophobic rhetoric to rally the masses within their respective nations, the assertions by Archbishop Akinola and President Obasanjo were directed primarily at their fellow Nigerians. In an interview with historian Philip Jenkins published in the *Atlantic Monthly*, the Archbishop explained that his vocal opposition to homosexuality was motivated not by anti-colonial fervor or a desire to turn the worldwide Church's attention to his congregants' material suffering, but by the competitive threat of Islam. "Across the continent," Jenkins wrote, "Muslims have tried to make converts by arguing that the Christian West is decadent and sexually irresponsible."[30] If Akinola and his Church were perceived to be condoning homosexuality, he risked losing his flock to other Christian churches or, even worse, to Islam.[31] Far from renouncing the legacy of colonialism, Akinola and other Nigerian Christians view the acceptance of homosexuality by liberal Western churches as a betrayal of the values taught by the missionaries.[32] This sense of betrayal is heightened by Nigerian Christians' sensitivity to accusations from cultural nationalists, including practitioners of indigenous religions, that they have forsaken authentically African traditions in order to 'imitate' the West.[33]

Islamic reformists use a version of this discourse that paints virtually any (Nigerian) Christian or secularist, or any Muslim who deviates from the 'true' Islamic path, as an 'imitator' of the West. This version does not involve appeals to authentic African traditions, however, for from an orthodox Islamic perspective such traditions, like Bori, are typically seen as 'pagan.'[34] Indeed, most Hausa Muslims respect 'traditional customs' [*al'adun gargajiya*] only insofar as these are compatible with Islam. When asked to comment on the Anglican debate over same-sex marriage, for example, Hakeem Baba-Ahmed, the head of Northern Nigeria's Shari'a council, declared simply that condoning homosexuality "will lead to a further erosion of our accepted principles of morality."[35] In so doing, he expressed solidarity with his (homophobic) Christian counterparts without endorsing or opposing their appeal to "the African way of life."

Appeals to cultural (as opposed to religious) tradition are especially problematic for Northern nationalists in the context of debates about gay rights, for among southern Nigerians it is widely rumored that homosexuality is widespread in the North. As early as 1965, a character in Wole Soyinka's novel *The Interpreters* referred to Northern Nigerian "Emirs and their little boys."[36] More recently, Festus Eriye, a Yoruba journalist writing for a South African newspaper, asserted that "homosexuality thrives" in Northern Nigeria, and that "it is a common practice among some in the elite classes to make use of the services of male homosexual prostitutes know as 'Dan Daudu' in the Hausa language."[37] Nigerian and African gay-rights activists have appropriated this stereotype as evidence for the existence of homosexuality in 'traditional' African cultures. In an interview with a Radio Netherlands reporter, the president of Alliance Rights, a gay-rights organization based in Ibadan, in southwestern Nigeria, was quoted as saying:

> Looking at [the subject of homosexuality] from cultures in Africa, like in the northern part of Nigeria. We find out that there are people they call *dan daudus. Dan daudu* is a typical Hausa term. It has been existing even before the advent of the Europeans. It means "men who are wives of men."[38]

Such reports are circulated widely on the internet thanks to organizations like Behind the Mask, which publishes an African gay-rights website (www.mask.org.za) from its headquarters in Johannesburg, and GlobalGayz.com, whose owner is based in California and Massachusetts.

Reporters for the Lagos-based newspaper *The News* offered an alternative historical interpretation, claiming that, although Kano's "notoriety for homosexuality is legendary . . . [g]ay culture was never a tradition in Kano or any part of Nigeria. The belief was that it was introduced into Northern Nigeria by two influences, beginning from the Arabs, who brought Islam and then the British who colonised the country."[39] While this attempt to paint all of Nigeria's regions as 'traditionally' free of homosexuality may seem desirable from the standpoint of national unity, it relies on a narrative of Northern culture as sexually 'tainted' by contact with Arabs. As noted in Chapter 5, such narratives circulate informally among some Hausa Muslims, but they coexist with a more powerful narrative that views Hausa society as enriched by its historical contacts with Arab-Islamic civilization.

In light of these statements, it seems likely that the hisbas' efforts to prosecute Aunty Maiduguri and the Bauchi 18 – and popular support for these efforts – were incited not by Northern Nigerian activists affiliated with a supposed 'Gay International,' nor by an intrinsic cultural or religious hostility towards homosexuality, but by a nationalistic desire to defend the North's reputation against negative sexual stereotypes. (By the same token, the Muslim Brothers' failure to whip up support for prosecuting the alleged same-sex 'wedding' in 1994 may have been due in part to their anti-nationalist ideology.) Despite their shared antipathy towards homosexuality, Islamic Northern nationalists and the nation's southern and Christian leaders seem locked in a competitive cycle of sexual innuendo, as each camp struggles to live down the other's implicit accusations of homosexuality by stepping up its own antigay rhetoric.

In critiquing these representations of Hausa sexual culture, it is not enough to point out the linguistic errors in translating the word *dan daudu* or the lack of historical and ethnographic evidence for Northern Nigerians' alleged homosexual practices. The textual medium and genre must also be taken into account. In particular, it is significant that most of the statements cited above were published in journalistic venues. News articles are a discourse genre that demands a particular linguistic register (in this case, some form of standard English) and a particular rhetorical style (ostensibly factual, direct, and sincere). In this regard, journalistic discourse is similar to the genre of academic writing. By comparison, a fiction writer like Soyinka has more freedom to vary the registers and styles he deploys in his texts. The relative freedom of fiction makes it possible to re-imagine gender, desire, work, faith and other dimensions of human experience in ways that nonfiction usually does not. It is for this reason that Hoad and Massad pay extensive attention to fiction writing, especially novels, in their work.[40]

The playful everyday discourses of 'yan daudu and other masu harka offer a similarly rich set of imaginative possibilities, frustrating the efforts of journalists, scholars, theologians and lawyers who would try to fix their meanings. The *Al-Mizan* story about the alleged same-sex 'wedding,' for example, failed to appreciate the campy humor inherent in the name Madhuri Mairawa, which everyone at the party (and presumably many of the newspaper's readers) recognized was not the host's 'real' name. Yet the party-goers did not all share the same sense of the name's affective and moral significance. This lack of consensus became poignantly apparent a few months after the party when Madhuri Mairawa died in an automobile accident. I heard the news at a friend's home where a group of masu harka were trading accounts of the tragedy and wistfully reminiscing about their friend. In the course of narrating one amusing story, a 'shirted' ɗan daudu referred to Madhuri as 'she.' He was immediately interrupted by a 'civilian' who chastised him for using the feminine pronoun now that Madhuri was dead. (The 'civilian' did not object to the name Madhuri.) The narrator insisted that he meant no disrespect, that Madhuri had been his 'girlfriend,' and that the feminine pronoun was consistent with the way they had always talked with each other (at least in private). The other 'shirted' 'yan daudu supported this explanation and stressed the love [*soyayya*] that is shared between 'girl-friends.' The 'civilian' got quiet, but looked unconvinced.

The *Al-Mizan* reporter also seems to have interpreted the organizer's bragging about 'bridal gifts' too literally. Based on my experience at that party and others like it, any talk of a 'groom' and 'bridal gifts' was almost certainly tongue-in-cheek. Although some participants may well have described their intimate same-sex relationships as 'marriage,' no one, as far as I know, seriously considered them morally equivalent to a 'real' heterosexual marriage. Yet, as we saw in Mansur and Lami's argument over Usman and the ring (see Chapter 3), the similarities and differences between a metaphorical 'marriage' and a 'real' one cannot be enumerated with any kind of precision. This indeterminacy was apparently lost on the *Al-Mizan* reporter, as was the possibility that the organizer may simply have been fooling with him. A similar misapprehension may have occurred when Islamist hisbas and international gay-rights organizations colluded in defin-ing the parties of Aunty Maiduguri and the Bauchi 18 as 'same-sex weddings.' In all cases, the rhetorical norms of journalism, law enforcement, and political advocacy came into conflict with those of what I might call the 'playful talk' of Hausa *homos*. In the case of the Bauchi 18, the representatives of ILGHRC seem to have realized the incongruity between their discourse and that of the accused men, and attempted to adjust their own discourse accordingly. Whether their efforts will ultimately help or hurt the men's case remains to be seen.

The notion of a Hausa Muslim gay political movement akin to the queer Muslim movements that emerged in North America and Great Britain in the late 1990s – and that, as Massad notes, have been enthusiastically supported by organizations like IGLHRC – seems unlikely for the near future. Ideologies of language are central to this disparity. Whereas politicized queer Muslims publicly proclaim that there is no contradiction between being gay and being a good Muslim,[41] 'yan daudu and other masu harka generally do see such a contradiction; they just hope that their 'shame' [*kunya*] and faith in God will attract His ultimate mercy and forgiveness. This emphasis on 'shame' – keeping inappropriate feelings and unpleasant truths out of sight and out of earshot – has long been accepted, in Hausaland and other Islamic societies, as a basic requirement of cultural citizenship. Yet this 'will not to know,' as Steven Murray[42] calls it, is being increasingly challenged by the ideological commitment to rhetorical explicitness – to naming, defining, describing, and evaluating – that characterizes Islamist and secular movements alike. As the global competition between and within these movements intensifies, 'yan daudu and others like them, whose gender and sexual practices have been calibrated to balance 'shame' and 'play,' may find themselves further excluded from participation in Northern Nigerian public life.

Notes

1   Albakri (1994).
2   I translate the phrase *wanda aka aura* as 'male bride' by analogy with the more usual expression *wadda aka aura* ['the one[f] taken in marriage']. The groom would be described as 'the one[m] who took her in marriage' or 'the one[m] who married her' [*wanda ya aure ta*]. Note that Madhuri Mairawa is a pseudonym; the actual name printed on the invitation card and in the *Al-Mizan* article was that of a different Indian film actress.

3 BBC (2007).
4 IGLHRC (2008).
5 Despite the similar nomenclature, Nigeria's Muslim Brothers have no known formal ties to the Muslim Brotherhood in Egypt or other countries. See Kane (2003); Umar (1993).
6 Izala is short for *Jamaʿatul izālat al-bidʿa wa iqāmat al-sunnah* [Arabic: 'Society for the removal of innovation and the reinstatement of tradition']; see Kane (2003).
7 See the Islamic Movement's website: www.islamicmovement.org.
8 A number of Nigerian NGOs address the problems faced by sexual minorities, but they have generally done so discreetly. Nigerian supporters of gay rights became more vocal *after* the government started focusing on the issue, not before.
9 Dunton and Palmbert (1996: 24); Hoad (2007: 163).
10 Hoad (2007: Chapter 4).
11 Massad (2007).
12 Massad (2007: 163).
13 Massad (2007: 265).
14 Massad (2007: 189, his emphasis). The word *necessarily* was added to a previous version of this chapter and acknowledges that some 'poor and nonurban men' in Egypt *might* identify as homosexual or gay (cf. Massad 2002: 363).
15 Hoad (2007: 83).
16 Hoad (2007: 84).
17 Massad (2007: 417). Donham (1998) and Epprecht (2004) are theoretically sophisticated examples of the historical emergence of 'gay' identities in South Africa and Zimbabwe, respectively, but were not cited by Hoad or Massad.
18 Foucault (1990).
19 Bleys (1996); McClintock (1995); Stoler (1995); Malinowski (1929); Mead (1923).
20 Said (1979); Bhabha (1994).
21 Lutz and Collins (1993).
22 Cited in Murray and Roscoe (1998: xii).
23 White (1990); Hansen (1992); Ferguson (1999).
24 Kakaki (1993).
25 Leap (1996); Leap and Boellstorf (2004).
26 For ethnographic accounts of the appropriation of global iconographies of glamour by feminine men, see Newton (1972); Besnier (2002); Johnson (1997); Manalansan (2003). For an ethnographic account of the circulation of Indian films in Nigeria, see Larkin (2008).
27 Hoad (2007: Chapter 3).

28 Quotations in this paragraph are from Hoad (2007: 66–67).

29 BBC (2004).

30 Jenkins (2003).

31 BBC (2004).

32 Timberg (2005).

33 Examples of such cultural nationalism include the academic writings of Amadiume (1987); Aremu (1991); and Oyěwùmí (1997).

34 The idea that Bori is uniquely African is widespread among Hausa Muslims and certain Western scholars (such as Miles 2003), but is contradicted by research that shows the extent to which contemporary Bori has embraced Islamic, Western and other African elements (Greenberg 1946; O'Brien 2000).

35 Bryant (2004).

36 Cited in Hoad (2007: 33).

37 Eriye (2003).

38 Beauchemin (2002).

39 Sulaiman and Adebayo (2002).

40 Another scholar who has used literary analysis to shed critical light on the ways sexuality is being reimagined in postcolonial African and Arab settings is Jarrod Hayes (2000), whose work focuses on sexuality and nationalism in French-language novels from the Maghreb.

41 See, e.g., the website of Al-Fatiha, a queer Muslim organization in the United States (www.al-fatiha.org) and the documentary film *A Jihad for Love* (2007), directed by Parvez Sharma.

42 Murray (1997b).

EPILOGUE

MAY GOD KEEP A SECRET

I hadn't seen Alhaji Zinari since 1997. Over the next nine years he'd continued traveling back and forth to Saudi Arabia, and I'd missed him on my two previous visits. So I was delighted to find out he was in town when I returned to Kano in 2006. My delight was dampened, however, by the news that Alhaji Damina, his closest 'girlfriend,' had recently passed away. I'd last seen Damina in 2002, when he was running a restaurant in Rijiyar Kuka a few blocks away from the neighborhood's main market. Some time after that he too traveled to Saudi Arabia, where he stayed for a while with Zinari in Jiddah. Damina came back from that trip noticeably thin and weak. He died within a year at the age of 38, leaving a wife and five daughters, including two from his first marriage.

After listening to Zinari describe Damina's symptoms, I asked whether he had died of *cutar AIDS* ['AIDS disease'].

"It's not AIDS!" Zinari exclaimed. "It's illness, that's all."

His outburst surprised me and put me on the defensive. "You said he got thin . . ."

Zinari wouldn't hear it. "Every time a *dan daudu* dies," he complained, "people say it's AIDS. It's not AIDS. It's illness, that's all."

Readers and audiences of earlier versions of this project have asked why the HIV/AIDS epidemic does not figure more prominently in my accounts of the lives of 'yan daudu and their associates. The question is apt. In the three decades since it was first identified, the human immunodeficiency virus, facilitated by scientific ignorance, social intolerance, governmental inaction and economic inequality, has had a disproportionately devastating impact on poor people, gender and sexual minorities (including sex workers), and people of African descent. As members of all these demographic categories, 'yan daudu have not escaped this holocaust. By 2006, most of the 'yan daudu I had known since the 1990s, most of them my age or younger, had died. I learned of some of these deaths through letters and phone calls, but since most of my friends had no access to these media, in most cases I received the sad news in person. Every time I returned to Nigeria I would make the rounds to my old haunts, where I was told about friends and acquaintances who had moved or died since my last visit. Judging from the symptoms described to me, I estimate that about half the deaths in my social circle were due to HIV. Yet AIDS, or *kanjamau* ['slimming disease'], was rarely mentioned as the cause of death.

My friends' relative silence around AIDS contrasted with the increasing attention the epidemic was receiving in the Nigerian public sphere. A turning point in this regard occurred in the summer of 1997 when the family of Fela Kuti, the most celebrated Nigerian musician of the twentieth century, announced that he had died of AIDS. Fela's politically and sexually charged performances had brought him international respect and notoriety, as well as periodic trouble with the Nigerian authorities. One of the many controversies he ignited before he got sick involved his infamous statement that AIDS was an '*oyinbo* disease,' *oyinbo* being Yoruba for 'white man.' Fela's death, which happened while I was in Kano, made the HIV/AIDS epidemic an urgent topic of public discourse nationwide, yet rates of infection and mortality continued to mount. Meanwhile, Nigerians of all ages, including men who have sex with men, remained vulnerable to a host of additional health problems. 'Tropical' diseases such as malaria and yellow fever, 'lifestyle' and 'environmental' diseases like diabetes and cholera, along with a pervasive lack of access to clean water, medical care and safe transportation, conspire to limit the average Nigerian's life expectancy to 47 years.[1]

If AIDS seems missing from the stories recounted here, then, it is not because 'yan daudu have been unaffected by the pandemic. Rather, its absence reflects the silence I observed in people's everyday discourse and the discomfort I encountered when I tried to raise the issue. This silence was due partly to the stigma attached to AIDS, but it also reflected the high rates of illness and premature death generally, as well as the value most Hausa Muslims place on personal discretion. With those sensitivities in mind, this epilogue describes the fates of the people and places discussed in this book, as I have been able to determine at the time of this writing. My aim is not simply to lament the passing of individuals and communities, though given so many losses, the sadness I share with my surviving friends is real, as is our occasional nostalgia. But loss is not the only theme.

An equally important theme, and a frequent refrain in Hausa conversations, is patience. To 'exercise patience' [*yi haƙuri*] is to endure pain, to refrain from letting your passions get the better of you, and to put your trust in God. Patience is a personal virtue, but it is also profoundly social. I learned this, as I learned so many other lessons, by inadvertently violating a social norm. An example occurred when I went to find the brother of a neighbor of mine with whom I'd had a disagreement. I knew the brother sympathized with my point of view, and was hoping he would talk some sense into my neighbor. When I perceived that the brother was not going to intervene on my behalf, I lost my temper and began yelling about the wrongs I felt my neighbor had done to me. We were standing outside during the middle of the day, and my loud voice began to turn heads.

"I'm giving you patience" [*Ina ba ka haƙuri*], my neighbor's brother pleaded, repeating himself several times as I continued to yell. I had not heard this expression before, and had no idea what it meant. In my mind's eye, patience couldn't be given; you either had it or you didn't. I assumed he was simply trying to defend his brother, and this exacerbated my ire.

"I don't want any patience!" I retorted.

My anger didn't get me anywhere, of course. All it did was to confirm what I later found out was my reputation for having 'hotness of heart' [*zafin zuciya*]. I didn't begin to appreciate the concept of 'giving patience' until I heard it used in a different, less volatile context. Iliyasu, an assistant at Alhaji Lawan's restaurant in Rijiyar Kuka, was seriously ill and had gone to convalesce in the village where his family lived. Since I had a car, I drove with Alhaji Lawan and some others to visit him. We found Iliyasu asleep with a small group of women around his bed. Alhaji Lawan took the lead in offering prayers.

"May God heal."

"Amen."

"May God increase your^{pl} patience."

"Amen."

"May God keep a secret."

"Amen."

My initial impulse had been to think of patience as a band-aid which covers up an injury without healing it. Looking back on the incident with my neighbor's brother, I realized that the proverbial band-aid was underrated: to cover an injury is to protect it so the body's innate healing capacities can do their work. By the same token, patience isn't passive. It protects us from the social, physical and spiritual injuries that come from 'hotness of heart' and allows us to use our God-given talents to their maximum potential. Sitting and praying with Iliyasu and his relatives, I understood how patience could be experienced as a gift, for it is with the support of our neighbors and loved ones that we are able to endure hardship and to hope that, with God's grace, our burdens might be lifted.

But what did Alhaji Lawan mean by "May God keep a secret"? As a child of twentieth-century suburban America, where time was money and self-expression was the key to happiness, I found it difficult to exercise patience, but I could understand its virtues. Secrecy, on the other hand, made me think of taboos. "May God keep a secret" [*Allah ya rufe asiri*, literally 'May God cover a secret'] seemed to suggest that Iliyasu's illness was a sign of something too shameful to mention. How could his relatives take comfort in such an ominous accusation? Alhaji Lawan's prayer also seemed to contradict the value I had learned to place – as a scholar, a gay man, and a cultural citizen of the modern Western world – on forthrightness and clarity. Only later did it dawn on me that, no matter how direct and honest we might be, we all have some secrets that are best kept covered. In that light, 'May God keep a secret' was another kind of gift, reminding us all of the need for discretion so that God alone is left to judge our secrets. Iliyasu recovered from his illness and came back to work at the restaurant a few months later.

With the death of Alhaji Damina, Alhaji Zinari became the only surviving member of the group of 'yan daudu I had gotten to know in Rijiyar Kuka. In 2006, he was divorced and living in a single rented room, spent most of his days at the nearby home of an older 'girlfriend,' and was making plans to return to Saudi Arabia. His one child, a teenage daughter, was living with an uncle in a village outside Kano. Zinari was pleased when I gave him copies of some photographs I had taken of Damina in 2002, and offered to give one of them to Damina's wife. Alhaji Lawan, a grandfather several times over, died in 2001. He'd closed the restaurant a few months earlier when he became too sick to manage it. Iliyasu and another assistant died shortly after him; his youngest assistant had died in the late 1990s.

Alhaji Balarabe, who had helped Damina and Zinari get their start as 'yan Kano-Jiddah, was quite ill with diabetes when I left Nigeria in 1994 and died shortly thereafter. Upon his death a controversy arose over a house he owned in Sabon Gari. (His primary residence had been his Arabian-style house in Rijiyar Kuka.) Damina and Zinari had lived in the house before they were married and claimed Alhaji Balarabe had wanted them to have it, while Balarabe's biological children, represented by their mother's brother, claimed the house as part of their inheritance. The case dragged on for several years and was finally settled in the children's favor, though Zinari and Damina did receive a small sum of cash.

When he wasn't in Jiddah, for many years Alhaji Zinari had commuted between Rijiyar Kuka and Sabon Gari. He spent most of his time at a large women's house managed by an older independent woman, Hajiya Kyauta, who with the help of her 'daughters' and a few 'sons' like Zinari, served expensive meals, played board games, and provided other forms of entertainment to the 'big men' who came to relax at the house. Zinari's specialty was a sweet peanut porridge [kunun gyada].

By 2006, his visits to Sabon Gari had become so rare that, when I asked after him to Hajiya Kyauta, she thought he was still in Saudi Arabia and was hurt to find out he'd been back for some time without calling on her. The next time I visited Rijiyar Kuka I insisted that Zinari accompany me to her house. Their reunion clearly made her happy, but it was also an occasion of sadness: a large part of their conversation was devoted to trading stories about mutual friends who had died, almost all of them independent women and 'yan daudu. Indeed, it was because he had lost so many friends that Alhaji Zinari no longer cared to visit Sabon Gari. "There's no one," he told me. At the age of 44, he had outlived most of his peers and a number of his juniors. On my way to the airport I stopped by Rijiyar Kuka so we could say good-bye. Zinari gave me a videotape of a biki for my research along with the cellphone number of one of his neighbors. When I called the number in early 2007, the neighbor told me Zinari had gone back to Saudi Arabia. He did not know when he'd return.

Apart from Hajiya Kyauta and her 'daughters,' my own social circle in Sabon Gari was also decimated. Mai Kwabo, my assistant, friend and drinking buddy, died of tuberculosis in 1995. Hajiya Asabe saved up enough money to host a biki in 1996, but took ill soon afterwards and was reportedly staying with friends in Lagos when I returned the following year. He died in 1998. Alhaji Yaro Faransa and his 'daughters' (including Dan Zaria, the one who joked about his 'breasts') kept his house going until 2000, when their landlord evicted them, allegedly under pressure from the newly constituted hisbas. When I went back in 2002 to see if they had returned, a teenage Igbo girl who now lived in the house did not recognize Alhaji Yaro's name. An Igbo tailor whose shop was a few doors down told me he had died. From other sources I found out about the deaths of two of Alhaji Yaro's 'daughters,' a couple who had long been teased for being 'lesbians' ['yan kifi]. I did not find out what happened to the house's other residents.

My friends in Katsina dispersed even more quickly. In 1997, the dan daudu who had worked at the restaurant next door to Lami's told me Lami had gone to Lagos, Mansur to Kano, and Haruna to Kaduna. He did not know what happened to Barbado. Before I left, he asked me if I still had the cassette [kaset].

"What cassette?" I asked.

"The one you made with Lami and the rest. Does it still exist?"

"Oh, that one!" I nodded, recalling the audiotape discussed in Chapter 4. "Yes, it still exists. It was very helpful." I was surprised he remembered it and even more surprised that he brought it up, since he had refused to join us when we recorded it.

"Good," he replied.

By 2006, Katsina had changed so much I had trouble finding the street where Lami's restaurant had been. Both that storefront and the one next to it now housed other businesses, and no one I asked knew of Lami, Mansur or Haruna. A 'shirted' friend from Kano who had moved to Katsina took me to a restaurant in a different neighborhood, where the proprietor, a frail-looking man in his seventies, greeted me warmly and, when he ascertained from my friend that I was a kind of *ashi*, introduced himself by both his 'man's name' [*sunan namiji*] and his 'ɗan daudu name' [*sunan ɗan daudu*].

"What's your name?" he asked me.

I told him my man's name was Rudi in English or Sani in Hausa, while my ɗan daudu name, given to me by some 'shirted' friends, was Rudiya. He was the oldest ɗan daudu I'd ever met. His 'daughter' was a Christian Igbo who had grown up in the North, and sat at a table writing in what looked like a schoolbook. I wanted to spend more time with them, to ask about the history of daudu, but the friend who had brought me was in a rush. Before we left, the proprietor told me that Mansur and Haruna had died within the last few years and that Lami had gone to Sudan. His 'daughter' corrected him and said Lami was in Saudi Arabia.

The fates of my friends and acquaintances in Rijiyar Kuka, Sabon Gari and Katsina suggest that HIV/AIDS and other public health problems have taken a far greater toll on 'people of the bariki' than the reinstatement of Shari'a. Although Shari'a remains popular as a symbol of Northern Nigerian identity, many Hausa Muslims have grown cynical about the way its enforcement has focused on policing 'un-Islamic' practices in barikis and other working-class areas at the expense of social justice. As a result, while the spaces within which 'yan daudu and others are able to 'play' have been curtailed, they have not been entirely eliminated. The life that goes on at Hajiya Kyauta's house in Sabon Gari and at the restaurant I visited in Katsina points to the limits of the hisbas' reach. So do stories I heard about the employees and customers who fought back when hisbas tried to close down some of the bars in Zakawa, and the bikis that continue to take place in rural areas or just over the border in the Republic of Niger. Even the cases of Aunty Maiduguri and the 'Bauchi 18' index resistance to the new Islamic legal code. Though hisbas managed to shut down both parties and arrest some of the participants, the fact that the parties were organized at all suggests a defiant desire for 'playing and laughing.'[2]

My visits to Madari were equally bittersweet. Alhaji Tasidi, the town's senior ɗan daudu and my first host there, died sometime before 1997. His assistant died soon afterwards, but over the next few years the town's bariki population remained relatively stable. Jamilu came back to his uncle's farm every rainy season, and Kabiru expanded his business after returning from Kano, where he'd spent several months working at a friend's restaurant while male relatives in his home village helped him find a bride. After Shari'a was 'launched' in Kano in 2000, the state that had jurisdiction over Madari was scheduled to follow suit, and the bariki was abuzz with rumors about what the new law would mean for the town's independent women, 'yan daudu, Bori practitioners, and the Christian southerners who ran the hotel-bars.

The effect was dramatic. Within two years the town's independent women were forced to give up their businesses for the sole reason that they were unmarried. Most of them moved away, including Hajiya Zara, who with the help of one of her boyfriends enrolled in a women's business course in the state capital. She did not give up her lease in the Madari market, however, in the hope that she would eventually be able to reopen her restaurant. One independent woman with nowhere else to go was taken in, along with her children, by Alhaji Ado, who continued serving food at his 'Play and Laughter Hotel.' As men with an Islamically legitimate, if unconventional, occupation, he and the town's other 'yan daudu were allowed to keep their businesses. Some 'yan daudu even benefited from the new law. When two independent women were forced to abandon their restaurants, Kabiru and another ɗan daudu, Rilwan, took over their leases, a clear step up from the tables they had been renting for their food-stands.

Shari'a hurt 'yan daudu's businesses in other ways, however. The new law forced the hotel-bars to stop selling alcohol and banned the 'traditional play' – music, dancing and Bori – that often took place at night in the open areas adjacent to the market. Coupled with the absence of independent women, this ban on entertainment meant fewer visitors to the market; fewer visitors meant fewer customers and fewer opportunities to make intimate connections with and for those men who might want them. Yet Shari'a did not extinguish 'traditional play' altogether. It simply became less frequent and less obvious as the 'players' – along with practitioners of other forbidden activities, like drinking, gambling and 'prostitution' – sought other venues outside town or behind closed doors.

Within the space of a year in 2005–2006, Kabiru died of emaciation and Rilwan was murdered – stabbed in his bed in the middle of the night. They were both in their thirties. After the murder, according to Alhaji Ado, he and some other 'yan daudu were detained for questioning and kept in jail for several days. The police then dropped the case, ostensibly for lack of leads, though Alhaji Ado suspected they lost interest because the victim was a ɗan daudu. With the murderer at large, the town's 'yan daudu lived in fear that one of them might become his next victim. Meanwhile, Kabiru's and Rilwan's assistants, both in their early twenties, took over their respective businesses and hired new assistants of their own. At the time of my visit in 2006, Kabiru's assistant was embroiled in a legal dispute with Kabiru's family, who were claiming possession of both his house and his business. The family was expected to win the case, and Kabiru's assistant was unsure where he would go next.

I timed my visit to coincide with Madari's market day, when I could count on seeing old, and not-so-old, friends and acquaintances. Though dismayed by the news about Rilwan and Kabiru, I enjoyed seeing Alhaji Ado, Jamilu, and Kabiru's assistant, whom I had first met only in 2002, and took a special pleasure in meeting the younger 'yan daudu who had arrived more recently. One of them, Gambo, was no older than seventeen, yet he sashayed through the market with the graceful confidence of a woman twice his age. Sitting on a bench in the motor-park, I found myself staring at him, mesmerized by the way he flitted his eyes and cocked his head as he went about tending to Alhaji Ado's customers.

"Do you have women like that in your city?"[3]

The voice seemed to come out of nowhere. I was so caught up watching Gambo that I hadn't noticed the man sitting on the bench next to me. I looked at him quizzically.

"What kind of women?" I asked.

"That kind," he said, pointing with his chin. I followed his gaze to a group of women who were sitting on a mat under a tree. They seemed to be waiting for a bus, but I couldn't see what distinguished them from any other women in the motor-park.

"Women . . . what do you mean?"

"That kind," he repeated, still pointing his chin. "Men who do women's work!" His raised voice caught the attention of Gambo. The man had been pointing at him all along.

"What is it?" Gambo shouted.

"Girl, will you[f] give me some rice?" the man teased.

Gambo rolled his eyes and smirked. "You^m want to eat, is that it?"

The naughty pun made him laugh. "You hear?" the man said, turning back to me. "Now tell me: Do you have women like that in your city?"

Notes

1 Life expectancy for a child born in 2006; see UNICEF (2008).

2 *Defiant Desire* is the title of Mark Gevisser and Edwin Cameron's (1995) ground-breaking anthology on sexual minorities in South Africa.

3 Statements about place of origin are usually expressed with plural pronouns. Thus, English 'my city' vs. Hausa 'our city.' This question was posed both times using second-person plural pronouns: 'Do you^{pl} have women like that in your^{pl} city?' [*Kuna da mata irin wannan a garinku?*].

GLOSSARY OF HAUSA TERMS

Hausa terms are written according to standard Hausa orthography. Thus, words beginning with the letters ɓ, ɗ, ƙ and 'y follow those beginning with b, d, k and y, respectively. Plural forms are in parentheses.

Underlining indicates a term which has no conventional meaning in Hausa outside of the 'harka dialect'.

Asterisk (★) indicates a term whose meaning in the 'harka dialect' is different from that in conventional spoken Hausa. ★The English translation of the in-group meaning is preceded by an asterisk.

alhaji (alhazai) 'pilgrim (m.), man who has performed the *hajj*'; masculine title of respect (see also *babban mutum*).

<u>aras</u> sex between men, anal intercourse.

<u>ashi</u> ɗan daudo.

aure marriage.

auren kulle 'locked-up marriage'; purdah, wife-seclusion.

babban mutum (manyan mutane) 'big person'; big-man, prominent person.

ba da ruwa★ 'give water'; ★impress, make a positive impression on someone.

balbela the buff-backed heron or cattle egret, renowned for its beauty and whiteness.

banza nonsense, worthlessness, uselessness.

bariki 'barracks'; the area of a Hausa town in which un-Islamic practices, such as drinking alcohol, gambling and *karuwanci*, are usually tolerated.

biki (bikukuwa) party, especially in celebration of a wedding or naming.

birni★ the Old City area enclosed by an ancient Hausa city's walls; a very large city; ★anus.

Bori Hausa cult or practice of spirit-possession.

boye hide; **a boye** in hiding, covertly.

dadaro★ long-term extramarital sexual relationship; mistress (*karuwa* or ★*dan daudu*).

daudu phenomenon or practice of men acting like women.

dan ('yan) 'son of'; one who does (an activity).

dan aras ('yan aras) masculine man who has sex with other men.

dan daudu ('yan daudu) man who acts like a woman.

dan daudun riga ('yan daudun riga) 'dan daudu of the shirt'; man who acts like a woman only in private (*a boye*), otherwise maintaining an ordinary masculine identity.

dan Kano-Jiddah ('yan Kano-Jiddah) person who travels frequently between northern Nigeria and Saudi Arabia.

farar-hula★ (fararen-hula) 'civilian'; ★any masculine man (i.e., one who is not a *dan daudu*); more specifically, a *dan aras*.

fili★ 'field, open space, chance'; ★beauty, attractiveness.

fitacce★ (fitattu) '(having) emerged, someone or something that has come out'; ★refers to overt *'yan daudu* as opposed to *'yan daudun riga*.

fito fili 'come out in the open'; reveal something in public.

gargajiya tradition.

gidan mata (gidajen mata) 'women's house'; house where *karuwai* and *'yan daudu* live, and where they receive and entertain male guests.

gugag gida final festivities of a biki [literally 'wipe up the house'].

habaici innuendo, insinuation.

haja★ 'goods, merchandise'; ★the younger partner in a male – male sexual relationship, expected to be receptive in terms of both sex and the exchange of material gifts; see also *kwazo*.

hajiya★ 'pilgrim (f.), woman who has performed the *hajj*'; feminine title of respect; ★used by *'yan daudu*.

hajj pilgrimage to Mecca.

hakuri patience.

harka★ 'business, affair, matter'; ★sex between men, homosexuality; anal intercourse.

jama'a community, the public.

iskanci frivolity, craziness, vice.

Jumma'a Friday, the Islamic day of rest and collective prayer; the weekly prayer performed (by men) at a Friday mosque.

Kano-Jiddah frequent travel, usually for commercial reasons, between northern Nigeria and Saudi Arabia.

karin magana 'folded speech,' proverb.

karuwa★ (karuwai) 'prostitute, courtesan'; single adult woman who lives on her own; ★*ɗan daudu* who practices *karuwanci*.

karuwanci 'prostitution, courtesanship'; practice of providing social and sexual companionship to men, extramaritally, in exchange for material gifts and favors.

kawali (kawalai) 'pimp, procurer'; intermediary who introduces men to *karuwai* and/or *'yan daudu* in exchange for material gifts.

kirki honor, respectability.

kifi★ 'turn one thing over onto another (of similar nature or quality)'; ★sex between women, lesbianism.

kishiya★ 'co-wife'; ★a *ɗan daudu* who is or has a rival for the affection of a man.

kunya shame, modesty, self-restraint.

ƙauye★ countryside, village; ★space between a person's thighs.

ƙawa★ (ƙawaye) 'girlfriend'; the platonic female friend of a woman, girl or ★*ɗan daudu*.

ƙawance★ 'girlfriendship'; platonic friendship between women, girls or ★'yan daudu.

ƙwazo★ 'diligence, hard work'; ★the older partner in a male–male sexual relationship, expected to be active in terms of both sex and the giving of gifts.

lemo★ 'citrus fruit, soda pop'; ★penis.

luɗu, luwaɗi sodomy, male homosexuality.

maɗigo lesbianism, sex between women.

mai (masu) one who has (a possession or quality); one who does (an activity).

mai harka (masu harka) 'one who does the business'; man who has sex with men, homosexual man.

maiwasa 'performer' at a biki.

malam (malamai) (Islamic) teacher/scholar.

manya see *babban mutum*.

masu see *mai*.

mata★ (mata) wife; ★*ɗan daudu* who takes the role of feminine-identified partner of a *ɗan aras* in the context of *dadaro*.

matar aure (matan aure) married woman.

meka ɗan ɗaudu.

miji★ (mazaje) 'husband'; ★masculine partner of a *ɗan daudu* in the context of *dadaro*.

mutum (mutane) person, man.

namiji★ (maza) 'man, male, masculine'; ★masculine man, one who is not a *ɗan daudu* (see also *farar-hula*).

rashi deficiency, lack.

rayuwa★ 'life'; ★social life of *masu harka*.

riga 'shirt, (man's) gown' (see *ɗan daudun riga*).

salla Islamic prayer ritual performed five times daily.

sana'a occupation, trade, craft.

saurayi (samari) young man; (with possessive suffix:) boyfriend.

shewa loud, jeering laughter done by women or 'yan daudu in groups; cackling.

soro small room at the entrance of a house or compound in which a man receives and entertains his guests.

uban biki 'father of the biki.'

uwa★ 'mother, aunt'; ★term of respect and affection used by a younger *ɗan daudu* to address or refer to an older *ɗan daudu*.

uwar biki 'mother of the biki.'

waje 'outside'; the area outside a traditional Hausa city's walls.

waka (wakoki) song, poem.

wasa play, game, joke.

'ya★ 'daughter, niece'; ★term of affection used by an older *ɗan daudu* to address or refer to a younger *ɗan daudu*.

'yan see *ɗan, 'yar*.

'yar ('yan) 'daughter of'; one who does (an activity).

'yar kifi ('yan kifi) woman who has sex with other women, lesbian.

yare★ 'mother-tongue, dialect, language variety'; ★the in-group code of 'yan daudu and other *masu harka*.

yarinya girl; (with possessive suffix) girlfriend (romantic or erotic). (Cf. *Kawa*.)

yawon duniya 'roaming the world'; leaving home to live catch-as-catch-can.

zance conversation, discourse; courtship preceding marriage.

BIBLIOGRAPHY

'Abd al-Wahhāb, Muhammad Ibn, n.d. Kitāb al-Tawhīd: Essay on the Unicity of Allah, Or What Is Due Allah from His Creatures. Isma'īl Rājī al Fārūqī, trans. Salimiah (Kuwait): International Islamic Federation of Student Organizations.

Abdullahi, Salisu A., 1984 A Sociological Analysis of the Institution of'Dan Daudu in Hausa Society. M.A. thesis, Bayero University, Kano.

Abu-Lughod, Lila, 1986 Veiled Sentiments: Honor and Poetry in a Bedouin Society. Berkeley, CA: University of California Press.

Abu-Lughod, Lila, 1990 The Romance of Resistance: Tracing Transformations of Power Through Bedouin Women. American Ethnologist 17(1): 43–55.

Abu-Lughod, Lila, 1993 Writing Women's Worlds: Bedouin Stories. Berkeley: University of California Press.

Adamu, Abdalla U., 2002 Ibro Dan Daudu – Hilarious! Film review posted to internet listserv Finafinan_Hausa@yahoo.com, May 18.

Adamu, Abdalla U., 2006 Private Sphere, Public Wahala: Gender and Delineation of Intimisphäre in Muslim Hausa Video Films. Paper presented at conference entitled, Negotiating Culture in the Context of Globalization, Dakar, Senegal, April 5.

Adamu, Mustafa, 2003 Akilu Aliyu: A genius remembered. BiafraNigeriaWorld, March 15. http://news.biafranigeriaworld.com/archive/2003/mar/15/127.html (Accessed July 8, 2005).

Ahmed, Leila, 1992 Women and Gender in Islam. New Haven, CT: Yale University Press.

Aken'ova, Cesnabmihilo Dorothy, 2002 Reproductive Health Research in Nigeria. Paper presented at Women's Health and Action Research Centre Seminar, University of Benin, June 25.

Albakri, Muhammad, 1994 Namiji ya auri namiji a Kano ['Man marries man in Kano']. Al-Mizan (Zaria), 4 Zul-hajji 1414 (May 14, 1994): 1.

Aliyu, Aƙilu, 1976 Dan Daudu. *In* Fasaha Aƙiliya. Dalhatu Muhammad, ed. pp. 67–69. Zaria: Northern Nigerian Publishing Co.

Amadiume, Ifi, 1987 Male Daughters, Female Husbands: Gender and Sex in an African Society. London: Zed Books.

Anderson, Benedict, 1991 Imagined Communities: Reflections on the Origin and Spread of Nationalism, 2nd edn. London: Verso.

Aremu, P. S. O., 1991 Between Myth and Reality: Yoruba Egungun Costumes as Commemorative Clothes. Journal of Black Studies 22(1): 6–14.

Askew, Kelly M., 2002 Performing the Nation: Swahili Music and Cultural Politics in Tanzania. Chicago: University of Chicago Press.

Austin, John, 1975 How to Do Things with Words, 2nd edn. J. O. Urmson and Marina Sbisà, eds. Cambridge, MA: Harvard University Press.

Babankano, Mohammed Y. Abdul, 1993 Littattafan ƙagaggun labarai a da da kuma yanzu ['Fictional Written Literature in the Past and Now']. Gaskiya Ta Fi Kwabo, June 24, 1993: 2.

Bachrach, Judy, 2003 It's a Mad, Mad Miss World. Vanity Fair, March 2003.

Bakhtin, Mikhail, 1981 The Dialogic Imagination: Four Essays. ed. Michael Holquist, trans. Caryl Emerson and M. Holquist, Austin, TX: University of Texas Press.

Baldick, Julian, 1989 Mystical Islam: An Introduction to Sufism. London: I. B. Tauris.

Barber, Karin, John Collins, and Alain Ricard, 1997 West African Popular Theatre. Bloomington: Indiana University Press.

Bargery, G. P., 1934 A Hausa-English Dictionary and English-Hausa Vocabulary. London: Oxford University Press.

Barkindo, Bawuro, 1993 Growing Islamism in Kano City since 1970: Causes, Form and Implications. *In* Muslim Identity and Social Change in Sub-Saharan Africa. Louis Brenner, ed. pp. 91–105. Bloomington, IN: Indiana University Press.

Barkow, Jerome H., 1973 Muslims and Maguzawa in North Central State, Nigeria: An Ethnographic Comparison. Canadian Journal of African Studies 7(1): 59–76.

Barlet, Olivier, 2000 The African Audience Is Anything But Homogeneous. *In* African Cinemas: Decolonizing the Gaze, trans. Chris Turner. pp. 232–250. New York: Zed Books.

Basso, Keith H., 1979 Portraits of "the Whiteman": Linguistic Play and Cultural Symbols among the Western Apache. Cambridge: Cambridge University Press.

Bauchi, Sadik, 2005 Wani matashi ya gamu da ajalinsa a gidan kallo [Youth Meets Death at Video Parlor]. Al-Mizan (Zaria, Nigeria), Feb. 14. <http:www.almizan.faithweb.com> (Accessed May 28).

Bauman, Richard, and Charles L. Briggs, 1990 Poetics and Performance As Critical Perspectives on Language and Social Life. Annual Review of Anthropology 19: 59–88.

Bauman, Richard, and Charles L. Briggs, 2003 Voices of Modernity: Language Ideologies and the Politics of Inequality. Cambridge: Cambridge University Press.

BBC (British Broadcasting Corporation), 2004 Obasanjo Backs Bishops Over Gays. BBC News website, Oct. 27. http://news.bbc.co.uk/2/hi/africa/3955145.stm (Accessed May 28, 2005).

BBC (British Broadcasting Corporation), 2007 Nigerian 'Lesbian Wedding' Denied. BBC News website, April 28. http://news.bbc.co.uk/2/hi/africa/6603853.stm (Accessed May 22, 2008).

Beauchemin, Eric, 2002 The Nigerian Closet. Program broadcast on Radio Netherlands. http://www.bureauafrique.nl/autresdepartements/africa/Radionetherlandsturns60/_archivesafricaprogrammes (Accessed May 22, 2008).

Besmer, Fremont, 1983 Horses, Musicians and Gods: The Hausa Cult of Spirit Possession. South Hadley, MA: Bergin & Garvey.

Besnier, Niko, 1993 Polynesian Gender Liminality Through Time and Space. In Third Sex, Third Gender: Beyond Sexual Dimorphism in Culture and History. Gil Herdt, ed. pp. 285–328. New York: Zone Books.

Besnier, Niko, 2002 Transgenderism, Locality, and the Miss Galaxy Beauty Pageant in Tonga. American Ethnologist 29(3): 534–566.

Besnier, Niko, 2004 The Social Production of Abjection. Desire and Silencing Among Transgender Tongans. Social Anthropology 12(3): 301–323.

Bhabha, Homi, 1994 Remembering Fanon: Self, Psyche and the Colonial Condition. In Colonial Discourse and Post-Colonial Theory. Patrick Williams and Laura Christman, eds. pp. 112–123. New York: Columbia University Press.

Bivins, Mary Wren, 1997 Daura and Gender in the Creation of a Hausa National Epic. African Langauges and Cultures 10(1): 1–28.

Bleys, Rudi, 1996 The Geography of Perversion: Male-to-Male Sexual Behaviour Outside the West and the Ethnographic Imagination, 1750–1918. London: Cassell.

Boellstorf, Tom, 2005 The Gay Archipelago: Sexuality and Nation in Indonesia. Princeton, NJ: Princeton University Press.

Boyd, Jean, and Beverly Mack, 2000 One Woman's Jihad: Nana Asma'u, Scholar and Scribe. Bloomington: Indiana University Press.

Briggs, Charles L., 1986 Learning How to Ask: A Sociolinguistic Appraisal of the Role of the Interview in Social Science Research. Cambridge: Cambridge University Press.

Briggs, Charles L., 1998 "You're a Liar – You're Just Like a Woman!": Constructing Dominant Ideologies of Language in Warao Men's Gossip. *In* Language Ideologies: Practice and Theory. Bambi Schieffelin, Kathryn Woolard and Paul Kroskrity, eds. pp. 229–255. New York: Oxford University Press.

Briggs, Charles L., 2004 Theorizing Modernity Conspiratorially: Science, Scale, and the Political Economy of Public Discourse in Explanations of a Cholera Epidemic. American Anthropologist 31(2): 164–187.

Bryant, Elizabeth, 2004 Nigerian Anglicans leading resistance to gays in church. Toronto Star, February 1.

Bucholtz, Mary, and Kira Hall, 2004 Theorizing Identity in Language and Sexuality Research. Language in Society 33: 469–515.

Bucholtz, Mary, A. C. Liang, and Laurel A. Sutton, eds., 1999 Reinventing Identities: The Gendered Self in Discourse. New York: Oxford University Press.

Butler, Judith, 1990 Gender Trouble: Feminism and the Subversion of Identity. New York: Routledge.

Butler, Judith, 1993 Bodies That Matter: On the Discursive Limits of "Sex." New York: Routledge.

Butler, Judith, 2004 Undoing Gender. New York: Routledge.

Calhoun, Craig, ed., 1993 Habermas and the Public Sphere. Cambridge, MA: MIT Press.

Callaway, Barbara, 1987 Muslim Hausa Women in Nigeria: Tradition and Change. Syracuse, NY: Syracuse University Press.

Cameron, Deborah, and Don Kulick, 2003 Language and Sexuality. Cambridge: Cambridge University Press.

Cameron, Deborah, and Don Kulick, 2005 Identity Crisis? Language and Communication 25: 107–125.

Casey, Conerly C., 1998 Suffering and the Identification of Enemies in Northern Nigeria. Political and Legal Anthropology Review 21(1): 1–25.

Casey, Conerly C., 2008 "Marginal Muslims": Politics and the Perceptual Bounds of Islamic Authenticity in Northern Nigeria. Africa Today 54(3): 66–92.

Chauncey, George, 1994 Gay New York: Gender, Urban Culture, and the Making of the Gay Male World, 1890–1940. New York: Basic Books.

Clarke, Peter B., and Ian Linden, 1984 Islam and Modern Nigeria: A Study of a Muslim Community in a Post-Independence State, 1960–1983. Mainz: Grünewald; Munich: Kaiser.

Coles, Catherine, and Beverly Mack, eds., 1991 Hausa Women in the Twentieth Century. Madison: University of Wisconsin Press.

Cooper, Barbara M., 1995 The Politics of Difference and Women's Associations in Niger: Of "Prostitutes," the Public, and Politics. Signs 20(4): 851–882.

Cooper, Barbara M., 1997 Marriage in Maradi: Gender and Culture in a Hausa Society. Portsmouth, NH: Heinemann.

Coulmas, Florian, 1981 Introduction: Conversational Routine. *In* Conversational Routine: Explorations in Standardized Communication Situations and Prepatterned Speech. F. Coulmas, ed. pp. 1–17. The Hague: Mouton.

Crowder, Michael, 1964 Indirect Rule, French and British Style. Africa: Journal of the International African Institute 34(3): 197–205.

Daily Comet, 1959a Any Politics in Raid of Kano Prostitutes? Daily Comet (Kano), July 16: 1.

Daily Comet, 1959b NA Police and Prostitutes. Daily Comet (Kano), July 17: 2.

Diawara, Mamadou, 1997 Mande Oral Popular Culture Revisited by the Electronic Media. *In* Readings in African Popular Culture. Karin Barber, ed. pp. 40–48. Bloomington: Indiana University Press.

Doi, Abdur Rahman I., n.d. Western Civilization, Islam and the Muslim Youth. Ahmedabad: Muslim Publishing House.

Donham, Donald L., 1998 Freeing South Africa: The "Modernization" of Male–Male Sexuality in Soweto. Cultural Anthropology 13(1): 3–21.

Dunton, Chris, and Mai Palmberg, 1996 Human Rights and Homosexuality in Southern Africa. Uppsala: Nordiska Afrikainstituet.

Duranti, Alessandro, 1994 From Grammar to Politics: Linguistic Anthropology in a Western Samoan Village. Berkeley, CA: University of California Press.

Ebron, Paulla, 2002 Performing Africa. Princeton, NJ: Princeton University Press.

Eckert, Penelope, 2002 Demystifying Sexuality and Desire. *In* Language and Sexuality: Contesting Meaning and Theory in Practice. K. Campbell-Kibler, R. Podesva, S. Roberts, and A. Wong, eds. pp. 99–110. Stanford, CA: CSLI Publications.

Eckert, Penelope, and Sally McConnell-Ginet, 1992 Think Practically and Look Locally: Language and Gender as a Community-Based Practice. Annual Review of Anthropology 21: 461–490.

Epple, Carolyn, 1998 Coming to Terms with Navajo *Nádleehí*: A Critique of Berdache, "Gay," "Alternate Gender," and "Two-Spirit." American Ethnologist 25(2): 267–290.

Epprecht, Marc, 2004 Hungochani: The History of a Dissident Sexuality in Southern Africa. Montreal: McGill-Queen's University Press.

Eriye, Festus, 2003 Archbishop's Stance Draws Nigerian Approval. Sunday Times (Johannesburg), Nov. 9.

Evans, David T., 1993 Sexual Citizenship: The Material Construction of Sexualities. London: Routledge.

Fabian, Johannes, 1983 Time and the Other: How Anthropology Makes its Object. New York: Columbia University Press.

Ferguson, James, 1999 Expectations of Modernity: Myths and Meanings of Urban Life on the Zambian Copperbelt. Berkeley, CA: University of California Press.

Foucault, Michel, 1980 Power/Knowledge: Selected Interviews and Other Writings, 1972–1977. Colin Gordon, ed.; C. Gordon, Leo Marshall, John Mepham, and Kate Soper, trans. Brighton: Harvester Press.

Foucault, Michel, 1990 History of Sexuality: An Introduction. New York: Vintage Books.

Furniss, Graham, 1995 The Power of Words and the Relation Between Hausa Genres. *In* Power, Marginality and African Oral Literature. G. Furniss and Liz Gunner, eds. Cambridge: Cambridge University Press. 130–144.

Furniss, Graham, 1996 Poetry, Prose and Popular Culture in Hausa. Washington: Smithsonian.

Furniss, Graham, 2003 Hausa Popular Literature and Video Film: The Rapid Rise of Cultural Production in Times of Economic Decline. Institut für Ethnologie und Afrikastudien Working Papers, no. 27. Mainz: Johnnannes Gutenberg Universität.

Gal, Susan, 1991 Between Speech and Silence: The Problematics of Research on Language and Gender. *In* Gender at the Crossroads of Knowledge: Feminist Anthropology in the Postmodern Era. Micaela di Leonardo, ed. pp. 175–203. Berkeley, CA: University of California Press.

Gal, Susan, 1994 Gender in the Post-Socialist Transition: The Abortion Debate in Hungary. East European Politics and Societies 8(2): 256–286.

Gal, Susan, 1995 Language, Gender and Power: An Anthropological Review. *In* Gender Articulated. Kira Hall and Mary Bucholtz, eds. pp. 169–182. New York and London: Routledge.

Gal, Susan, and Gail Kligman, 2000 The Politics of Gender after Socialism: A Comparative Historical Essay. Princeton, NJ: Princeton University Press.

Gal, Susan, and Kathryn Woolard, 1995 Constructing Languages and Publics: Authority and Representation. Pragmatics 5(2): 129–138.

Gaudio, Rudolf P., 1997 Not Talking Straight in Hausa. *In* Queerly Phrased: Language, Gender, and Sexuality. Kira Hall and Anna Livia, eds. pp. 416–429. New York: Oxford University Press.

Gevisser, Mark, and Edwin Cameron, eds., 1995 Defiant Desire. New York: Routledge.

Gidley, C. G. B., 1967 'Yankamanci – the Craft of the Hausa Comedians. African Language Studies 8: 52–81.

Gidley, C. G. B., 1974 Karin Magana and Azanci As Features of Hausa Sayings. African Language Studies 15: 81–96.

Gilley, Brian Joseph, 2006 Becoming Two-Spirit: Gay Identity and Social Acceptance in Indian Country. Lincoln: University of Nebraska Press.

Goodwin, Marjorie H., 1990 He-Said-She-Said: Talk as Social Organization among Black Children. Bloomington: Indiana University Press.

Gora, Aminu A., 2002 Yadda Rabilu Musa Danlasan, Ibro ya kwace kasuwar finafinan Hausa ['How Rabilu Musa Danlasan, Ibro Cornered the Hausa Film Market']. Fim 32 (August). <http://www.fim.tvheaven.com/babbanlabari132.html> (Accessed Feb. 3, 2004).

Greenberg, David F., 1988 The Construction of Homosexuality. Chicago: University of Chicago Press.

Greenberg, Joseph H., 1946 The Influence of Islam on a Sudanese Religion. (Monographs of the American Ethnological Society 10). New York: J. J. Augustin.

Grégoire, Emmanuel, 1993 Islam and the Identity of Merchants in Maradi (Niger). In Muslim Identity and Social Change in Sub-Saharan Africa. Louis Brenner, ed. pp. 106–115. Bloomington: Indiana University Press.

Gregory, Steven, 1999 Black Corona: Race and the Politics of Place in an Urban Community. Princeton: Princeton University Press.

Habermas, Jürgen, 1989 [1962] The Structural Transformation of the Public Sphere: An Inquiry into a Category of Bourgeois Society. Thomas Burger, trans. Cambridge, MA: MIT Press.

Hale, Thomas A., 1998 Griots and Griottes. Bloomington: Indiana University Press.

Hall, Kira, 1995a Lip Service on the Fantasy Lines. In Gender Articulated. K. Hall and Mary Bucholtz, eds. pp. 183–216. New York: Routledge.

Hall, Kira, 1995b Hijra/Hijrin: Language and Gender Identity. Ph.D. dissertation, University of California, Berkeley.

Hall, Kira, 1997 "Go Suck your Husband's Sugarcane": Hijras and the Use of Sexual Insult. In Queerly Phrased: Language, Gender and Sexuality. K. Hall and Anna Livia, eds. Oxford: Oxford University Press.

Hall, Kira, and Mary Bucholtz, eds., 1995 Gender Articulated: Language and the Socially Constructed Self. New York: Routledge.

Hall, Kira, and Anna Livia, eds., 1997 Queerly Phrased: Language, Gender, and Sexuality. New York: Oxford University Press.

Hall, Kira, and Veronica O'Donovan, 1996 Shifting Gender Positions Among Hindi-Speaking Hijras. *In* Rethinking Language and Gender Research: Theory and Method. Janet Bing, Victoria Bergvall and Alice Freed, eds. pp. 226–228. London: Longman.

Hansen, Karen T., ed., 1992 African Encounters with Domesticity. New Brunswick, NJ: Rutgers University Press.

Harvey, David, 2006 Spaces of Global Capitalism: Towards a Theory of Uneven Geographical Development. London: Verso.

Hayes, Jarrod, 2000 Queer Nations: Marginal Sexualities in the Maghreb. Chicago: University of Chicago Press.

Haynes, Jonathan, ed., 2000 Nigerian Video Films. Athens, Ohio: Ohio University Press.

Heath, Shirley Brice, 1983 Ways with Words: Language, Life, and Work in Communities and Classrooms. Cambridge: Cambridge University Press.

Heath, Shirley Brice, 1986 What No Bedtime Story Means. *In* Language Socialization Across Cultures. Bambi S. Schieffelin and Elinor Ochs, eds. pp. 97–124. Cambridge: Cambridge University Press.

Heath, Shirley Brice, 1997 The Essay in English: Readers and Writers in Dialogue. *In* Dialogue and Critical Discourse: Language, Culture, Critical Theory. Michael Macovski, ed. pp. 195–214. Oxford: Oxford University Press.

Hill, Clifford A., 1971 A Study of Ellipsis Within Karin Magana. Ph.D. dissertation, University of Wisconsin-Madison.

Hill, Deborah, 1992 Imprecatory Interjectional Expressions: Examples from Australian English. Journal of Pragmatics 18(2/3): 209–223.

Hill, Polly, 1972 Rural Hausa: A Village and a Setting. Cambridge: Cambridge University Press.

Hiskett, Mervyn, 1975 History of Hausa Islamic Verse. London: University of London School of Oriental and African Studies.

Hiskett, Mervyn, 1984 The Development of Islam in West Africa. London: Longman.

Hoad, Neville, 2007 African Intimacies: Race, Homosexuality, and Globalization. Minneapolis: University of Minnesota Press.

Hochschild, Arlie Russell, 1983 The Managed Heart: Commercialization of Human Feeling. Berkeley: University of California Press.

Hutson, Alaine S., 1999 The Development of Women's Authority in the Kano Tijaniyya, 1894–1963. Africa Today 46(3/4): 43–64.

Hutson, Alaine S., 2001 Women, Men, and Patriarchal Bargaining in an Islamic Sufi order: The Tijaniyya in Kano, 1937 to the Present. Gender & Society 15(5): 734–753.

Hymes, Dell, 1974 Foundations in Sociolinguistics: An Ethnographic Approach. Philadelphia, PA: University of Pennsylvania Press.

IGLHRC (International Gay and Lesbian Human Rights Commission), 2008 Dispatch from Bauchi, Nigeria, February 15. http://www.iglhrc.org/ site/iglhrc/section.php?id=5&detail=831 (Accessed May 22, 2008).

Inoue, Miyako, 2003 Gender, Language and Modernity: Toward an Effective History of Japanese Women's Language. American Ethnologist 29(2): 392–422.

Inoue, Miyako, 2006 Vicarious Language: Gender and Linguistic Modernity in Japan. Berkeley: University of California Press.

Irvine, Judith T., 1989 When Talk Isn't Cheap: Language and Political Economy. American Ethnologist 16(2): 248–267.

Irvine, Judith T., 2008 Subjected Words: African Linguistics and the Colonial Encounter. Language and Communication 28(4): 323–343.

Irvine, Judith T., and Susan Gal, 2000 Language Ideology and Linguistic Differentiation. In Regimes of Language: Ideologies, Polities, and Identities. Paul V. Kroskrity, ed. Santa Fe: School of American Research Press. 35–84.

Jakobson, Roman, 1990 [1957] Shifters, Verbal Categories, and the Russian Verb. In On Language: Roman Jakobson. L. Waugh and M. Monville-Burston, eds. pp. 386–392. Cambridge, MA: Harvard University Russian Language Project.

Jang, Tae-Sang, 1999 A Poetic Structure in Hausa Proverbs. Research in African Literatures, March.

Jenkins, Philip, 2003 Defender of the Faith. Atlantic Monthly 292(4): 46ff.

Johnson, Mark, 1997 Beauty and Power: Transgendering and Cultural Transformation in the Southern Philippines. Oxford: Berg.

Kakaki, 1993 Ya bai wa sojojin ƙasar Amurka damar yin luɗu da maɗigo ['He Gives American Soldiers the Right to Practice Sodomy and Lesbianism']. Kakaki (Bauchi, Nigeria), July 30: 5.

Kane, Ousmane, 2003 Muslim Modernity in Postcolonial Nigeria: A Study of the Society for the Removal of Innovation and Reinstatement of Tradition. Leiden: Brill.

Kaplan, Morris, 1997 Sexual Justice: Democratic Citizenship and the Politics of Desire. New York: Routledge.

Kaplan, Morris, 2005 Sodom on the Thames: Sex, Love, and Scandal in Wilde Times. Ithaca, NY: Cornell University Press.

Keating, Elizabeth L., 1998 Power Sharing: Language, Rank, Gender and Social Space in Pohnpei, Micronesia. New York: Oxford University Press.

Kessler, Suzanne, and Wendy McKenna, 1985 Gender: An Ethnomethodological Approach. Chicago: University of Chicago Press.

Kleis, Gerald W., and Salisu A. Abdullahi, 1983 Masculine Power and Gender Ambiguity in Urban Hausa Society. African Urban Studies (New Series) 16: 39–54.

Korau, Muhammad, 1959 Kamen karuwa an bar jaki ana dukan taiki: 'Yan daudu fa? ['Arresting Prostitutes, Donkey Is Left While Sack Is Beat: What About 'dan daudu?']. (Letter to the editor.) Daily Comet (Kano), July 16: 3.

Krings, Matthias, 1999 On History and Language of the "European" Bori Spirits of Kano, Nigeria. In Spirit Possession. Modernity & Power in Africa. Behrend, Heike and Ute Luig, eds. pp. 53–67. Madison: University of Wisconsin Press.

Kroskrity, Paul V., 2000 Language Ideologies in the Expression and Representation of Arizona Tewa Ethnic Identity. In Regimes of Langauge: Ideologies, Polities, and Identities. P. V. Kroskrity, ed. pp. 329–359. Santa Fe: School of American Research.

Kulick, Don, 1998 Travesti: Sex, Gender, and Culture among Brazilian Transgendered Prostitutes. Chicago: University of Chicago Press.

Kulick, Don, 2000 Gay and Lesbian Language. Annual Review of Anthropology 29: 243–285.

Kulick, Don, and Margaret Willson, eds., 1995 Taboo: Sex, Identity, and Erotic Subjectivity in Anthropological Fieldwork. New York: Routledge.

Labov, William, 1972 On the Transformation of Experience in Narrative Syntax. In Language in the Inner City. pp. 354–396. Philadelphia, PA: University of Pennsylvania Press.

Larkin, Brian, 2000 Hausa Dramas and the Rise of Video Culture in Nigeria. In Nigerian Video Films, 2nd ed. Jonathan Haynes, ed. pp. 209–241. Athens, OH: Ohio University Press.

Larkin, Brian, 2002a The Materiality of Cinema Theaters in Northern Nigeria. In Media Worlds: Anthropology on New Terrain. Faye D. Ginsburg, Lila Abu-Lughod and B. Larkin, eds. pp. 319–336. Berkeley: University of California Press.

Larkin, Brian, 2002b Indian Films and Nigerian Lovers: Media and the Creation of Parallel Modernities. In The Anthropology of Globalization: A Reader. Jonathan Xavier Inda and Renato Rosaldo eds. Oxford: Blackwell.

Larkin, Brian, 2008 Signal and Noise: Media, Infrastructure, and Urban Culture in Nigeria. Durham, NC: Duke University Press.

Last, Murray, 1967 The Sokoto Caliphate. New York: Humanities Press.

Last, Murray, 1991 Adolescents in a Muslim City: The Cultural Contexts of Danger and Risk. Kano Studies (Special issue: Youth and Health in Kano Today): 41–70.

Last, Murray, 2008 The Search for Security in Muslim Northern Nigeria. Africa 78(1): 41–63.

Lave, Jean, and Étienne Wenger, 1991 Situated Learning: Legitimate Peripheral Participation. Cambridge: Cambridge University Press.

Lawuyi, Olatunde Bawo, 1997 The World of the Yoruba Taxi Driver: An Interpretive Approach to Vehicle Slogans. *In* Readings in African Popular Culture. Karin Barber, ed. pp. 146–150. Bloomington: Indiana University Press.

Leap, William L., 1996a Can There Be a Gay Discourse Without a Gay Language? *In* Cultural Performances: Proceedings of the Third Berkeley Women and Language Conference, M. Bucholtz, A. C. Liang, L. Sutton and C. Hines, eds. pp. 399–408. Berkeley Women & Language Group.

Leap, William L., 1996b Word's Out: Gay Men's English. Minneapolis: University of Minnesota Press.

Leap, William L., 2004 Language, Belonging and (Homo)Sexual Citizenship in Cape Town, South Africa. *In* Speaking in Queer Tongues: Globalization and Gay Language. W. L. Leap and Tom Boellstorf, eds. pp. 134–162. Urbana: University of Illinois Press.

Leap, William L. and Tom Boellstorf, eds., 2004 Speaking in Queer Tongues: Globalization and Gay Language. Urbana: University of Illinois Press.

Leap, William L., and Ellen Lewin, eds., 1996 Out in the Field: Reflections of Lesbian and Gay Anthropologists. Urbana: University of Illinois Press.

Levtzion, Nehemia, and Humphrey J. Fisher, eds., 1986 Rural and Urban Islam in West Africa. Boulder and London: Lynne Rienner.

Linde, Charlotte, 1993 Life Stories: The Creation of Coherence. New York: Oxford University Press.

Low, Setha, ed., 1999 Theorizing the City: The New Urban Anthropology Reader. New Brunswick, NJ: Rutgers University Press.

Lubeck, Paul M., 1986 Islam and Urban Labor in Northern Nigeria: The Making of a Muslim Working Class. Cambridge: Cambridge University Press.

Lutz, Catherine A., and Lila Abu-Lughod, eds., 1990 Language and the Politics of Emotion. Cambridge: Cambridge University Press.

Lutz, Catherine A., and Jane L. Collins, 1993 Reading *National Geographic*. Chicago: University of Chicago Press.

MacLeod, Arlene E., 1994 Accommodating Protest: Working Women, the New Veiling, and Change in Cairo. New York: Columbia University Press.

Mahmood, Saba, 2003 The Politics of Piety: The Islamic Revival and the Feminist Subject. Princeton, NJ: Princeton University Press.

Malinowski, Bronislaw, 1929 The Sexual Life of Savages in North Western Melanesia. London: Routledge and Kegan Paul.

Mamdani, Mahmood, 1996 Citizen and Subject: Contemporary Africa and the Legacy of Late Colonialism. Princeton, NJ: Princeton University Press.

Manalansan, Martin F., 2003 Global Divas: Filipino Gay Men in the Diaspora. Durham, NC: Duke University Press.

Masquelier, Adeline, 1995 Consumption, Prostitution, and Reproduction: The Poetics of Sweetness in Bori. American Ethnologist 22(4): 883–906.

Masquelier, Adeline, 2001 Prayer Has Spoiled Everything: Possession, Power, and Identity in an Islamic Town of Niger. Durham, NC: Duke University Press.

Massad, Joseph, 2002 Re-orienting Desire: The Gay International and the Arab world. Public Culture 14(2): 361–386.

Massad, Joseph, 2007 Desiring Arabs. Chicago: University of Chicago Press.

Matory, J. Lorand, 1994 Sex and the Empire That Is No More: Gender and the Politics of Metaphor in Oyo Yourba Religion. Minneapolis: University of Minnesota Press.

McClintock, Anne, 1995 Imperial Leather: Race, Gender and Sexuality in the Colonial Conquest. London: Routledge.

McElhinny, Bonnie, 1995 Challenging Hegemonic Masculinities: Female and Male Police Officers Handling Domestic Violence. In Gender Articulated, Kira Hall and Mary Bucholtz. eds. pp. 217–244. New York: Routledge.

McIlvenny, Paul, ed., 2002 Talking Gender and Sexuality. Philadelphia: John Benjamins.

McIntyre, Joseph A., 1980 The Language of Hausa Greetings: The Social Construction of Hierarchy. Afrika und Übersee 63: 39–67.

Mead, Margaret, 1923 Coming of Age in Samoa. New York: Morrow.

Mendoza-Denton, Norma, 2008 Homegirls: Latina and Cultural Practice among Latina Youth Gangs. Malden, MA: Wiley-Blackwell.

Miles, William F. S., 2003 Shari'a as De-Africanization: Evidence from Hausaland. Africa Today 50(1): 51–75.

Miller, Peggy, Randolph Potts, Heidi Fung, Lisa Hoogstra, and Judy Mintz, 1990 Narrative Practices and the Social Construction of the Self. American Ethnologist 17: 292–311.

Modan, Gabriella G., 2007 Turf Wars: Discourse, Diversity, and the Politics of Place. Malden, MA: Wiley-Blackwell.

Morgan, Marcyliena, 1991 Indirectness and Interpretation in African American Women's Discourse. Pragmatics 1(4): 421–451.

Murray, Stephen O., 1987 A Note on Haitian Tolerance of Homosexuality. In Male Homosexuality in Central and South America. S. O. Murray, ed. San Francisco: Instituto Obregón.

Murray, Stephen O., 1997a Gender-Defined Homosexual Roles in Sub-Saharan African Islamic Societies. *In* Islamic Homosexualities: Culture, History, and Literature. S. O. Murray and Will Roscoe, eds. pp. 222–229. New York: New York University Press.

Murray, Stephen O., 1997b The Will Not to Know: Islamic Accommodations of Male Homosexuality. *In* Islamic Homosexualities: Culture, History, and Literature, Stephen O. Murray and Will Roscoe, eds. pp. 14–54. New York: New York University Press.

Murray, Stephen O., 2000 Homosexualities. Chicago: University of Chicago Press.

Murray, Stephen O., and Will Roscoe, eds., 1997 Islamic Homosexualities: Culture, History, and Literature. New York: New York University Press.

Murray, Stephen O., and Will Roscoe, eds., 1998 Boy-Wives and Female Husbands: Studies in African Homosexualities. New York: St. Martin's Press.

Namadi, Halliru na A., 1957 'Yan daudu yafi kyau a matsa wa lam[b]a ['It Would Be Better to Put Pressure on 'Yan Daudu']. (Letter to the editor.) Daily Comet (Kano), May 23: 3.

Nanda, Serena, 1990 Neither Man nor Woman: The Hijras of India. Belmont, CA: Wadsworth.

Nast, Heidi J., 1994 The Impact of British Imperialism on the Landscape of Female Slavery in the Kano Palace, Northern Nigeria. Africa 64(1): 34–73.

Nast, Heidi J., 2005 Concubines and Power: Five Hundred Years in a Northern Nigerian Palace. Minneapolis: University of Minnesota Press.

New Nigerian, 2000 Shari'a Boosts Morals, Checks Vices. New Nigerian (Kaduna), June 23: 1.

Newton, Esther, 1972 Mother Camp: Female Impersonators in America. Chicago: University of Chicago Press.

Northern Star, 1959 Dandaudus Jailed. Northern Star (Kano), July 8: 1.

O'Brien, Susan M., 2000 Power and Paradox in Hausa Bori: Discourses of Gender, Healing and Islamic Tradition in Northern Nigeria. Ph.D. thesis, University of Wisconsin-Madison.

O'Brien, Susan M., 2007 La charia contestée: Démocratie, débat et diversité musulmane dans les "étas Charia" du Nigeria. Politique Africaine 106: 46–68.

Ochonu, Moses, forthcoming Colonialism within Colonialism: The Hausa-Caliphate Imaginary and British Administration of the Nigerian Middle Belt. African Studies Quarterly.

Ochs, Elinor, 1988 Culture and Language Socialization in a Samoan Village. Cambridge: Cambridge University Press.

Ochs, Elinor, and Lisa Capps, 2001 Living Narrative: Creating Lives in Everyday Storytelling. Cambridge, MA: Harvard University Press.

Okamoto, Shigeko, 1995 "Tasteless" Japanese: Less "Feminine" Speech Among Young Japanese Women. In Gender Articulated. Kira Hall and Mary Bucholtz, eds. pp. 297–325. New York: Routledge.

Okonta, Ike, and Oronta Douglas, 2001 Where Vultures Feast: Shell, Human Rights, and Oil in the Niger Delta. San Francisco: Sierra Club Books.

Onishi, Norimitsu, 1999 A Nigerian State Turns to the Koran for Law. New York Times, Dec. 8: A4.

Onishi, Norimistu, 2000 Islam Meets Africa and Islam Bows. New York Times, Jan. 9: WK20.

Ortner, Sherry B., 1995 Resistance and The Problem of Ethnographic Refusal. Comparative Studies in Society and History 37(1): 173–193.

Oyěwùmí, Oyèrónké, 1997 The Invention of Women: Making An African Sense of Western Gender Discourses. Minneapolis: University of Minnesota Press.

Paden, John N., 1973 Religion and Political Culture in Kano. Berkeley: University of California Press.

Pellow, Deborah, 1997 Male Praise-Singers in Accra: In the Company of Women. Africa 67: 582–601.

Pellow, Deborah, 2008 Landlords and Lodgers: Socio-Spatial Organization in an Accra Community. Chicago: University of Chicago Press.

Philips, Susan U., 1983 The Invisible Culture: Communication in Classroom and Communityon the Warm Springs Indian Reservation. New York: Longman.

Philips, Susan U., 2000 Constructing a Tongan Nation-State Through Language Ideology in the Courtroom. In Regimes of Language: Ideologies, Polities, and Identities. Paul V. Kroskrity, ed. pp. 229–258. Santa Fe: School of American Research Press.

Piamenta, M., 1979 Islam in Everyday Arabic Speech. Leiden: E. J. Brill.

Pierce, Steven, 2003 Farmers and "Prostitutes": Twentieth-Century Problems of Female Inheritance in Kano Emirate, Nigeria. Journal of African History 44: 463–486.

Pierce, Steven, 2005 Farmers and the State in Colonial Kano. Bloomington: Indiana University Press.

Pierce, Steven, 2007 Identity, Performance, and Secrecy: Gendered Life and the "Modern" in Northern Nigeria. Feminist Studies 33(3): 539–565.

Pittin, Renée I., 1979 Marriage and Alternative Strategies: Career Patterns of Hausa Women in Katsina City. Ph.D. thesis, University of London.

Pittin, Renée I., 1983 Houses of Women: A Focus on Alternative Lifestyles in Katsina. In Female and Male in West Africa. Christine Oppong, ed. pp. 291–301. London: George Allen & Unwin.

Pittin, Renée I., 2003 Women and Work in Northern Nigeria: Transcending Boundaries. New York: Palgrave Macmillan.

Plummer, Ken, 1995 Telling Sexual Stories: Power, Change, and Social Worlds. New York: Routledge.

Rain, David, 1999 Eaters of the Dry Season: Circular Labor Migration in the West African Sahel. Boulder, CO: Westview Press.

Reynolds, Jonathan T., 2001 The Time of Politics (Zamanin Siyasa): Islam and the Politics of Legitimacy in Northern Nigeria, 1950–1966, 2nd ed. Lanham, MD: University Press of America.

Rickford, John R., and Angela E. Rickford, 1976 Cut-Eye and Suck-Teeth: African Words and Gestures in New World Guise. Journal of American Folklore 89(353): 294–309.

Robinson, Charles H., 1969 [1900] Nigeria, Our Latest Protectorate. New York: Negro Universities Press.

Rosaldo, Renato, 1997 Cultural Citizenship, Inequality, Multiculturalism. *In* Latino Cultural Citizenship: Claiming Identity, Space, and Rights. William Flores and Rina Benmayor, eds. pp. 27–38. Boston: Beacon Press.

Roscoe, Will, 1991 The Zuni Man-Woman. Albuquerque: University of New Mexico Press.

Rudes, Blair A., and Bernard Healy, 1979 Is She for Real? The Concepts of Femaleness and Maleness in the Gay World. *In* Ethnolinguistics: Boas, Sapir and Whorf Revisited. Madeleine Mathiot, ed. pp. 49–61. The Hague: Mouton.

Rufa'i, Aisha A., 1986 Sexism and Language. M.A. thesis, Bayero University, Kano.

Said, Edward, 1978 Orientalism. New York: Vintage.

Said, Edward, 1981 Covering Islam: How the Media and the Experts Determine How We See the Rest of the World. New York: Pantheon.

Said, Edward, 1993 Culture and Imperialism. New York: Random House.

Sassen, Saskia, 2001 The Global City: New York, London, Tokyo. Princeton, NJ: Princeton University Press.

Schieffelin, Bambi B., 1988 The Give and Take of Everyday Life: Language Socialization of Kaluli Children. Cambridge: Cambridge University Press.

Schieffelin, Bambi, and Elinor Ochs, eds., 1986 Language Socialization Across Cultures. Cambridge: Cambridge University Press.

Schiffrin, Deborah, 1984 Jewish Argument As Sociability. Language in Society 13: 311–335.

Searle, John, 1969 Speech Acts: An Essay in the Philosophy of Language. Cambridge: Cambridge University Press.

Shuman, Amy, 1986 Storytelling Rights: The Uses of Oral and Written Texts by Urban Adolescents. Cambridge: Cambridge University Press.

Silverstein, Michael, 1976 Shifters, Linguistic Categories, and Cultural Description. *In* Meaning in Anthropology. K. H. Basso and H. A. Selby, eds. pp. 11–55. Albuquerque: University of New Mexico Press.

Silverstein, Michael, 1993 Metapragmatic Discourse and Meta-Pragmatic Function. *In* Reflexive Language: Reported Speech and Metapragmatics. John A. Lucy, ed. Cambridge: Cambridge University Press. 33–58.

Sinnott, Megan, 2004 Toms and Dees: Transgender Identity and Female Same-Sex Relationships in Thailand. Honolulu: University of Hawaii Press.

Sirriyeh, Elizabeth, 1999 Sufis and Anti-Sufis: The Defence, Rethinking and Rejection of Sufism in the Modern World. Richmond, Surrey: Curzon.

Skinner, Neil, ed. and trans., 1969 Hausa Tales and Traditions, vol. 1. Belfast: W. Erskine Mayne. [Originally published as Litafina Tatsuniyoyi na Hausa, Frank Edgar, ed., 1911.]

Skinner, Neil, 1980 An Anthology of Hausa Literature in Translation. Zaria, Nigeria: Northern Nigerian Publishing Co.

Smith, Mary F., ed. and trans., 1981 [1954] Baba of Karo: A Woman of the Muslim Hausa. New Haven, CT: Yale University Press.

Smith, Mary F., ed. and trans., 1991 Labarin Baba: Mutuniyar Karo ta Kasar Kano ['The Story of Baba: A Woman of Karo in Kano Emirate']. Madison: African Studies Program, University of Wisconsin-Madison.

Smith, Michael G., 1957 The Social Functions and Meaning of Hausa Praise-Singing. Africa 27: 26–43.

Smith, Michael G., 1959 The Hausa System of Social Status. Africa 29: 239–252.

Smith, Michael G., 1969 Institutional and Political Conditions of Pluralism. *In* Pluralism in Africa. Leo Kuper and M. G. Smith, eds. pp. 27–65. Berkeley: University of California Press.

Soares, Benjamin F., 2005 Islam and the Prayer Economy: History and Authority in a Malian Town. Ann Arbor: University of Michigan Press.

Stevenson, Nick, 1997 Globalization, National Cultures, and Cultural Citizenship. Sociological Quarterly 38: 902–926.

Stilwell, Sean A., 2004 Paradoxes of Power: The Kano "Mamluks" and Male Royal Slavery in the Sokoto Caliphate, 1804–1903. Portsmouth, NH: Heinemann.

Stoler, Ann Laura, 1995 Race and the Education of Desire: Foucault's History of Sexuality and the Colonial Order of Things. Durham, NC: Duke University Press.

Sulaiman, Tajudeen, and Bamidele Adebayo, 2002 Nation's Homosexuals. The News (Lagos), Apr. 22.

Timberg, Craig, 2005 Nigerian Churches Tell West to Practice What It Preached on Gays. Washington Post, Oct. 24: A16.

Trimingham, J. Spencer, 1968 The Influence of Islam upon Africa. New York: Praeger.

Umar, Muhammad Sani, 1993 Changing Islamic Identity in Nigeria from the 1960s to the 1980s: From Sufism to Anti-Sufism. *In* Muslim Identity and Social Change in Sub-Saharan Africa. Louis Brenner, ed. pp. 116–134. Bloomington, IN: Indiana University Press.

UNICEF (United Nations Children's Fund), 2008 At a Glance: Nigeria-Statistics. http://www.unicef.org/infobycountry/nigeria_statistics.html (Accessed: October 23, 2008).

Urla, Jacqueline, 1995 Outlaw Language: Creating Alternative Public Spheres in Basque Free Radio. Pragmatics 5(2): 245–261.

Valentine, David, 2007 Imagining Transgender: An Ethnography of a Category. Durham, NC: Duke University Press.

Warner, Michael, 2002 Publics and Counterpublics. Cambridge, MA: MIT Press.

Watts, Michael, 1999 Islamic Modernities? Citizenship, Civil Society, and Islamism in a Nigerian City. *In* Cities and Citizenship. James Holston, ed. pp. 67–102. Durham, NC: Duke University Press.

Wenger, Étienne, 1998 Communities of Practice: Learning, Meaning, and Identity. Cambridge: Cambridge University Press.

Werthmann, Katja, 1997 "Women of the Barracks": Muslim Hausa Women in an Urban Neighbourhood in Northern Nigeria. Africa Today 72(1): 112–130.

Werthmann, Katja, 2000 Nachbarinnen: die Alltagswelt muslimischer Frauen in einer nigerianischen Großstadt. Frankfurt: Brandes & Aspel.

West, Candace, and Don H. Zimmerman, 1987 Doing Gender. Gender and Society 125–151.

White, Luise, 1990 The Comforts of Home: Prostitution in Colonial Nairobi. Chicago: University of Chicago Press.

Whitehead, Harriet, 1981 The Bow and the Burden Strap: A New Look at Institutionalized Homosexuality in Native North America. *In* Sexual Meanings: The Cultural Construction of Gender and Sexuality. Sherry B. Ortner and Harriet Whitehead, eds. pp. 80–115. Cambridge: Cambridge University Press.

Whitsitt, Novian, 1998 The Literature of Balaraba Ramat Yakubu and the Emerging Genre of Littattafai na Soyayya: A Prognostic of Change for Women in Hausa Society. Madison: African Studies Program, University of Wisconsin-Madison.

Williams, Walter L., 1986 The Spirit and the Flesh: Sexual Diversity in American Indian Culture. Boston: Beacon Press.

Works, John A., 1976 Pilgrims in a Strange Land: Hausa Communities in Chad. New York: Columbia University Press.

Yahaya, Ibrahim Yaro, and Abdulƙadir Dangambo, 1986 Jagoran nazarin Hausa ['Hausa Research Guide']. Zaria (Nigeria): Gaskiya Corp.

Yahya, D., 1989 Kano Intellectual History: Mapping the Intellectual Landscape. *In* Kano and Some of Her Neighbors. Bawuro M. Barkindo, ed. Zaria: Ahmadu Bello University Press.

Yusuf, Ahmed Beitallah, 1974 A Reconsideration of Urban Conceptions: Hausa Urbanization and the Hausa Rural-Urban Continuum. Urban Anthropology 3(2): 200–221.

INDEX

Note: Pseudonyms of people and places are indicated in **bold**; "n" and a number after a page number refers to a note number on that page.

address, forms of 2, 67, 72, 74, 76, 85, 92, 105–7, 129, 134, 147, 148, 152

Ado (Alhaji Ado) 93, 95, 203–4

aesthetics 8, 18, 25, 51, 92, 93, 171

affect 39, 67, 79, 80, 85, 89, 90, 91, 106, 129, 137, 141, 179

Africa and Africans, representations of 11, 13, 33, 37, 38, 39, 55, 140, 178, 179, 182, 184

age 7, 65, 66, 91, 131, 147, 165, 166, 167, 169, 172, 197, 200, 204

agency 56, 79

AIDS (*see*) HIV/AIDS

Akinola, Peter 188–9

Al-Fatiha (organization) 195n41

Al-Mizan (newspaper) 175–7, 179, 183, 192, 193n1, 193n2

alhaji (*see also* big men) 107, 134, 162

Aliyu, Aƙilu 48–52, 63, 153–4

Allah
faith in 125, 133, 141, 147, 164, 169, 193, 198, 199

judgment of 6, 46–7, 119, 127, 161, 199

name of xiv, 118, 125–6

will of 32, 50–2, 77, 81, 101–2, 121–2, 125

ambiguity (*see also* indirectness, habaici) 33, 100, 132, 139, 152, 155, 192

ambivalence 67, 72, 127, 132, 157

America (USA), cultural norms of 8, 66, 67, 72–3, 84, 110, 198, 199

Anglican Church 188–9

anthropology 37, 41, 72, 182, 183, 185

Arab people 16, 38, 129, 138–9, 140, 181–2, 190–1

Arabic language 15, 19, 35, 38, 70, 76–8, 97, 125–6, 138, 147, 170
used by 'yan daudu 3, 20, 81, 111, 127–9, 135

architecture 36, 113, 114, 134

Asabe (Hajiya Asabe) 1, 2, 3, 29–31, 74, 108–12, 134, 163–4, 186, 201

attractiveness (*see also* desire) 6, 61, 71, 79, 85, 103, 121, 134, 157

Baba of Karo 40–4, 55, 64, 81

Balarabe (Alhaji Balarabe) 134–5, 138, 145, 200

balbela (buff-backed heron) 101–3

banza (worthlessness) 7, 19, 32, 49–51, 100–1, 104, 131

Barbado 75–6, 80–5, 89, 91–5, 100–4, 118–20, 201

bariki
  history of 18, 39, 64
  life in 30, 40, 53, 72–3, 85, 86, 94, 117, 202
  moral status of 19, 55, 92, 112, 131
  people of 21, 25, 32, 42, 68–9, 86, 88n15, 124, 143, 146–7, 165

'Bauchi 18' 13, 178–80, 183, 191–2, 202

Bayero University, Kano (BUK) 14, 15, 17

big men (*manyan mutane*) 6, 69, 132, 134, 143, 145, 162, 163, 168, 170, 171, 176, 200

bikis (celebrations)
  economic aspects 63, 152, 165, 168–9
  videos of 22, 145–7, 163–4, 166–70, 172–3, 176
  women's 19, 55, 96, 163
  'yan daudu's 59n31, 72, 74, 94, 121, 159, 164–6

bisexuality 10

Bori (spirit-possession) 18–19, 21, 36, 38–40, 44, 58n21, 59–96, 124, 131, 140, 189, 195n34, 203
  and 'yan daudu 17, 32–4, 41–2, 48, 52–3, 55, 57n5, 84, 94, 97, 163, 165–6

Borno (*see also* Kanuri) 26n1, 33–5

boyfriends (*see also* '*yan aras*) 1, 74, 79, 81, 85, 89–90, 105, 112, 121, 203

capitalism 25, 44, 64, 124

children 10, 42, 51, 59n31, 61, 63, 76, 96, 99, 115n1, 117, 132, 134, 143, 147, 153, 158, 171, 200, 203

Christianity 7, 33, 37–8, 48, 175, 188

Christians 12, 18, 20, 23, 30, 69, 123, 126, 179, 182, 189–91, 202–3

citizenship 3, 7, 8, 13, 124, 167–9, 188, 193, 199

city (*see bariki*, Kano city, urban life)

city-states (*see* Kano emirate, Hausa city-states)

Civil War 52, 54

'civilians' (*fararen-hula*) (*see also masu harka, homos*) 9, 20, 29, 93, 110, 112–14, 136–7, 164, 176, 192

class (*see also daudu*, occupation, poverty, wealth) 8, 21, 24, 40, 45, 48, 61, 64–5, 86, 168, 182–3, 188
  class distinctions among 'yan daudu and masu harka 92–3, 115, 124, 136, 140, 147, 156, 158, 190, 202

clothing (*see also* dress) 14, 62, 74, 76, 128, 135, 142n12, 161
  women's 6, 42, 47, 55, 145, 147–8, 158, 166, 169

co-wives 91–2, 96, 105, 148

codeswitching (*see also* Arabic language, English language) 128, 141n2, 170

colonialism 6, 11, 140, 183–4, 188–9
  in northern Nigeria 18, 30–1, 37–42, 44–5, 55, 58, 64, 87n4, 133, 168

coming-out stories 66–7, 84

communicative competence 108

competition, among 'yan daudu 79, 91, 105, 112, 172

concubines (*see also* independent women, prostitutes) 18, 36, 58n20

conflict, among 'yan daudu 73, 79–80, 85, 90, 110–11, 122, 147, 172

contradictions
  ideological 24–5, 73, 87, 122, 127, 131, 133, 141, 146, 171, 172, 193
  in 'yan daudu's stances towards dominant norms 38, 92, 120, 122, 131, 152

corruption (*see also* big men) 6, 54, 171, 179

counterpublic 124, 147, 167, 172, 173

cross-dressing (*see* 'Bauchi 18', clothing, dress, transvestites)

customs (*see* play, tradition)

Damina (Alhaji Damina) 107–8, 130, 134–8, 145–7, 158–70, 172–5, 186, 196, 199–200

dancing 6, 33, 38, 46, 55, 59n31, 74, 94–6, 145, 163, 165–7, 169–70, 187, 203

dan daudu
  origin and use of term 31, 33–4, 42–3, 83–3, 151, 153–4, 178, 185, 190–1
  synonyms for 90, 93, 186–7

Dan Zaria 120, 201

daudu, as occupation 25, 55, 61, 65–7, 86–7, 95, 186, 203

desire (*see also* attractiveness) 9–10, 25, 66, 147, 181–3, 191, 202

dialect (*see* harka dialect)

discretion (*see also* indirectness, shame) 43, 67, 75, 86, 106, 112–14, 141, 144, 158, 194n8, 198–9

divorce 12, 86, 105, 115n1, 163, 199

domestic sphere 92, 130, 148, 170

dress (*see also* clothing) 1, 3, 7, 14, 134

drinking (alcoholic beverages) 1, 2, 18, 69, 84, 95, 109, 115, 117, 118, 119, 140, 203

economics
  of daudu 56–7, 65, 67, 69, 86, 165
  of Nigeria 6, 54

education
  Islamic 15, 36, 156
  Western (*boko*) 15, 156
  'yan daudu's attainment of 56, 20, 61, 81, 84, 186

emirates (*see* Kano emirate, Hausa city-states)

English language (*see also* codeswitching) 15, 18, 19, 20, 31, 37, 72–4, 169, 170, 178, 184
  used by 'yan daudu and masu harka 9, 56, 110–11, 131, 156, 158, 165, 186

entextualization 67, 146, 173

ethnicity (*see also* Hausa ethnicity) 12, 19, 37, 58n20, 170–1
  of 'yan daudu 20, 70, 202

explicitness 26, 112, 119, 121, 129, 131–2, 172, 193

faith 3, 26, 97, 121–8, 140–1, 168, 179, 193

family relations (*see also* children, fathers, kinship, mothers) 24, 61, 68, 115, 119, 134–6, 140, 145, 147–54, 156, 198, 200, 204

farming 18, 61, 63–5, 95–6, 203

fathers 56, 64, 65, 114, 153–4, 170, 177
  fatherhood 10, 63, 64, 93, 148, 158, 200

fellowship (*zumunci*) (*see also* solidarity)
72, 86
feminine practices (*see also* gesture,
women's talk, women's work)
6, 8, 25, 51, 56, 82, 99, 102,
114, 146, 148, 149, 152, 153,
155, 157, 158, 159, 169, 170,
171
feminine referents (*see also* grammatical
gender, masculine referents,
names, pronouns) 68, 74, 76,
82, 91–2, 100, 102, 105–6, 107,
131, 149–50, 151, 152, 175, 185,
187, 192
femininity 9, 10, 43, 79, 84, 92, 96,
132, 152, 163, 166
feminist scholarship 16, 35–6
film (*see also* video) 122–3
Hausa 21, 24–5, 91, 143–61,
167–73
Indian (Bollywood) 175, 186–7
Fodio, Usman dan 35–6, 159–60,
168
food, cooking and serving 4, 6, 31,
34, 51, 52, 55, 62, 65, 82–3, 86,
118, 162, 203
Fulani people 20, 35, 37–8, 58n20,
70
Funtuwa, Yadudu Hamisu 52–4, 71

gay (*see also* homosexuality, same-sex
marriage)
gay-rights activism 13, 178–84,
186, 188–93
as identity label 9, 181–4
Western gay life 9–10, 16, 66, 73,
84, 185–6, 199
gender
grammatical (*see also* feminine
referents, masculine referents,
names, pronouns) 76, 88n17,
92, 102, 152, 185
as social-theoretical category 7–8,
10–16, 21, 31, 35, 45, 55, 57,

66, 87n8, 96, 169–70, 172–3,
184
gender segregation 14–16, 97, 164
genre (*see also* proverbs, habaici, songs,
poetry, oral literature) 21, 49,
51, 67, 90–2, 96–7, 101, 104–5,
121, 130, 154, 167, 183, 191
gesture 6, 102, 145, 148, 154, 157,
159
girlfriends (*kawa*) 62, 68, 72–86, 89,
108–10, 134, 192, 196
glamor 71, 95–6, 171, 186
globalization 8, 26, 124, 181–2, 186,
188–90, 193
God (*see* Allah)

habaici (*see also* ambiguity, indirectness)
21, 90–2, 96–106, 121, 130–1,
148–9, 151
hajj 2, 107, 129, 111, 135, 138,
161
Hamza 69–72, 81, 86
harassment (*see* police)
harka dialect (*yaren harka*) 87, 93,
106, 112–14, 137, 185–6
Haruna 73–5, 94, 100–6, 118–19,
121–2, 127–33, 141, 201–2
Hausa
city-states (emirates) 4, 6, 20,
34–6, 44, 48, 74n20, 190
ethnicity 2, 21–2, 33, 38, 51, 86,
96–7, 127–31, 155, 159, 161,
166, 185
language 15, 21, 31, 35, 37, 76,
110, 127, 130, 190
heteroglossia 171–2
heterosexuality 3, 10, 54, 72, 92,
159, 181, 183, 188, 192
heterosexuals, terms for 93, 113
hisbas 23, 30, 168, 177–9, 191–2,
201–2
history 22, 31, 34–57
HIV/AIDS 7, 22–4, 139, 196–7,
202

homos (*see also* civilians, *masu harka*)
9–10, 112–15, 139, 183
homosexuality 2–3, 5, 9–10, 16–17,
32–4, 42–3, 55, 57, 92, 106,
120, 124, 132, 136, 141, 150–1,
177–86, 188–93
honor (*kirki*) 2, 16, 17

Ibro Dan Daudu (film) 144–61,
168–73
identity 7, 25, 33, 57, 63–7, 82,
87n8, 92, 151–2, 163, 181–3
ideology (*see also* language ideologies)
political 48, 124, 126, 134, 140,
176, 191
Igbo people 58n17, 69, 111, 201,
202
imams (*see also malamai, ulama*) 126,
136–7, 144, 146–8, 161, 168,
170, 172
immigrants to northern Nigeria 18,
20, 35, 110, 111
indexical meaning 46, 68, 79, 85,
92, 113, 124, 127, 129–32,
154, 165–6, 169–70, 185–6,
202
Indirect Rule (*see also* colonialism)
37, 38
indirectness (*see also* ambiguity, *habaici*)
90, 92, 98–9, 105, 107–8, 154,
169
International Gay and Lesbian Human
Rights Commission (IGLHRC)
178, 181, 193
internet 10, 12, 51, 154–5, 178,
190
intertextuality 170, 172
Islam
in Hausaland 17–18, 34–6, 168,
190–1
and northern Nigerian nationalism
7, 15, 25, 124, 146, 160, 170–1,
173, 191

Islamic law (*see* Shari'a)
Islamic mysticism (*see* Sufism)
Islamic reformism 7, 8, 11, 25,
27n8, 35, 48, 54–5, 124, 146,
179–81, 189, 191
Islamic scholars (*see* imams, *malamai*)
Islamist movements (*see also* Islamic
reformism) 60n49, 126, 136,
140, 159, 171, 178–83, 192–3
Izala (*see also* Islamic reformism) 54,
136, 140, 179, 194n6

Jamilu 61–3, 65–9, 72, 86, 158,
202–4
jealousy 75, 89–91, 105, 108, 172
Jihad for Love (film) 195n41

Kabiru 62–3, 65–6, 69, 72, 86,
203–4
Kaduna 12, 41, 76, 81–4, 201
Kano city (*see also bariki*) 3–4, 35,
44–7
reputation for homosexuality
16–17, 190
social geography of 14, 17–18,
29–30
Kano emirate 4, 18, 36, 38, 41,
45–6, 98–9
Kano state government 4, 15, 23–4,
97, 163, 176
Kano-Jiddah (*see* Saudi Arabia, '*yan
Kano-Jiddah*)
Katsina 12, 20, 35, 55, 73–6, 80–1,
83–4, 88, 90, 94, 118, 201–2
kawalai (prostitutes' agents) 6, 34,
42, 55–6, 171
'yan daudu as 'pimps' 5, 17, 55
kinship (*see also* children, family
relations, fathers, mothers) 26,
63, 68, 86, 188

labor (*see daudu*, farming, occupation,
prostitution, work)

Lagos   36, 72, 81, 84, 190, 201
Lami   73–86, 89–91, 94–5, 100,
   118–19, 121, 192, 201–2
language
   language ideologies   97–9, 126–7,
      129, 168–73, 193
   language socialization   104,
      88n22
   'yan daudu's linguistic skills   20–1,
      99, 130
laughter (*see also shewa*)   93, 95,
   104–5, 120, 122, 148, 152,
   155–8, 202–3
law (*see also* Shari'a)   45, 179, 192
lesbians   16, 66, 73, 177–8, 180,
   183–5, 201
lexicon (*see* harka dialect)
life stories   41–3, 67, 84, 86, 88n19

Madari (town)   20, 24, 61–3,
   69–72, 93–4, 98–9, 107–8,
   121, 158, 202–5
Madhuri Mairawa   175–80, 183,
   186
Maguzawa (non-Muslim Hausa)   34,
   97, 130
Mai Kwabo   20, 67, 69–71, 73–5,
   80, 85, 89–91, 93–4, 98, 100,
   104, 107–10, 185, 201
malamai (Islamic scholars)   3, 14–15,
   17, 20–1, 35, 140–1, 168
Mansur   73–86, 90–2, 94–5, 100,
   118–19, 121, 128, 131–2, 192,
   201–2
markets, 'yan daudu's presence at   4,
   18, 20, 39, 62, 69, 93, 107, 113,
   145, 161, 196, 203–4
marriage (*see also bikis*, co-wives,
      divorce, women)
   heterosexual   15–16, 34, 43, 107,
      135, 148–51, 179
   same-sex   13, 150, 175–80,
      188–9, 191–2

masculine referents (*see also* feminine
      referents, grammatical gender,
      names, pronouns)   70, 72, 74,
      76, 79, 92, 150, 152
masculinity   9, 26, 86–7, 90, 115,
      132
   of 'yan daudu   145–6, 152, 156,
      159, 163
masu harka (*see also* civilians, *homos*)
      9–10, 20, 23, 92, 112–14, 132,
      137, 141, 155–7, 164, 176,
      185–6, 192–3
Mecca teeth   123–4, 135
media (*see also* newspapers, film,
      video)   24, 167, 172
   media coverage of Shari'a   12, 123,
      178–9
migration   24, 54, 64, 69, 72, 76, 82,
      95, 197, 203
missionaries (*see also* Christianity)   37,
      58n16, 189
modernity   8, 20, 37, 39–40, 52, 55,
      188
mosques   18, 19, 125, 161
mothers, 'yan daudu as   62–3, 68, 72,
      134–5, 143, 152
music   1, 3, 19, 38, 59n43, 61, 156,
      165–6, 169, 187, 203
musicians   29, 32, 55, 64, 94, 145,
      163–6, 169, 175, 197
Muslim Brothers (Islamic Movement)
      (*see also* Islamic reformism)   5,
      136, 140, 175–6, 179–80, 191,
      194n5
Muslim identity   2, 7, 16, 46,
      96, 121–34, 136, 140–1, 189,
      193

names
   author's   2, 129, 141n11, 202
   feminine   1, 10, 51, 74, 92, 100,
      107, 112, 134, 151, 175, 192,
      202

naming celebrations (*see also bikis*) 19, 50, 55, 75, 95, 119

narrative (*see also* coming-out stories, life stories) 104n22

  cultural narratives 35, 38, 156, 191

  'yan daudu's narratives 57, 65–7, 69–71, 75–6, 79–80, 82–6, 192

nationalism (*see also* publics, public sphere)

  African 8, 151, 180, 181, 188, 189, 190

  northern Nigerian 7, 25–6, 44–5, 55, 151, 190–1, 202

Native Authority (*see also* colonialism, Indirect Rule) 37–8, 45, 48

neoliberalism 188

networks 4, 7, 68–9, 86, 124, 146, 156, 158, 165–6, 172, 176

newspapers 12, 17, 22, 45–7, 123, 167, 176–7, 179, 185, 190, 192

Niger, Republic of 36, 60n53, 202

Nigeria

  federal government of 6, 7, 15, 23, 25, 44, 54, 60n49, 71, 124, 133, 138, 171, 173, 175, 179–80, 197

  national politics of 23, 44–5, 47–9, 54, 170–1, 175–6

northern Nigeria 26n7

  northern states 4–6, 12, 23–4, 26n1, 29, 48, 60n49, 63, 69, 179–80, 203

oaths (*see also* prayer, swearing) 77, 126, 170

Obasanjo, Olusegun 23, 189

occupation (*sana'a*) (*see also daudu*) 9, 18, 21, 24–5, 51, 55–6, 63–4, 67, 95, 103, 112, 136, 167, 203

oil economy 6, 52–4

Old City (*see* Kano city)

oral literature 96–8

Orientalism 11–12, 123, 181

pagans (*arna*) 17, 38, 128, 132

parliaments (*majalisai*) 113–15

participation 8, 124, 167, 172–3, 193

patience (*hakuri*) 78–80, 98, 109, 141, 147–9, 153, 168, 198–9

performance of identity 8, 65, 67, 76, 84, 87n8, 92–3, 100, 104, 114, 119–20, 124, 138, 146, 169–70, 186

pilgrimage (*see hajj*)

pimps (*see kawalai*)

Pittin, Renée I. 26nn, 28n31, 55, 60n56, 88n24

play (*wasa*) 6–7, 32, 61, 93, 95–7, 130, 141, 165, 193

  'traditional play' (*wasan gargajiya*) 61, 202–3

poetry (*see waka*)

police 6, 17, 23–4, 29–31, 39, 45, 48, 86, 168, 171, 176–7, 183, 204

polygamy (*see* co-wives)

poverty 6–7, 19, 24, 57–8, 65, 73, 86, 115, 136, 181–2, 188

praise-shouters 55, 64–5, 94, 96–7, 145, 163–6, 168–9

prayer 1, 3, 41, 117–21, 140, 147, 161, 165, 198–9

precolonial era 18, 34–6, 38, 44–5, 64, 87n4

pronouns (*see also* grammatical gender) 74, 76, 79, 88n17, 92, 100, 105, 115n3, 152, 192

prostitutes (*karuwai*) (*see also* independent women) 2, 5, 6, 19, 23, 29, 32, 41–8, 52–4, 64–6, 69–71, 171, 187

  'yan daudu as 1, 5, 70–1, 84, 190

prostitution (*karuwanci*) (*see also* kawalai) 2, 3, 17–18, 21, 24, 31, 39–43, 51–2, 55–7, 156, 203

proverbs (*karin magana*) 21, 90–1, 96–103, 110, 117, 121, 130–1, 148–9, 159

public sphere 8, 32, 35, 52, 197

publics 47, 48, 166, 168, 170
  Islamic public 124, 170
  northern Nigerian public 7, 25, 51–2, 146, 167, 170–1, 173, 193

queer Muslims 193, 195n41

race 7, 8, 37–40, 58n16, 124, 140, 181–4

religion (*see Bori*, Christianity, Islam, *Maguzawa*) 7, 8, 21

Rijiyar Kuka (neighborhood) 19, 107, 130, 134, 158, 161–2, 196, 198–202

roaming the world (*yawon duniya*) 44, 54, 64, 65, 71, 81, 82, 84

romance novels (*labarun soyayya*) 21, 150

Sabon Gari (neighborhood) 1, 2, 17, 18, 19, 21, 29, 30, 31, 68, 70, 110–12, 117, 120, 164, 185, 186, 200–2

Saudi Arabia 23, 48, 107, 126
  'yan daudu's travels to 2–3, 24, 72, 127, 129, 133–6, 138, 140, 158, 161, 162, 197, 200–2

secrecy 66, 112, 113, 199

secrets 87, 110–13, 176, 199

sex (activity) 6, 19, 25

sex (category) 10

sexual citizenship (*see also* citizenship, counterpublic, publics) 8, 13, 188–93

sexuality
  colonial discourses of 39
  and northern Nigerian nationalism 7–8, 11–13, 21, 45, 146, 170
  as social-theoretical category 8–9, 65–6, 181–3
  of 'yan daudu and masu harka 55–7, 86, 92, 115, 131, 136–8, 158, 161

shame (*kunya*) 20, 67, 92, 94, 119, 120, 144, 148, 154, 167, 169, 171, 176, 193

Shari'a (Islamic law) 4, 5, 29–30, 32, 35, 48, 60n49, 69, 94, 160, 171
  effect on 'yan daudu 7, 23, 24, 63, 164, 168, 172, 173, 202
  with respect to gender and sexuality 3, 12, 19, 36, 63, 113, 115, 179–80, 190

shewa (*see also* laughter) 50–1, 82–4, 92, 100, 102, 118, 137

shirted 'yan daudu (*'yan daudun riga*) 9, 87, 108, 155, 186, 192, 201, 202, 203

silence 66, 85, 145, 146, 149, 165, 168–70, 197

slang (*see* harka dialect)

slavery 35, 64, 87n4

social networks (*see* networks)

socialization (*see also* language socialization) 88n22, 72, 85, 152

sodomy, sodomites 9, 13, 178, 180, 184, 185

Sokoto Caliphate 35, 36, 37, 38, 40, 44, 58n10, 160

solidarity (*see also* fellowship) 91, 93, 105

songs (*see also* poetry) 6, 92, 94, 95, 96, 119, 120

South Africa 180, 188, 190, 194n17, 205n2

southern Nigerians   1, 12, 15, 16, 20, 44, 55, 87n1, 190, 191, 203

space (*see also* Kano city)   17, 92, 113–15, 129, 147, 163–8, 172, 202

spirit-possession (*see Bori*)

state (*see* Nigeria, northern Nigeria)

status   2, 9, 33, 42, 54, 64–5, 87, 96, 130–1, 135, 145, 162, 166, 168, 170, 185

Sufism, Sufi orders   25, 45, 101, 124, 140

swearing (*see also* oaths, prayer)   122, 125–8

talk (*see* women's talk)

tape-recording (audio)   20, 69, 71, 73, 75, 85, 94, 100, 102, 118, 124, 128, 130, 144–6, 201

Tasidi (Alhaji Tasidi)   107–8, 202

thieves   19, 64, 65

tradition (*gargajiya*) (*see also* play)   17, 19, 52, 55, 65, 96, 97, 131, 146, 166, 170, 189, 203

scholarly constructions of   33, 34, 37–40, 188–91

transgender   10, 11, 66, 84

translation   5, 17, 34, 41, 42, 43, 44, 55, 56, 70, 72, 73, 132, 137, 184, 185, 187, 191

transnationalism   4, 124, 133, 136, 170

trans-Saharan trade   4, 35, 133

transsexualism   88n9

transvestites   10, 17, 33, 34, 155

urban life (*see also bariki*, Kano city)   17–19, 29, 37, 39–40, 45, 47, 53, 125, 136, 165, 170

urbanites   9, 16, 18, 61, 64–5, 96

violence   12, 56, 84, 123, 180, 200

towards 'yan daudu   6, 24, 29, 168, 178

voice quality   89, 92, 110, 127, 143, 147–8, 153, 168

Wahhāb, Muhammad Ibn 'Abd al-   126, 141

Wahhabism   48

waka (song-poetry)   35, 48–54, 63, 71, 97, 153–4, 167

wealth   6, 25, 61, 65, 112, 115, 121, 136, 140, 143, 171, 181, 185

of 'yan daudu   3, 133–6, 146, 162, 165, 169, 172

weddings (*see bikis*, marriage)

Western culture

negative representations of   7, 15, 48, 51, 139, 151, 175, 185–6, 188–9

Western representations of Islamic and/or African cultures   8–13, 21, 123, 134, 178–9, 181–3, 188–9

white men, white people   21, 37, 40, 74, 85, 107, 139–40, 180, 183, 185, 197

whiteness, metaphorical   101–3, 167

women

independent women (*see also* prostitutes)   4, 6, 19, 21, 24, 34, 62–3, 68–9, 71–2, 74, 82, 86, 87n1, 94–5, 97, 103, 109, 111–12, 115, 124, 133, 142n18, 145, 163, 165–6, 169, 200

married women (*see also* co-wives)   19, 65, 86, 97, 165

women's houses   5–6, 19, 24, 29, 41–2, 48, 55, 73, 117

women's talk   6, 25, 91–4, 100, 102, 118, 145, 170–1

work 2, 8, 18, 64, 86–7
  women's work 15, 65
  'yan daudu's performance of 6,
    62, 65–6, 76, 82, 159, 204

'yan aras (*see also* boyfriends) 9, 76,
  79–80, 84–5, 91, 93
'yan daudu (*see also dan daudu*)
  representations of 51–2, 54–5,
    103, 117, 121–2, 128, 130–2,
    143–73, 175–6

social role of 32, 55–7,
  65–6
Yaro Faransa (Alhaji Yaro
  Faransa) 109, 120, 201

Zakawa (town) 19, 69–70, 74, 117,
  167, 202
Zara (Hajiya Zara) 62–3, 73,
  203
Zinari (Alhaji Zinari) 134–40,
  196, 199–201